25910

KU-490-423

BI 0769627 2

This

You

2 6

Preventing
Classroom Failure

Preventing Classroom Failure

An Objectives Approach

Mel Ainscow
Headteacher, Castle School, Walsall

David A. Tweddle
Senior Psychologist, Birmingham

David Fulton Publishers
London

UNIVERSITY OF
CENTRAL ENGLAND

Book no.   07696 272

Subject no.   371.926 Ain

INFORMATION SERVICES

Copyright© 1988 by David Fulton Publishers Ltd.

Reprinted 1983
Reprinted 1984
Reprinted 1985
Reprinted 1986
Reissued in paperback 1988

All rights reserved.

No part of this book may be reproduced by any means, or
transmitted, or translated into a machine language without the written permission of the publisher.

British Library of Cataloguing in Publication Data:

Ainscow, Mel
    Preventing classroom failure: an
    objectives approach.
    1. Learning disabilities
    I. Title   II. Tweddle, David A.
    371.9′043   C4704
    ISBN 1-85346-092-3

Typeset by Computacomp (UK) Ltd., Fort William, Scotland.
Printed and Bound in Great Britain

Foreword

Teachers have, for long, written 'he could do better' on children's reports. The authors of this book ask 'can teachers do better?' The Warnock Committee estimated that the vast majority of children with special educational needs were to be found in the classrooms of ordinary schools and stated that this was where their needs should be met. The authors face this challenge, and try to build up a framework in which teachers can ask themselves what their aims for their children are, and how they can set about achieving these aims. In this book, teachers are regarded as professionals who see themselves accountable for the educational progress of the children entrusted to them, who see their children's performance as providing on-going information about how their teaching can be developed and improved.

The authors do not put these aims forward as pious exhortations to starry-eyed endeavour. They are concerned with the nuts and bolts level of practical methodology – and furthermore, a methodology which they themselves have tried out. Mel Ainscow and the teachers in the school of which he is headmaster have worked along the lines set out in this book, and have no illusions about the effort involved in doing so. Dave Tweddle is a Senior Educational Psychologist who is developing these approaches with the schools in his area. Together they have produced a book which systematically enables teachers to ask themselves how effectively they teach.

The attempt to assess effectiveness in education is, of course, anathema to many; but Tweddle and Ainscow are not proposing a brave new world for the training of automata. They are simply stating that there are certain basic tool skills which children can expect teachers to help them master, to give them access to the wide world of understanding and of expressing ideas. Nor do the authors deny the handicapping effect which physical, social, and emotional factors may have on children's opportunity and capacity to respond to teaching. But the authors rightly point out that, at the end of the day, teachers for their part still have to ask themselves how they can help children to make progress. It is at this point that this book will provide not only a challenge but also a practical source of help.

K. WEDELL

University of Birmingham

Contents

Preface

The purpose of this book is to describe in detail an objectives approach to designing and implementing teaching programmes for children with learning difficulties. No attempt is made to provide a textbook account of the many other approaches to educational difficulty, nor do we see the book as a primer of teaching method. The presented approach is unique only in so far as it leans heavily on our own practical experience, but it is based upon the tried and tested principles of behavioural psychology.

Throughout the text the terms 'slow learners' and 'children with learning difficulties' are used interchangeably. We see no need of a precise definition of these terms because the ideas which are described are as applicable to the mentally handicapped child as they are to the junior school pupil with a spelling problem. Therefore, although the book was written particularly for teachers in primary schools and ESN (M) schools and units (at least in so far as this emphasis is reflected in the examples used), it should contain some material which is relevant to the needs of adolescents in normal secondary school and even of severely subnormal children.

It is suggested that the newcomer to the objectives approach should read Chapters 1 to 8 in sequence, as the ideas are presented and developed in a logical fashion. The first two chapters examine the usual approach to dealing with slow-learning children at the primary stage, suggesting an alternative, more positive orientation. Chapters 3 and 4 provide the theoretical framework necessary for developing teaching programmes using objectives, and Chapter 5 discusses some of the important issues involved in implementing a programme in the classroom. Chapter 6 consists of a selection of programmes in basic subject areas which serve as examples of the approach for study, and which may be adapted for classroom use, and Chapter 7 develops the ideas presented in earlier chapters and describes a procedure for dealing with more extensive learning problems involving some specialist techniqués. Finally, Chapter 8 is concerned with evaluating a teaching programme.

Whereas Chapters 1 to 8 focus on writing and implementing programmes for individual children, the last two chapters introduce some broader issues. Chapter 9 describes the use of the objectives approach in developing a curriculum in a special school, and the final chapter provides an overview of the use of the approach in a wide range of settings, including work with slow learners in secondary schools and with children having severe learning difficulties.

The text has been rewritten a number of times during the past three years and bears little resemblance to our original synopsis. Since we are daily involved in the practical use of the objectives approach, we find our ideas regularly being modified by experience. Indeed only the existence of a publisher's deadline has enabled us to bring the work to this conclusion. No doubt in years to come further experience will lead us to reject or adapt some of the suggestions made here. *All we can say is that at this time this is as far as we have got.*

In conclusion, while we accept responsibility for the content of the book, we must acknowledge the help and advice of a great many friends and colleagues. In particular we must thank Professor R. Gulliford who has always been willing to provide advice; Roger Cocks, who has provided advice on particular aspects of the text; the staff of Castle School, Walsall, many of whose ideas are incorporated in this book; and the many teachers, inspectors, psychologists, and students with whom we have worked and from whom we have learnt so much.

We owe a special debt to Dr Klaus Wedell for his invaluable advice and encouragement, and his attention to detail in reading through this text. Finally, we must thank our wives, Jacky and Sandra, for their support, tolerance, and understanding throughout the writing of this book.

Mel Ainscow and David A. Tweddle
1978

CHAPTER 1

Peter

Chapter Goal: *To describe, using a case study, the usual orientation to the educational problems of slow learners.*

This is the story of Peter Blakey's first year in the junior department of a primary school. Most teachers who have taught in a primary school will probably know a child like Peter – some may know many.

Peter moved into Mrs Jones's class in September. Fairly quickly she realized that Peter was some way behind the others and raised the subject in conversation with Miss Nolan, Peter's previous class teacher. Miss Nolan confirmed that this had always been the case, but said that Peter seemed happy enough and had made some progress during his year with her, albeit rather slow. Mrs Jones decided to keep a careful eye on the situation.

As time went on the problem seemed to grow steadily worse. It was true that Peter was making some progress, but it was painfully slow and the gap between him and the rest of the class seemed to be growing by the day. Perhaps even more worrying was that Peter's behaviour seemed to be deteriorating. He had been very rude once or twice when told to get on with his work, and was frequently finding excuses not to work. Books and pens had been lost, requests to go to the toilet had become more frequent, and Peter was always first to volunteer for any job that would take him out of the classroom.

Mrs Jones decided to ask the headteacher's advice. She described the problems she was having with Peter to Mr Walker, the headteacher, who decided first to talk to Miss Nolan and then later asked Mrs Jones to prepare a full written report over the Christmas holidays so that consideration could be given to Peter's needs. Mrs Jones presented the following report to the headteacher on the first day of the new term:

REPORT ON PETER BLAKEY

Peter is a pleasant and likeable little lad, despite the fact that it is almost impossible to keep him working for more than a few minutes at a time. He needs constant one-to-one supervision. Otherwise his mind seems to wander and eventually he begins interrupting the other children. I feel as though I have tried absolutely everything. I have shouted at him and tried kindness, but it doesn't seem to make much difference to his attitude.

As far as work is concerned Peter can only read six or seven words on the Burt Word Recognition Test. He can recognize his own name and is currently reading Ladybird 2A, although he doesn't always seem to understand what the book is about. In arithmetic it is much the same story! He is a long way behind the rest of the class, he can count reasonably well and do simple sums (on a good day and provided he can use counters), but again he doesn't seem to really understand the processes involved. In group and class language lessons Peter rarely contributes.

I have thought a lot about Peter in an attempt to get to the bottom of his problem by finding what is really the matter with him. I have wondered whether he has difficulty hearing because his speech is still very immature and he invariably fails to carry out any instructions that I give him. I just cannot decide whether he has difficulty hearing properly, doesn't understand what is said to him, or is simply lazy.

I have not met Peter's mother as she did not turn up to the parents' meeting last term. Miss Nolan told me that Peter has no father − apparently he died before Peter was three. I have wondered whether this may have affected his work in some way.

Peter's favourite activities in school are painting and PE, and he says that he likes watching TV at home. He loves to paint or crayon and he will sit doing this all day if I let him.

I hope that some special help can be provided for Peter as soon as possible. I feel very sorry for him, but I am afraid I just don't understand his difficulties and don't know how best to help him. I think that it is an urgent problem because his behaviour in class is getting steadily worse.

Mrs P. Jones, Classteacher

The headteacher, who had met Mrs Blakey only once, decided to invite her to school to discuss Peter's problems. He wanted to find out more about the family background and thought he might persuade Mrs Blakey to do some work with Peter at home. In any event, he needed her permission to refer Peter to the Remedial Service and the school medical officer.

Eventually, a meeting was arranged between Mr Walker, Mrs Jones, and Mrs Blakey. Apparently, Mr Blakey had died in a road accident just before Peter's third birthday and whilst Mrs Blakey was pregnant. Susan, Peter's sister, was now nearly five and attended a local nursery school full-time. It appeared that Mrs Blakey had not attended parents' evening because she had been let down by the baby-sitter at the last minute. Both Mr Walker and Mrs Jones were impressed by Mrs Blakey's genuine concern for Peter and her eagerness to help as much as possible at home. Mrs Blakey was not surprised to learn that Peter was some way behind the other children in his class because, in her words, he had 'always been slow to catch on'. She explained that he was one and a half before he could walk properly, and well over two before he could say more than two or three words clearly. Mr Walker was particularly interested to hear that Peter's birth had been a difficult one. Mrs Blakey said that forceps had been used and 'his head was a funny shape'. He wondered if mild brain damage had been sustained, or if Peter was suffering from dyslexia. He said nothing about this to Mrs Blakey, however, but decided to mention these details to whoever subsequently came to see Peter. Mrs Blakey agreed to Mr Walker's suggestions that advice should be sought from the Remedial Service. She was less happy about referring him to the school medical officer, since she was sure that Peter's hearing was normal and felt that the exercise was rather pointless. Nevertheless, consent for the referral was given.

Afterwards, Mrs Jones and Mr Walker discussed the interview, which they both felt had been helpful. A number of points had been raised which might at least partly explain Peter's problems. It was possible that Mr Blakey's death had had some kind of long-lasting effect upon Peter, and Mrs Blakey had said that 'Peter often asks about him'. Mr Walker felt sure that the difficult birth was an important factor and thought that mild brain damage had probably been sustained. And finally, while Mrs Blakey seemed a caring and well-intentioned mother, she clearly was not very bright herself, and maybe this was a factor. Whatever the cause of the problem, Mr Walker agreed with Mrs Jones that expert help should be sought immediately, and so he wrote to the Remedial Service and asked the school medical officer to check Peter's hearing.

Whilst Mr Walker received prompt acknowledgements to his requests, it was some time before he heard anything further. He knew that the school medical officer and the Remedial Service had quite long waiting lists and therefore did not expect Peter to be seen by either much before Easter. Eventually, Mrs Blakey was asked to take Peter to the school clinic for a hearing test. This she did, and the results of a thorough audiometric investigation indicated, as Mrs Blakey had anticipated, that Peter's hearing was normal. A letter confirming these findings was sent to the school.

In the meantime a speech therapist had visited the school to see another child and Mr Walker took the opportunity of mentioning Peter. The speech therapist kindly agreed to see him that morning and, after talking to him for some time, reported back to the headteacher that, although Peter's speech was rather immature for an eight-year-old, there was certainly no sign of any abnormal articulation. The problem would solve itself with time, she said, and she could not justify giving him regular, individual, speech therapy.

Just before the Easter holidays, Mr Thompson, a teacher from the Remedial Service, visited the school to see Peter. He took him into the medical room and administered a number of tests. Throughout the session Peter worked well for Mr Thompson and showed no signs of distractibility. This did not surprise Mrs Jones because she knew that Peter was capable of concentrating for quite long periods if he was really interested and she was prepared to give him her individual attention. This was one of the main problems – she had thirty-two children in her class and she could not ignore them to deal with Peter.

Before leaving, Mr Thompson discussed his findings with Mr Walker and Mrs Jones, and later submitted a detailed written report. A number of interesting points came out of the discussion. First of all, test results indicated that Peter might be in need of special education. Mr Thompson had administered the English Picture Vocabulary Test (Full Range), and Peter had a standard score of 76. Mr Thompson explained that sophisticated intelligence tests could be administered only by a psychologist but the EPVT, which measures 'receptive vocabulary', 'correlates' highly with IQ. If Peter's IQ was also 75–80 he would be very close to the range of IQ which was usually associated with educationally subnormal children. He therefore suggested that a referral for a full psychological assessment should be made immediately, but pointed out that this could only be done with parental consent.

Mr Thompson listened to Mr Walker's information about Peter's home circumstances and the difficult birth. He agreed that these factors might well be the cause of Peter's learning difficulties, but again felt that an educational psychologist would be better qualified to judge.

A number of useful suggestions were made by Mr Thompson. He had used Stephen Jackson's Phonic Skills Test with Peter. This test attempts to identify which of a wide range of phonic skills have been acquired, and which have not. In actual fact, Peter could not manage much of the test and most of the information it yielded was already known to Mrs Jones. Nevertheless, a booklet is supplied with the test which contains a variety of teaching suggestions as well as instructions for administration, and Mr Walker felt that the test would be useful with other children who had reading difficulties. In addition, Mr Thompson suggested that D. H. Scott's Programmed Reading Kit contained a wide range of materials which would be appropriate for Peter, and said that he would loan one to the school so that they could evaluate its usefulness.

By now Mrs Jones had mixed feelings about all that had happened. On the one hand the school medical officer, the speech therapist and the remedial teacher had presumably acted as promptly as their work load had permitted, and each had done their job properly. The medical officer and the speech therapist had answered the questions they had been asked about Peter's hearing and speech, and Mr Thompson had made a number of useful and practical suggestions. On the other hand, Mrs Jones was aware that Peter's problems still existed, the gap between him and the rest of the class was still growing, and his behaviour, if anything, had further deteriorated. Peter's name was now to be placed on yet another waiting list. In all probability, by the time he was seen by the psychologist the end of the Summer Term would be in sight, and then Peter would be moving into someone else's class. She was frustrated, believing that more should be done for Peter but not knowing who to blame.

It was late June before the psychologist arrived at the school. Mrs Blakey had consented to the referral which was made in writing by Mr Walker soon after the Easter holidays. Mrs Armitage, the educational psychologist, saw Peter in the medical room and the interview lasted most of the morning. A meeting was held that afternoon after school between Mrs Armitage, Mr Walker and Mrs Jones to discuss the results of the assessment. The first important point to come out of the discussion was that Peter apparently did not need special education. He was not educationally subnormal. Mrs Armitage had used the Wechsler Intelligence Scale for Children, a test which provides a Verbal Scale IQ and a Performance Scale IQ. Peter's VS IQ was 79. The Verbal Scale, the psychologist explained, consists of a number of subtests which involve the child's using and understanding language. Hence the close correlation between the VS IQ and the EPVT standard score produced by Mr

Thompson. However, Peter's PS IQ was 94, nearly average. The Performance Scale consists of the same number of subtests but requires the child to respond non-verbally by doing puzzles, coding exercises and so on. Peter's Full Scale IQ was 'well within the normal range', Mrs Armitage felt that segregating Peter would not be in his best interests. She pointed out that 'sending Peter to a special school would deprive him of the opportunity to interact with normal children'. Peter was apparently a good deal brighter than the children at the local ESN school and anyway, 'his reading age is now over six, and so he is obviously making some progress'.

The recommendation not to transfer Peter to a special school was not contested by either Mr Walker or Mrs Jones. After all, they were not wanting to off-load their problems, but were more concerned to learn what could be done to help Peter within their school.

Mrs Armitage asked about Peter's home circumstances, and Mr Walker provided the background information he had collected during his interview with Mrs Blakey six months earlier. The psychologist then explained that it was difficult to determine exactly *why* a child was having learning difficulties in the same way as a doctor, for example, might diagnose a physical ailment. The truth was, she explained, that all of these factors were probably involved in some way.

Mrs Jones then raised the question of dyslexia. Was Peter dyslexic? Mrs Armitage explained that she had reservations about the use of this term, again because it was difficult to know exactly what people meant by it, and in any event, she said, 'there are no special teaching methods which are particularly suitable for the treatment of dyslexia'.

Three practical suggestions were made by Mrs Armitage before she left. First, she said that she could probably arrange for a peripatetic remedial teacher to visit the school once a week from September to take Peter out of his class for individual reading lessons. Secondly, she suggested that language work for Peter was as important as reading, and in a subsequent written report to Mr Walker she listed three books containing useful suggestions and a language development programme which she felt would be appropriate. And, finally, regarding Peter's deteriorating classroom behaviour, Mrs Armitage emphasized that the classteacher should praise Peter's efforts generously, no matter how modest his achievements were, compared to his peers. Mr Walker ordered the books and the language programme immediately in the hope that they would arrive before Peter began his second year in the junior department.

Mrs Jones ended the year as she had started it – worried about Peter. The remedial teacher, the school medical officer, the speech therapist, and the psychologist had all seen him. They had all either answered the questions they had been asked, or made useful suggestions about what might be done with him in the classroom. Various books, a language programme and a test had been recommended and ordered, and a remedial teacher was to visit Peter once a week from the start of the following term. Although Peter had made some progress during his year with her and was still manageable in the classroom, albeit at times rather awkward and most of the time easily distracted, Mrs Jones was still apprehensive about his future.

6

Recommended Further Reading

Cleugh, M. F. (1968). *The Slow Learner, Some Educational Principles and Policies*. London: Methuen.

An introduction to the policies and principles underlying the accepted approach to the education of slow learners.

Furneaux, B. (1969). *The Special Child*. Harmondsworth: Penguin.

A useful and readable survey of work with exceptional children in special schools and ordinary schools.

Gulliford, R. (1969). *Backwardness and Educational Failure*. Slough: National Foundation for Educational Research.

An introductory text dealing with the nature and sources of educational failure.

Presland, J. (1970). Who should go to ESN schools?, *Special Education*, **59**, 1, 11–16.

A psychologist examines the issues involved in deciding which children should be placed in ESN schools.

CHAPTER 2

Teaching Slow Learners

Chapter Goals: *To describe the weaknesses of the traditional approach represented in Chapter 1, and the essential features of the approach that is being recommended.*

What happened to Peter Blakey is probably not unlike what happens to many other slow-learning children in primary schools throughout the country. It represents the accepted approach to the identification and assessment of children with learning difficulties, and provides some insights into the special efforts which are made on their behalf. There are, no doubt, considerable variations in approaches to this problem from area to area, and even from school to school, but the case study of Peter represents what might typically happen in many areas to a young child who is seen to be having serious learning problems.

It must be stressed at this point that there is no intended criticism of any of the characters who are involved in the case or, for that matter, the professional groups they represent. The teachers and specialists are all seen to be conscientious and well-intentioned persons who respond to Peter's problems in a caring and professional manner. Stating that a child has to wait to be seen by a psychologist, for example, represents what is usually the case in most areas. No criticism is intended, and none should be inferred.

Despite the conscientious attention of the classteacher, the prompt and proper attention of the headteacher, and the helpful suggestions from all those who eventually become involved, our system for dealing with slow learners seems somehow to fail Peter Blakey. Is Peter's case typical or exceptional in terms of the success of this form of intervention? Unfortunately, there is a lamentable lack of objective data on the effectiveness of this traditional approach, but the limited evidence which exists (e.g. Collins, 1961) seems to support the impression that, despite the skill and commitment of teachers and specialists involved in this kind of work, the success rate is suprisingly low. While it is, of course, undeniable that successes do occur, readers with extensive teaching experience, who have seen young children resist special attempts to accelerate progress, will probably support this conclusion.

The purpose of this chapter is to look closely at some of the important features of the approach adopted in the case study, with a view to identifying those aspects that might be improved. In order to do this, a distinction will be made between those factors which are *within* the teacher's control and those which are *outside* the teacher's control. There are clearly certain factors which influence a child's educational progress over which the teacher can have little or no influence. Since nothing can be done about these, there seems to be little point in focusing too much attention in their direction. It is factors which are within teacher-control that must be our primary concern. This is a practical classification with which to structure the development of the argument, and one which leads to interesting conclusions.

Factors Outside the Teacher's Control

There is a natural desire among those who teach slow learners to know *why* a particular child is having learning problems. The discussion between Mrs Jones and Mr Walker was probably fairly typical in that they were speculating about the reasons for Peter's difficulties. The death of Mr Blakey, Mrs Blakey's subsequent struggle to raise two children, her own limited ability, the difficult birth and the possibility of mild brain damage were all mentioned as possible contributory factors. It will also be recalled that the issue was never clearly resolved, the psychologist suggesting that probably *all* these factors in some way influenced Peter's development.

What if Mrs Armitage had been able to solve the riddle and specify which of the suggested possible causes was largely responsible for Peter's difficulties? How useful would this information have been? Certainly the staff of the school could do little to improve Mrs Blakey's domestic situation, and significantly influencing Mrs Blakey's intellectual competence was also outside their control. Although parent–teacher co-operation can, to some extent, influence a domestic situation or parental attitudes towards schools, it is unrealistic to have expected Mr Walker to do much more than he had already done in that direction. There already existed good parent–teacher liaison and special efforts had been made to have Mrs Blakey continue at home the work which Mrs Jones was doing in her classroom. It seems that in Peter's case at least, if family history or domestic circumstances were a significant causal factor, there was little more that Mr Walker or his colleagues could do about it.

What about the question of mild brain damage, or 'minimal cerebral dysfunction' as it is sometimes called, possibly caused in Peter's case by the forceps delivery? If Mrs Armitage could have confirmed that this was at the root of his difficulties, would any particular action or treatment necessarily follow from the diagnosis? The condition is a difficult one to diagnose reliably, it is not something which can be rectified surgically, and there is no evidence to suggest that children with minimal cerebral dysfunction should be taught differently from those without it. (Bateman, 1974). Even if we were able to confirm that this was the root cause of Peter's problem, therefore, we would still be no further forward in knowing how best to help him. In other words, brain damage might or might not be a significant causal factor, but in any event it is beyond the control of the classteacher.

It would appear that the causes, or aetiology, of Peter's problems in particular, and of mild to moderate learning difficulties generally, are elusive. Furthermore, in the search for a cause, there seems to be a tendency to speculate about factors which are largely beyond teacher control and consequently have minimal prescriptive value. If this is true, why do teachers persist in seeking the cause? It is as if there is an implicit assumption that a knowledge of the cause will lead directly to an understanding of what to do about it. This kind of approach resembles the medical model of diagnosis and prescription, and in fact may have derived from that source. Whilst it may suit medicine admirably, it seems to lead teachers up a series of blind alleys, and succeeds only in setting questions to which invariably there are no definitive answers and in inadvertently focusing attention on factors which are outside teacher influence.

A medical-style approach is apparent too in other ways. Mrs Jones thought that Peter might be dyslexic, and Mrs Armitage addressed herself to the question of whether or not he was educationally subnormal. Classifying children's difficulties by the use of descriptive labels, such as 'dyslexia', 'ESN', 'maladjusted' or whatever, is not unlike the medical labelling of physical ailments. But again there are problems, since what seems to work in medicine is not automatically useful in the field of education. First of all, there are enormous problems of definition. Very often there exists no commonly agreed, specific definition of terms such as 'dyslexia' or 'educationally subnormal'. Consequently, a child classified as ESN by one psychologist may not be so deemed by another. And the same is true of dyslexia. Secondly, and perhaps more important, there are no specific prescriptive implications associated with either diagnosis. That is to say, there is no evidence that ESN children learn, or should be taught, in a fundamentally different way from children who are not ESN. And the same with dyslexia. In fact Keogh (1975) wrote '... with the possible exception of children with sensory deficits or severe physical conditions, where modification of curricular materials is required to enhance availability of information, there is little evidence that exceptional children learn differently from normal children, or that they require dramatically modified instructional techniques.'

To sum up, therefore, what are the practical implications of labelling a child with terms such as 'ESN' or 'dyslexic'? First, it seems that there may be considerable differences of opinion between experts as to what constitutes an ESN or dyslexic child. And secondly, it seems to tell us little or nothing about how best to help the child. There is another important repercussion of the labelling process. The work of Rosenthal and Jacobsen (1968), Pidgeon (1970), and Nash (1973) seems to indicate that providing teachers with information about a child's *predicted* progress may influence the progress that is *actually* made. It has been demonstrated that children described to their prospective teacher as 'bright' seem to make more progress than those described as 'rather dull' − even when no such differences exist. If this is so, describing a child as ESN, dyslexic or brain-damaged not only has the disadvantage of telling us little or nothing about what or how he should be taught, but may also establish expectations of slow progress and limited achievement.

In Peter's case, attention was focused on the likely causes and possible classifications of his difficulties, and a number of factors were identified as being of possible significance. There was the social history and domestic circumstances, the question of the difficult birth and possible mild brain damage, and the question of whether he was 'ESN' or 'dyslexic'. Throughout this chapter the usefulness of this orientation has been questioned and it has been argued that the reason for the apparent dearth of prescriptive implications is simply that teachers are tending to focus on aspects of the problem that are largely, or even totally, beyond their control. The same criticism is sometimes made of intelligence tests. Mrs Armitage used an intelligence test with Peter, and, as a result, stated that he was not educationally subnormal. It is important, therefore, to spend some time examining this aspect of the psychologist's contribution.

The fortunes of intelligence tests have varied dramatically during the past 30 years, and inexplicably continue to be the subject of heated debate. An intelligence test usually consists of a wide range of tasks that have been standardized on a large number of randomly selected children of various ages. The purpose of doing an intelligence test with a child is to see how he or she performs on those tasks compared to all the other children of a similar age who were tested during the standardization. IQ scores, therefore, are a fairly reliable means of comparing children's general mental ability, and were consequently useful to Mrs Armitage in deciding whether or not Peter would be better placed in a special school. It is important to realize, however, that this is all an IQ can do. It does not purport to indicate what, or how, a child should be taught, and again there is no evidence to suggest that a child with an IQ of 69 learns, or should be taught, differently from a child with an IQ of 91.

It seems, therefore, that IQ is another factor beyond the teacher's control. In this case Mrs Armitage noticed that there was a considerable discrepancy between Peter's performance on verbal and non-verbal tasks and, as a result, recommended intensive language work. However it must be said that, although this is probably a reasonable interpretation of those test results, it is using the test for a purpose for which it was not designed, and in any event does not provide any detailed or specific indication of the *kind* of language work required.

So far a number of important aspects of the approach used with Peter have been examined. They have been found to have one important feature in common in that none of them seem to provide any detailed indication of what, or how, Peter Blakey should be taught, and it has been suggested that the reason for this is that they involve focusing on factors which are outside the teacher's control. Is it reasonable to assume, therefore, that the efforts of Mrs Jones and the specialists who eventually became involved would have been no less effective if these factors had been ignored?

Factors Within the Teacher's Control

The analogy between medicine and the traditional remedial style of intervention can be extended a little further. Both approaches are curative. When a child is seen to be having difficulties the remedial expert or psychologist is called in to diagnose the problem and prescribe appropriate remedial treatment, rather like the GP who is called in to the sick patient to diagnose the complaint and prescribe a treatment. Both situations represent a curative orientation in that the expert waits for the complaint to develop and then tries to cure it. There are considerable dangers involved in exposing children to prolonged classroom failure. Peter was starting to avoid that which he found difficult and his classroom conduct was beginning to deteriorate in other ways. Those readers who have taught slow learners will no doubt confirm this tendency from their own experiences.

Slow learners often develop a poor opinion of themselves, lose confidence and bring an expectation of failure with them into the classroom. Experienced teachers will recall dealing with children who hesitate at every step, who seek constant reassurance from the teacher and seem almost to know that they will fail. Keogh (1975) quotes research indicating that '... children with long histories of school failure ... bring a generalized expectation of failure to new problem-solving tasks. Self-perceived inadequacy and a "set" for failure may explain at least part of their school problems'.

If a complaint can be made against Peter's school it would be that it was two years before help was called, and almost a further year before any practical change occurred in Peter's circumstances. For almost three years he made 'painfully slow' progress, and was exposed to the failures and frustrations which that involved. This is a factor over which it is possible to have complete control. The headteacher could have referred the problem at least a year earlier, and it is even possible that the reception classteacher may have been able to predict that these difficulties were likely to occur. The point being made is that whatever provision is made for the slow learner, it is better for the intervention to occur as early as possible, thus eliminating unnecessary exposure to failure.

Considerable attention has recently been paid to procedures for identifying 'educationally at risk' pupils at an early age, and it has been consistently found that the most reliable system for spotting children liable to have learning difficulties is to structure the classroom observations of experienced teachers (Wedell and Raybould, 1976; Marshall, 1976). The material presented later in this book will provide a basis for this kind of observation. Meanwhile, teachers in primary schools should be aware that it is their responsibility to be on the look out for children who display signs of having difficulty with any aspect of the curriculum. Had this been the prevalent orientation in Peter's area, what eventually happened to him could have occurred at least one, and maybe even two or three, years earlier. This then represents the first fundamental difference between the approach used with Peter and the approach described in later chapters of this book. Instead of waiting for failure to occur and using external support services to formulate curative strategies, the intervention should be geared toward preventing failure by taking immediate action as soon as it is seen that a child is having difficulty.

It must be mentioned that the notion of early identification has been criticized because this too can influence teacher expectation, the prediction of failure becoming a self-fulfilling prophecy and actually limiting the child's prospect of success. This is a real danger, but one which can be overcome. It is being suggested that children with learning difficulties should be spotted as early as possible in order that subsequent classroom failure can be averted. It is certainly *not* suggested that we predict educational failure and then wait to assess the accuracy of our predictions.

A good tip that can be gained from Peter's story concerns the question of his possible hearing loss. The headteacher's swift action in calling for Peter's hearing to be checked must be applauded. Very often problems of learning can be avoided if an observant teacher, or parent, can pick out possible signs of hearing difficulty and an early investigation is made. The same, of course, applies with regard to possible visual abnormalities. It is vital that even a slight doubt in these directions should always be followed up.

Thus, the timing of the intervention is within the control of the teacher and might be modified to good effect, and possible problems of hearing or vision can be investigated. What are the other important factors which are within teacher-control and might be manipulated to benefit the child with learning difficulties? There is one which perhaps supersedes all others in importance. Look into most primary school classrooms and you will find a wide range of ability, with a few children working very quickly and accurately, the majority working steadily despite occasional problems, and a few, like Peter, experiencing difficulties in most subjects. Most class work is geared to the large middle group, their needs, interests, and rate of progress. As a result, while some children find their work easy, there are others who work and learn at a slower rate and find it increasingly difficult to produce the level of work required. As time goes on these children fall further and further behind, as the deficiency accumulates. The problem is amplified in some subject areas where a mastery of the first step is required before progressing to the next. If the first step has not been successfully accomplished, failure at subsequent stages becomes almost inevitable.

An influence on the thinking of many teachers is the notion of the natural distribution of ability which assumes that, given children of a full range of ability for whom a standard lesson is prepared, some will succeed with ease, some will steadily plod through, and others will be largely incapable of success. This kind of thinking is detrimental to the child with learning difficulties in many schools, where subjects are taught for a set amount of time, at a predetermined point in the child's primary school career. Given this kind of organization the natural distribution of ability does, in fact, become a 'natural distribution of attainment', where some children achieve a great deal, most children learn more or less what the teacher sets out to teach, and the likes of Peter are not given sufficient time to master much of the provided material.

Bloom (1975), at the University of Chicago, has developed the idea of 'mastery learning'. It is an approach which is helpful in producing learning programmes geared to the individual pupil. It recognizes that children have different aptitudes for learning. In other words, children need different periods of time to master a particular topic. Bloom suggests that we should *not* teach a topic for a predetermined time, assuming that all the children in the class will learn it to a varying degree of competence. Instead, in mastery learning, the amount of material to be learnt thoroughly is held *constant* and teaching time becomes the *variable* which is manipulated. Thus the emphasis is switched from consideration of ability, and other factors which imply limited potential, to that of aptitude, which suggests that all the children will achieve mastery of the topic provided the teacher allows sufficient time and matches other classroom conditions to the needs of the individual child.

This is the second factor over which teachers have a direct control and which might be manipulated to benefit the child with learning difficulties. He can be given enough time to master essential areas of learning.

Not a great deal was said about Mrs Jones's classroom, and so we are unaware of the extent to which the idea of mastery learning featured in her planning. In fact, not a great deal was said about any of a multitude of classroom variables which may have been influencing Peter's progress. Let us look even closer at Mrs Jones's classroom and consider other aspects of her methods and organization which might be modified to good effect.

If Peter was beginning to improvise strategies to avoid work, it may be that too much was being asked of him. Perhaps the tasks he was being set were too difficult, involving skills or knowledge which he did not possess. If this was the case then Peter's distractability and deteriorating classroom conduct were actually being caused, albeit inadvertently, by the teacher. This is certainly a potentially fruitful line of enquiry, but again one which was largely overlooked by the people in the case study.

What about the way in which Mrs Jones introduced the work and presented the tasks to Peter? Very often children who have difficulty with learning do so because, for whatever reason, they fail to understand the instructions that are given. It will be recalled the Mrs Jones was worried about Peter's hearing because of his apparent lack of understanding or oral instructions. Understanding of language is an area of crucial difference from pupil to pupil. Therefore, it is vital that teachers pay careful attention to the way that tasks are explained, ensuring that each pupil understands the vocabulary used.

What records were being kept in the classroom about Peter's progress? Again there was no mention of this in the case study. If there existed an accurate record of the work set, the teaching methods used, the skills already acquired, the areas of particular difficulty to Peter, it could provide invaluable data for the formulation of an appropriate programme of intervention. What about Mrs Jones's management of Peter on those occasions when he was being rude, interrupting other children or avoiding settling down to do his work? Could praise be used more effectively to maintain Peter's interest for longer periods and encourage his efforts?

This brief discussion of aspects of Mrs Jones's classroom is not intended to imply that she was necessarily doing anything wrong. It is merely suggested that her planning, teaching methods, and classroom organization are within her control but were not considered in any detail when Peter was being investigated. Instead there was a preoccupation with Peter himself, the state of his brain, his family background, test results, diagnosis, and classification – none of which provided Mrs Jones with any specific and detailed practical advice.

Summary

Throughout the analysis of the identification and assessment of, and the intervention in, Peter Blakey's difficulties an attempt has been made to vindicate the personalities and professional groups involved. Each was seen to act professionally and properly with Peter's best interests in mind, and in some way each contributed positively to the situation. The fault lies in the general approach which seems, in a number of ways, to emulate a medical model quite unsuitable for the treatment of children with learning difficulties. It allows children to fail before action is taken and is then preoccupied with factors outside the classteacher's control in an attempt to ascertain the cause of the problem or to fit the child to a descriptive label or category of handicap. In so doing attention is taken away from the multitude of variables within the teacher's control which might be manipulated to the benefit of the child.

The rest of this book attempts to focus on controllable classroom factors and ignores those things which are beyond teacher-influence. It is not denied that brain damage, a broken home, or a low IQ may have a direct and detrimental effect on a child's educational achievements. However, these things are largely, or entirely, beyond the teacher's control, and consequently provide no specific prescriptive information. Therefore there seems to be no point in focusing attention upon them. Instead, the theme throughout is on manipulating aspects of classroom organization and teaching methods in an attempt to prevent educational failure. Hopefully, the ideas and suggestions presented will help teachers to do a better job for the slow learner.

Recommended Further Reading

Bateman, B. (1974). Educational implications of minimal brain dysfunction, *Reading Teacher*, **27**, 662–668.
Argues that there are *no* educational implications in a diagnosis of minimal brain dysfunction.

Bloom, B. S. (1975). Mastery learning and its implication for curriculum development in Golby, M., Greenwald, J., and West, R. (Eds), *Curriculum Development*. London: Croom Helm.
Outlines the fundamental issues involved in mastery learning.

Brophy, J. E., and Good, T. L. (1974). *Teacher-Student Relationships*. New York: Holt, Rinehart & Winston.
Reviews recent research that has demonstrated the effects of teacher expectation.

Delamont, S. (1976). *Interaction in the Classroom*. London: Methuen.
Includes an introduction to teacher and pupil expectations and the notion of the self-fulfilling prophecy.

Holt, J. (1964). *How Children Fail*. Harmondsworth: Penguin.
Uses classroom observation to argue that 'school is a place where children learn to be stupid'.

Nash, R. (1973). *Classrooms Observed*. London: Routledge and Kegan Paul.
The behaviour of teachers and pupils observed in an attempt to demonstrate and explain how teacher expectations can act as self-fulfilling prophecies.

CHAPTER 3

The Objectives Approach

Chapter Goal: *To explain the importance of careful forward planning, and describe the techniques and advantages of writing teaching goals and objectives.*

A critical examination of what happened to Peter has helped us to identify a number of aspects of the usual orientation to the education of slow-learning children which might be modified to some advantage. In general terms these amount to de-emphasizing those aspects of the problem over which we have little, or even no, control such as domestic circumstances, family history, the condition of the brain, IQ scores, and non-prescriptive diagnostic labels, and focusing our attention on the classroom and the classteacher's own behaviour. What the teacher needs to know is: Is it possible to help the young child with learning difficulties by changing teaching methods and tactics, or by rearranging some aspects of classroom organization? It should not be disguised that what is being proposed is, in some aspects at least, considerably different to traditional practice. For example, it is suggested that classteachers are responsible for the early identification of educationally 'at risk' children, and that whatever can be done to help these children will take place in the classroom. For the support services, such as remedial specialists and psychologists, it means that they must concentrate their efforts in helping and advising the classteacher where the problem is occurring – in the classroom – and perhaps spending less time with the individual child.

What *can* the classteacher do to help the young child with learning difficulties? There are, of course, a number of fundamental classroom requirements that have been described and discussed at length elsewhere, in books, in journals, and at conferences, and about which experienced teachers now scarcely need reminding. For example, the importance of providing a bright and stimulating setting in which to work and learn – plenty of pictures on the wall, interesting objects around the classroom for the children to touch, see, and smell, and opportunities to interact with, and explore the environment. One needs only to observe a group of infant or nursery school children in a well-designed and attractive classroom. They appear to have an almost insatiable appetite to learn, and actively seek to acquire new skills and fresh knowledge. The role of the classteacher in this situation is largely one of the provider, skilfully creating learning opportunities and then guiding, prompting, and encouraging. The energy and the desire to learn come from the children, while the teacher tries to harness the energy and capitalize on the desire.

Then there are the personal qualities of the good teacher – patience, commitment, and understanding. It is fine to be technically competent, to have read the latest books and attended plenty of courses, but how useful is the theory without an ability to get on well with the children and develop a close rapport? There is of course no doubt that children with learning difficulties need a classteacher who is sensitive to their problems and who will provide a positive and encouraging atmosphere in which to learn.

In 1975 the Bullock Committee presented a report entitled 'A Language for Life' (DES, 1975) which emphasized 'language across the curriculum' and led teachers at all levels to look closely at the language they use in the classroom and the opportunities provided for their students to develop language skills. Like Peter in Chapter 1, many children with learning difficulties have retarded language development, and so the need for a linguistically stimulating setting becomes even more acute.

All of these things are aspects of the classteacher's own behaviour and classroom organization which might be modified to help the young child with learning problems. It is not our intention, however, to dwell on any of these issues. They are well-trodden areas, the importance of which we do not seek to undermine. Instead, it is suggested that the classteacher has a fundamental responsibility over and above those already briefly described which regrettably, in recent years, seems to have been relegated in importance and even overlooked entirely at times. That is to plan and implement carefully graded, appropriate teaching programmes for children who might have difficulties in learning.

One of the most consistent and educationally significant characteristics of children with learning handicaps is their reduced capacity for unplanned, incidental learning. Merely setting them loose in a well-planned and attractive setting is not enough. This is perhaps most noticeable with mentally handicapped children who are extremely dependent on carefully planned teaching, in contrast to children at the other end of the scale who learn almost despite adult interference. Within the context of this book, of course, we are not talking of the severely subnormal, but about children with mild to moderate learning difficulties. Nevertheless, the same argument applies. The greater the learning handicap, the greater is the need for a carefully planned intervention by the teacher if the pupil is to learn successfully.

What about the personal qualities of the effective teachers as referred to above? Again, we are seeking to complement rather than replace them. There are adults in all walks of life who possess similar virtues, but as teachers we would presumably argue that 'something extra' is required for entry into a specialized profession. The 'something extra' should include an expertise in formulating and implementing appropriate programmes of work for children with learning problems, for without this, patience and understanding – despite their obvious desirability – are not enough.

The importance of a linguistically stimulating environment is also undeniable. But the Bullock Report which brought our attention to the crucial role of language in learning, also points out that for some children there is a need for 'a more precise definition of linguistic objectives and for the provision of a more carefully planned language experience than is evident in most nursery and infant work at the present time'. (Para. 5.24). This is of course a much less frequently quoted section of the Report but one which was prompted by 'a number of the submissions of evidence', and was based on the unequivocal truth that simply to expose a child to material or even putting him into a one-to-one situation with an interested adult will not necessarily bring about the language growth we are seeking.

In all of these matters we wish to add to and complement, rather than substitute or replace. It would be foolish to challenge the importance of a well-designed classroom, language development, or the teacher's sensitivity and commitment. But these things alone are not enough. There is a missing ingredient – an additional priority requirement. Slow learners need a teacher who has worked out in detail and in advance what she is going to teach, how she is going to teach it, and how she is going to check that learning has occurred.

The thesis being presented is simple and, hopefully, consistently developed. A fundamental requirement of those responsible for the education of children with learning difficulties is clear, unconfused thinking, and an ability to plan and implement carefully graded teaching programmes.

To illustrate the point we can return briefly to the case of Peter. Throughout the account of his first year in the Junior Department, we are conscious of the commitment, and desire to help, of the people around him. In school, members of staff have spent a great deal of time thinking about and discussing Peter's problems. The visiting speech therapist, remedial teacher, and psychologist have brought their considerable expertise to bear on the subject and provided a lot of relevant and detailed information. But perhaps the overriding impression gained from the account is that despite all this expertise, the time spent and inter-professional discussion that has taken place, no detailed and clearly worked out programme of intervention has emerged. There is an abundance of useful suggestions, but when the complete story has unfolded, Mrs Jones is still left with the original problem of what to do with Peter.

Deciding on Teaching Goals

Where then do we start when planning a suitable teaching programme for a pupil such as Peter? The first step is to decide upon one or more teaching goals. In this context, a teaching goal is a description of our *priority teaching intentions*. In other words, which broad subject or skill areas are to be the focus of our teaching programme? And, within each subject area, what do we intend to teach? This will not be a final or irrevocable decision, but it is a crucial one without which we would be unable to develop our programme. For example, you might try to decide what you would aim to achieve during the next one or two terms. Then, at the end of that period, you can review the situation and possibly modify your priorities for the pupil in the light of that experience.

In talking to teachers it is not uncommon at this stage to hear that a child '... isn't much good at anything. In fact, she's miles behind the rest in everything'. Well, it may well be true that one child is less competent than her peers in all basic subjects, but we have to start work somewhere, and it would be extremely unusual if we could not decide, after some thought perhaps, the areas of most acute need.

Let us try to be more specific. It is suggested that you first decide which basic skill area(s) is to be the focus of your immediate attention. You might consider gross motor development, fine motor development and handwriting, language development, reading and spelling, numeracy and self-help skills such as feeding, dressing, and toileting. These broad headings probably cover the skills and knowledge generally considered to be essential for young children who are not severely mentally handicapped. It may be that one or several of these areas is considered a priority concern for a particular child. Just how many are chosen will be influenced not only by the extent and severity of the child's difficulties, but also by the kind of provision that exists in the classroom in terms of such factors as group size, withdrawal facilities, and the number of available auxiliary helpers.

Next, for each subject area chosen you will need to write down one or more priority teaching intentions. These are brief, general descriptions of what you, the teacher, intend to teach. Returning to the case of Peter, for example, you will recall that in reading he had not developed an adequate initial sight vocabulary, while in number he was struggling with simple computation, possibly because of lack of understanding of basic number concepts. Thus, it would make sense to emphasize our intentions in these areas by deciding upon the following teaching goals for Peter:

(1) To develop an initial sight vocabulary;
(2) To teach an understanding of simple numbers.

Thus we have taken the first steps in developing a teaching programme by simply selecting the subject areas of greatest need and deciding, albeit in rather vague terms, what we intend to teach within each.

Let us take another example to illustrate the point further. Here we have the case of a five-and-a-half-year-old admitted to a special school for ESN(M) children. It is quite likely that he is severely retarded in all basic skills, but again we need to decide upon our priorities. What are we going to concentrate on first? Possibly self-help skills and expressive language. Suitable teaching goals might be:

(1) To teach essential skills of toileting, feeding, and dressing;
(2) To teach the use of one- and two-word phrases.

In suggesting that the 'formulation of teaching programmes for children with learning difficulties should always begin with a clear statement of teaching intentions' we may seem to be labouring an obvious point. It is probably true that most teachers could describe in general terms the purpose of a particular teaching activity in which they are engaged. The important point is that this statement must be made *before* commencing the lesson. That the teaching goal can be deduced retrospectively is irrelevant. This is the first essential decision in a logical sequence of decisions, which will dictate what is eventually done with the child in the classroom.

To undermine its importance by saying that it is implicit in, or can be inferred from, the activity, is to miss the point entirely. Subsequent planning depends upon teaching goals being clearly stated, and these should represent a studied reflection of the immediate educational needs of the child.

To take these first steps in developing a teaching programme involves the classteacher in a preliminary assessment of the child's present competence in basic skills. The example of Peter showed that this does not involve taking the child out of the classroom, using normative tests, or calling in an expert. In fact, the teaching goals for Peter presented earlier were written on the basis of Mrs Jones's own observations. This kind of assessment is not beyond the expertise of any classteacher. It involves having an adequate knowledge of the child's relative strengths and weaknesses, and his attainments in the basic skills. No more. All classteachers have this kind of knowledge of the children in their class and, at this stage in the planning, this is all that is required.

To summarize so far, it is suggested that one of the priority educational needs of a young child with learning difficulties is a teacher who can formulate, and implement, carefully structured programmes. The first step in this process is to select the subject areas which are to be the main focus of attention and write down one or more teaching goals for each. The goals should describe priority teaching intentions and should be written in terms of what the teacher intends doing. The next step is to translate these goals into specific objectives which will form the basis of our programme.

Writing Objectives

Objectives are the cornerstone of the approach presented in this book. They will provide a basis for classroom assessment, teaching method, and record-keeping. It is important, therefore, to be clear exactly how the word 'objective' is being used. Reference can be found in the literature on curriculum development and evaluation to 'behavioural', 'performance', and 'instructional objectives'. There is, in fact, no clear distinction between any of these and so we have opted to reduce the confusion by simply referring to 'objectives'.

The fundamental characteristic of an objective is that it describes a pupil's behaviour. Because the word '*behaviour*' also describes an important concept in our approach we must again take time to ensure that reader and writers are talking about the same thing. Behaviour in this context does not necessarily refer to classroom conduct as, for example, we might describe a child as being 'badly behaved' or 'well behaved'. It is, instead, *any observable action*. Talking, pointing, writing, painting, and matching are all actions which are observable. They are all behaviours. On the other hand, thinking, understanding, and appreciating are not observable and, as a result, cannot be referred to as behaviours. This is not an easy idea to grasp at first, but it is an important one that should be fully understood before proceeding further. Remember that there are two important qualities to a behaviour:

(1) It must be an *action*;

(2)   It must be *observable*.

It was stated earlier that an objective describes a pupil's behaviour. Now we have defined this term we can look at an example of an objective:

The pupil copies his name from a model placed directly above.

In this objective the behaviour required is that of copying. So this is an appropriately written objective. For purposes of brevity, it will be easier from now on if we leave out and take for granted the phrase 'the pupil' at the beginning of the objectives.

Now test yourself by identifying the objectives in the following list of statements. Remember that the true objective *must* include a description of a pupil's observable action.

(1)   Writes down the cardinal numbers 1–10 from memory;
(2)   Swims 50 yards using any stroke;
(3)   Reads aloud any 20 words of the child's choice presented on flashcards;
(4)   Knows the meaning of the words *over* and *under*;
(5)   Matches the members of two equivalent sets containing less than ten members.

The fourth statement begins with the word 'knows'. Since it is not possible directly to observe a pupil knowing the meaning of a word, this is not an objective. Writing, swimming, reading aloud, and matching are all actions which can be observed. Statements using these verbs are, therefore, adequate objectives.

Look again at some of the teaching goals cited as examples earlier in this chapter:

To develop a basic sight vocabulary.
To teach essential skills of toileting, dressing, and feeding.

The distinction between our use of the terms 'goals' and 'objectives' should now be quite clear. Goals are general statements of priority teaching intention, expressed in terms of what the teacher intends to teach, while objectives are descriptions of specific pupil behaviours, indicating what the child should be able to do *after* teaching. The relationship between the two can best be illustrated by taking a goal and deriving some objectives from it.

Goal	To teach an understanding of simple numbers.
Objective 1.	Points to a set of between one and nine objects when asked to do so.
Objective 2.	States the cardinal property of presented sets of between one and nine objects.

The goal describes what the teacher intends to teach and the objectives are just two of what could be a longer list describing what the pupil should be able to do after he has been taught.

As will become clear when we come to the stage of implementing our programme of objectives in the classroom, it is important to make objectives as precise and unambiguous as possible. In Chapter 5 guidelines will be given for writing detailed objectives that will be necessary when detailed assessment is to be carried out on a pupil. Suffice it to say here that when writing an objective try to make it so clear that other teachers and, if possible, your pupils will be able to understand what is intended.

We now know that an objective should describe the end product of learning in terms of a pupil's behaviour. Furthermore, it should be unambiguous or, at least, as precise as possible given that obviously some constraints of space and time must apply.

Why Write Objectives?

Why is it necessary, or even desirable, to spend so much time and effort writing specific objectives for children with learning difficulties? Hopefully, wider benefits of this style of planning will emerge throughout the book. However, it is perhaps appropriate to mention certain important ones here in the knowledge that they will be considered in greater detail later.

First of all it must be said that some teachers would argue against the notion of using explicit objectives. They consider it to be time-consuming, leading the teacher to waste valuable efforts which could be more usefully allocated to the preparation of classroom materials. It is also felt by some teachers that planning with objectives is a cold, dehumanized approach which leads to stereotyped teaching, limiting the option of the teacher to be creative and spontaneous in the classroom. Hopefully such arguments will be adequately counteracted when we come to describe how the programme can be implemented.

The major case for having clear objectives concerns teacher effectiveness. Experience of in-service training for teachers in both primary and special schools fully confirms our belief that giving teachers skills of writing objectives and encouraging them to do so before planning teaching methods significantly increases the probability that the objectives will in fact be achieved. In other words, the teacher who knows where he is going is more likely to determine a suitable system for getting there and, ultimately, is more likely to arrive. The point is perhaps lightheartedly illustrated by this excerpt from 'Alice in Wonderland':

Alice asked the Cheshire Cat:
'Would you tell me, please, which way I ought to go from here?'
'That depends a good deal on where you want to get to', said the Cat.
'I don't much care where ...', said Alice.
'Then it doesn't matter which way you go', said the Cat.

Teachers who have not had the experience of teaching to clear objectives often find it difficult to accept the benefits that are proposed. The only real answer to the doubter is to recommend a trial. Take a child's problem of the type we have outlined and follow the sequence recommended in this chapter. Try to decide on one clear objective for the child. Then, when you have done this, plan and implement teaching methods geared to achieve the objective. Finally, ask yourself the question, did the time spent in formulating a clear purpose significantly improve the effectiveness of your intervention?

Another important argument in favour of clearly stated objectives concerns the distinction between *learning* and *teaching*. It must be accepted that simply because a teacher is teaching does not necessarily guarantee that the child is learning. And conversely, a child often learns when the teacher is not teaching. This being so, it is not enough for a teacher to plan work in terms of goals, which by their nature focus on what the teacher is doing and do so in rather vague terms. It is necessary to ask, 'How will I know that what I set out to teach has actually been learnt?', thus translating the goal into objectives. Only if this question is carefully answered can we be sure that the programme will stop when learning has occurred, and not simply after teaching has taken place.

It is probably true that most teachers would automatically attempt to check that learning has occurred at each important step in the teaching of a new skill or idea. The suggestion being made here does not mean extra work but simply requires that the 'checks' are worked out *before* the programme begins and are made explicit in the form of pupil objectives. This kind of specific, advanced planning will have profound implications for teaching methods and materials chosen, as well as adding clarity of purpose to the whole teaching process.

If the teacher's intention is to teach 'left and right', how is the child to demonstrate his mastery of the concept? A further important benefit of this style of planning was demonstrated when the authors recently asked a group of teachers this question. Amongst their answers were:

(1) Raises left or right hand when requested to do so;
(2) Points to left- or right-hand toy when requested to do so and presented a row of toys;
(3) Moves to the left or right when requested to do so.

It should be clear now that one goal may generate a range of different objectives. It would be unwise to assume that because a child has mastered the skill in objective (1), he can necessarily generalize his new-found competence to the situation described in objectives (2) and (3). The teacher must decide whether he requires the child to perform one or all of these objectives. The list, of course, need not end there. Readers could no doubt add several of their own to the two below:

(4) Points to the left or right of a facing person when requested to do so;
(5) Says that an object is to the left or to the right of a facing person.

These are different and arguably more difficult tasks, although they are still derived from the same teaching goal.

The point being made is that by making objectives explicit before the programme begins, the teacher is thinking more carefully, not only about what the child is expected to be able to do, but under what conditions he will most frequently be expected to do it. For example, in what circumstances will the pupil need to use concepts of left and right both inside and outside the classroom? That is, are objectives (4) and (5) essential at this stage, or will the achievement of objectives (1) to

(3) suffice? How important is each objective in terms of the child's present needs? The objectives which are derived from a particular teaching goal represent important curriculum decisions for the young child with learning difficulties.

Summary

In dealing with slow-learning children one of the important features of a teacher's approach should be on appreciation of the need for, and an ability to plan, carefully graded teaching programmes. This involves isolating subject areas of greatest need, deciding on priority teaching goals and generating clearly written objectives in terms of observable pupil action, *before* considering aspects of teaching methods. Time and effort spent on this form of detailed planning are likely to make the teacher's work far more effective.

Recommended Further Reading

Brennan, W. K. (1974). *Shaping the Education of Slow Learners*. London: Routledge & Kegan Paul.
  Includes an argument for the use of behavioural objectives when planning curricula for slow-learning children.
Gronlund, N. E. (1970). *Stating Behavioural Objectives for Classroom Instruction*. New York: Collier-Macmillan.
  Inexpensive and concise account of the mechanics of writing objectives.
MacDonald-Ross, M. (1975). Behavioural Objectives: a critical review, in Golby, M., Greenwald, J., and West, R., *Curriculum Design*. London: Croom Helm.
  Argues a strong case against the use of behavioural objectives, although accepting they may have value in skill training.
Mager, R. F. (1962). *Preparing Instructional Objectives*. San Francisco: Fearon.
  The classic work on writing clear objectives.
Popham, W. J. (1972). Probing the validity of arguments against behavioural objectives, in Gnagey, W. J., Chesebro, P. A., and Johnson, J. J. (Eds), *Learning Environments*. New York: Holt, Rhinehart, & Winston.
  Popham, an influential proponent of objectives in education, gives an emotional reply to criticisms.
Vargas, J. S. (1972). *Writing Worthwhile Behavioural Objectives*. New York: Harper & Row.
  A very detailed account of how to write objectives including lots of do-it-yourself exercises.

CHAPTER 4

Writing a Teaching Programme

Chapter Goal: *To discuss some of the issues involved in writing a teaching programme as a basis for step-by-step teaching.*

Most teachers with experience of teaching slow-learning children of various ages will probably confirm that the problems posed by older children are usually more complex and resistant to remedial efforts than those of younger children. If a child spends four or five years in the classroom, and at the end of that period is only as competent in basic academic skills as an average six-year-old, it is likely that he will have experienced considerable failure and frustration and, as a consequence, negative attitudes towards learning and school may have developed. In fact, it would hardly be surprising if such a child decided that reading and writing were not for him, and opted for alternative pursuits to bolster a deflated self-esteem. Like most adults, children thrive on praise and success. Ask a child what he most likes doing at school and he will probably tell you that which he sees himself as being best at; in other words, the activity from which he gains most kudos and approval from his teacher or peers. Ask a child what he dislikes and he will mention those subjects that are most problematic for him.

The problem for the teacher of the slow-learning child is knowing how to minimize exposure to failure and provide ample opportunities for successful classroom activity. The 'art' of the good teacher is the ability to set work which is at just the right level: not so easy that the child becomes bored by the lack of challenge, but not so difficult that the task appears daunting and out of reach. We are seeking to set work that guarantees a high level of success, but which also includes a modest challenge, representing a small but measurable step forward for the pupil. In so doing we would hopefully maintain interest and motivation by keeping the teacher's praise and approval within reach, but also move forward in small, carefully graded steps.

There are, of course, many teachers who are apparently blessed with an ability to pitch work consistently at just the right level. Is there any logical basis for their decision-making which can be rationalized and made explicit for the benefit of the less gifted or less experienced teacher? Or is it a matter of intuition and years of practical experience in the classroom – an amalgamation of skills which defy rational explanation? If it is the latter, it is small comfort indeed to the trainee, or probationer, teacher to have to say 'we don't really know how it's done, but in a number of years (if you are one of the gifted ones) you will be able to do it'. It is regrettable that experienced and effective teachers are rarely called upon to rationalize their expertise, thus allowing their decision-making processes to remain private and internalized. If this happens the inexperienced teacher is 'thrown in at the deep end' – left to find out for himself the best way of doing things, usually by trial and error. There are undoubtedly considerable difficulties involved in attempting to analyse teaching skills which have evolved over a number of years, but this is no justification for declaring the task impossible and making no attempt.

The teacher who has developed the art of presenting work at an appropriate pace, minimizing the likelihood of prolonged exposure to failure and ensuring success at each stage in the learning of a new skill, has developed skills of *task analysis*. By teaching the same basic skills over a number of years, the teacher learns how to break down complex tasks into small, carefully graded steps, each designed to take the pupil a little nearer the target. This is a difficult and complicated process which most teachers spend their entire careers considering, trying out alternative ways of teaching the same skills year by year. Obviously teachers evaluate the various methods they try, but this process tends to rely heavily on subjective impressions and is rarely documented or recorded in any systematic way. Instead, evaluation usually depends on a teacher trying out something with a class one year, and then, if it *seems* to work, using it and, perhaps, improving it the next year with another group of children.

Setting work at the right level, therefore, depends upon analysing the skill to be learnt into carefully graded steps. Such a teaching programme will then be a matter of leading the child with learning difficulties through the predetermined steps, allowing time for each stage to be thoroughly mastered before proceeding to the next. The objectives approach provides a framework for making this process logical, systematic, and explicit, and is consequently less dependent upon the indefinable personal qualities and intuition of the teacher.

The remainder of this chapter attempts to provide some broad guidelines for writing programmes of sequenced objectives which could be used as a basis for step-by-step teaching, and examines some of the issues and practical difficulties involved. Such a programme consists of a teaching goal, describing in general terms the priority teaching intention, and a number of objectives arranged to represent each important stage in the development of the goal, all of these being written in terms of pupil behaviour.

We cannot provide a do-it-yourself manual of instructions for writing programmes which can be applied easily to any learning problem. Writing detailed teaching programmes for children with learning difficulties is rather more complex than baking a cake or mending a puncture, where the steps in the process can easily be analysed. However, broad guidelines can be provided, and issues and problems likely to be encountered, raised and examined. But in the final analysis, the objectives approach to programme planning must not be regarded as a panacea, or a cure for all educational problems. However, while it cannot conjure instant solutions to all difficulties of classroom learning, it will certainly provide a sound basis for defining them and formulating a plan of positive action which can then be evaluated objectively. This at least would seem to be a significant step in the right direction.

Getting the Starting and Finishing Points Right

It is important that the programme begins *below* the level of the pupil's existing competency level. That is to say the first two or three objectives of the programme should already have been at least partially mastered by the child. There are very good reasons for this. The intention is to plan the programme so that the child progresses successfully from one step to the next. As soon as he seems to be having difficulty we will want to look closely at what he is being asked to do, what the task involves, and what existing skills are required for it to be accomplished successfully. It may be that this will involve reconsidering the programme itself, possibly even making modifications or extensions to it. In this kind of situation it would clearly be a nonsense if the pupils' existing competence was below the level of the first objective.

Including in the programme a few objectives already at least partially achieved has a further practical benefit. It provides a baseline − an account of where the pupil stands at the commencement of work on the programme. The benefits of this will be in terms of evaluating the success of the programme in achieving the target objectives.

In order to incorporate objectives already achieved the classteacher may need to look more carefully at the pupil for whom the programme is being written. So far, subject areas have been selected and teaching goals written on the basis of an existing knowledge of the child. At some stage, as planning becomes more detailed, it may be necessary to check in greater detail what the child can, and cannot, do. Nevertheless, extensive one-to-one assessment should not be necessary. It is merely a case of checking in the classroom whether a particular skill has already been acquired. For the teacher with a comprehensive knowledge of the child, who has perhaps been teaching him for some time, even this will probably be unnecessary at this stage.

It is equally important to define accurately where the programme ends. To a large extent this has been predetermined by the writing of the teaching goal. For example, consider the goal:

To teach the child to copy a manuscript style of handwriting.

The finish of this programme must surely be indicated by a target objective such as:

Copies a line of manuscript handwriting.

The relationship between a goal and the finish of the programme depends upon how specific the goal is, and the nature of the subject being taught. If reasonable care is taken to make the goal clear, problems of determining the targets of the programme should be largely eliminated. It must, of course, be stressed that a goal may lead to more than one target objective for a programme.

One of the possible dangers of this type of programme planning is that it might generate a limited expectation of the child. For example, it seems reasonable to plan a programme which, on the basis of the teacher's impression of how quickly the pupil grasps new ideas, might take a term, or two terms, to complete. Whilst it is very sensible to plan ahead for this period of time, it is important to be aware of the danger of *imposing* this predicted rate of progress on the child. The time to be spent on the teaching of a particular skill or idea is one of the variables which is entirely within the teacher's control. A pupil must be allowed just as much time as he needs to master an objective, whether this be more or less than the teacher's original prediction. It might be, therefore, that a pupil completes a programme, originally intended to take a term, in as little as five or six weeks, or else takes as long as two terms.

There is no easily available and reliable means of predicting a pupil's likely rate of progress. It is dangerous to *assume*, for example, that a child with an IQ of 87 will progress through a programme of objectives quicker than a child with an IQ of 68, although this may well be the case. Learning rate and IQ are *not* synonymous. A child can be said to have completed the programme when he has mastered the final objective, and all the preceding objectives, regardless of how long it was originally intended to last.

If this danger, that a programme has the potentiality actually to limit progress, is recognized, it is no longer a danger, and the finishing point of the programme is, in a sense, an arbitrary decision. When the programme has been completed by the child, work will continue, new goals will be created and fresh programmes generated.

To summarize, therefore, a programme should begin below the pupil's existing competence level with the first two or three objectives covering familiar ground. It is pointless to have the child faltering at some stage before the commencement of a carefully prepared programme. The decision of how far in advance to plan is an arbitrary one but there is a need to be aware of the dangers of imposing a predicted rate of progress on a pupil. If the programme is planned for a fixed period of time, care should be taken to ensure that the objectives reach well beyond even the most optimistic estimates of progress.

Getting the Sequence Right

Within the subject area chosen to be the focus of attention, we have now stated a teaching goal indicating the teacher's priority intentions, and objectives to represent appropriate starting and finishing points. The next phase of programme planning is to bridge the gap between the beginning and end with a carefully graded sequence of objectives. Each objective, of course, will be expressed in terms of observable pupil behaviour and should represent an important stage or aspect of the development of the teaching goal.

It would be folly to disguise the fact that the generating of programmes of this kind is extremely difficult. There may be some who would go further and claim it to be impossible, arguing that the present state of knowledge about how children acquire various basic skills, such as talking, reading, and writing, is inadequate for the purposes of reliably predicting the 'route' which a pupil will take in the development of such skills. This problem cannot be dismissed lightly and is worthy of further discussion. Neither of the authors, nor the objectives approach itself, has the capacity to generate definitive and detailed programmes of objectives which will undeviatingly represent the way in which each and every child will acquire complex educational skills. Such a state of affairs will ultimately only be possible when all questions about the *way* in which children learn have been answered. And this, of course, is a long way from being the case. The important point is even though theoreticians have not reached a unanimous explanation of how children learn certain complex skills, teachers still have a responsibility to get on with their job.

Let us take a simple example to illustrate the point. It is still far from clear how children acquire the skill of handwriting. It is not even known for certain whether children learn better using lined or unlined paper, whether manuscript print should be taught before a cursive style, or which is the best order to teach the different letters. Despite this incomplete state of knowledge, teachers must continue to teach children how to write.

All that is being suggested here is that we think about where we are going with a child, and try to plan out and write down the steps in advance. Teachers make decisions about the order in which they teach skills every day in classrooms throughout the country. The objectives approach merely requires the teacher to do this in a more systematic and thoughtful way, before teaching commences, writing down the steps in terms of the pupil's observable behaviour.

We have spent many interesting hours with groups of teachers discussing the question of the sequence of steps in different subject areas. This experience can be very enlightening, leading participants to question long-established personal beliefs. Often, individual teachers will agree to differ as to which is the best order for teaching particular skills, but nevertheless, it can be useful to hear the views of colleagues and to be aware that alternatives exist. An example that has been found to provoke heated debate concerns teaching children to tell the time. Consider the following sequence of objectives:

(1) Reads aloud hours from a clock;
(2) Reads aloud minutes from a clock;
(3) States that 60 minutes equals one hour;
(4) Reads aloud hours and minutes from a clock;
(5) States whether minute hand indicates 'to' or 'past' the hour;
(6) Reads aloud time by half and quarter hours.

Remember that the implication of the sequence is that the child should be taught the steps in this order and that this is meant to be the order most likely to lead to successful learning. Some readers will undoubtedly dispute this order of presentation. Many teachers would prefer to teach telling the time by half hours, then quarter hours and, finally, by hours and minutes. It is not the intention to resolve this issue but merely to point out that it is a matter of some importance. If there is an order of presentation in this area that is more likely to lead the child to learn successfully, then we need to know what it is.

We have worked extensively with groups of teachers from ordinary and special schools in workshop situations, devising programmes for children with learning difficulties. Even under simulated conditions in which a group has been presented with some contrived information, the resultant programmes have varied considerably and this would seem to suggest that a wide range of orientations are used by different teachers to teach the same set of skills in the classroom. This is not necessarily a bad thing unless there is overwhelming and unequivocal evidence demonstrating that a particular order is more effective than any other. Although this is invariably *not* the case, it is obviously beneficial that a teacher writing a programme should be informed of any relevant research evidence. There may be a need to read around the subject and it can also be very helpful to discuss aspects of the sequence with expert consultants – advisers, educational psychologists, or remedial specialists.

Are there any simple guidelines which can be applied to the question of sequencing objectives? For example, on what basis should the decision to include or exclude a particular objective be taken? Let us take an imaginary programme consisting of objectives (A), (B), and (C). Objective (C) in this programme is the *target* objective, but we teach objectives (A) and (B) *first* because we are speculating that with these additional skills the pupil will be in a better position to learn objective (C). This is the crux of the question of sequencing. By including an objective in a programme we are in effect saying that as a result of its acquisition the pupil will be better able to tackle subsequent objectives. Look at the following short '*number*' programme:

(A) Labels sets (0–10) by their cardinal property;
(B) Adds two sets (totalling less than 10) using concrete materials;
(C) Adds two sets (totalling less than 10) without using concrete materials and recording the sum in written form.

Notice that it is not absolutely essential that the pupil masters objectives (A) and (B) before learning (C) – he could memorize all the addition sums totalling less than 10 in written form and thus 'master' objective (C) without necessarily being able to perform (A) and (B). However, we are speculating that the pupil, having mastered objectives (A) and (B), will be in a better position to tackle objective (C).

Now look at the following *catching* programme:

(A) Catches a bean bag with two hands;
(B) Catches a tennis ball with two hands;
(C) Catches a tennis ball with one hand.

Notice again that a child could be taught to catch a tennis ball using one hand (C) without first learning to catch it with two (B). And similarly, he could be taught to catch a tennis ball with two hands (B) without first learning to catch a bean bag (A) What we *are* suggesting is that acquiring objectives (A) and (B) will help the pupil when he comes to tackle (C). In other words, if the pupil has practised catching bean bags and tennis balls with two hands, he will learn to catch a tennis ball with one hand more easily.

Therefore when sequencing objectives we are looking to include objectives which will make subsequent objectives easier to learn. In a sequence (A), (B), (C), acquiring

(A) should help the pupil acquire (B), which in turn should help him acquire (C). Sometimes this is relatively straightforward as, for example, in the 'number' and 'catching' programmes above. But not all programmes are as simple and this 'rule' cannot always be applied. Look at the following programme:

(A) Given two rods of different lengths, points to the appropriate rod when asked 'Which is the *short* rod?';

(B) Given several rods of different lengths, points to the appropriate rod(s) when asked: 'Which rods are *shorter*?';

(C) Given several rods of different lengths, points to the appropriate rod when asked: 'Which is the *shortest* rod?'.

In this case, while acquiring (A) is likely to make (B) easier to learn, the *reverse* is also possibly true. In fact you might even be able to teach these objectives in the order (C), (B), (A). They have been ordered in this way, therefore, merely because it seems *logical* to teach 'short' before 'shorter' before 'shortest'.

Finally look at this programme:

(A) States two ingredients of bread;

(B) States the names of four different meats;

(C) States the names of four different vegetables.

Here, although all three objectives are to do with the same topic, there is no reason at all to believe that teaching them in the order (A)–(B)–(C) will be better than any other order. Knowing the ingredients of bread will not help the pupil state the names of four different meats. The order is *arbitrary*.

To summarize therefore, *ideally* you should have reason to believe that including a particular objective in a programme is likely to make the next objective in the sequence more easily learnt. But this is not always possible and there are considerable variations from subject area to subject area. In some cases you will decide that one order merely seems more *logical* than any other, and at times the decision may even be *arbitrary*. It might help to reread this section *before* scrutinizing the wide range of programmes presented in Chapter 6, and to bear these points in mind. The question of sequencing is taken up again in Chapter 7 and a number of related issues are discussed in greater detail.

The Question of Step-Size

The final issue involved in sequencing the objectives is step-size. This refers to the 'gap' between any two objectives in the programme and is an issue of crucial importance. As an illustration of this, read and compare the following two short teaching programmes to do with dressing skills:

Programme 1:
(1) Holds out arms and legs to co-operate when being dressed;
(2) Dresses self with the exception of difficult fastenings (i.e. buttons, zips and shoe laces);

(3)   Dresses self including difficult fastenings.

Programme 2:
(1)   Pulls up trousers from the thighs;
(2)   Pulls up trousers from the ankles;
(3)   Puts on, and pulls up, trousers when one foot is already in trouser leg.
(4)   Puts on trousers unaided.

The step-size in programme 1 is bigger than the step-size in programme 2. In other words, the objectives in programme 2 are more finely graded. Whilst the first takes the pupil from co-operating in being dressed to dressing competently and independently in only three steps, the second programme takes four steps merely to teach the child to put on a pair of trousers.

Both of these programmes are expressed in terms of observable pupil behaviour, and the order of the objectives in each case is likely to hold true for most children. However, both programmes would not be suitable for the same child. Programme 2 was clearly designed for young children who are either physically or mentally handicapped, and who would probably experience considerable difficulties in learning to dress. Consequently the task has been broken down into very small steps. Programme 1 is part of a more extensive programme with a larger step-size, designed for children who, one might predict, would learn dressing skills more quickly. In other words, while a mentally handicapped child may require a programme of six or seven objectives simply to learn how to take off a sweater or pull on a pair of pants, another child may require a programme of fewer objectives to learn a more complex skill. Step-size therefore, must be related to the learning rate of the pupil for whom the programme is written.

What are the practical classroom implications of using a programme of grossly inappropriate step-size? If the step-size is too small the programme, if used inflexibly, may actually limit, rather than promote, progress. This could happen if a skill were broken down into unnecessarily small steps and the teacher insisted that a fixed amount of time be spent on each objective. On the other hand, if step-size is too big, it may be that a pupil becomes 'stuck' between two objectives for a prolonged period and the programme, in this situation, would be of little value as a basis for detailed planning.

It has already been suggested, within the context of discussing suitable starting and finishing points for the programme, that there is no reliable means of predicting learning rate, and step-size is clearly related to the predicted rate of learning. It cannot be *assumed*, for example, that 'high-IQ children' will always learn quicker than 'low-IQ children'. The only way of finding out how quickly a child will progress through a sequence of objectives is to 'try it and see'. This means that, in practice, the teacher speculates how quickly the child will learn, and consequently how small the step-size will need to be, implements the programme and, if necessary, modifies the step-size in the light of that experience. Regrettably, there is no simple solution to this dilemma, but appreciating the dangers and being prepared to review and if necessary modify the programme, goes a long way towards overcoming the problem.

The question of step-size will be raised again in Chapter 7 when more sophisticated aspects of the approach are discussed within the context of its application in special schools and units. Suffice it to say at this point that the step-size should be such that the objectives provide a useful basis for planning teaching activities – not so small that the pupil bounces through the sequence seeming to miss out whole sections of the programme, and not so big that he gets 'stuck' for long periods between objectives.

The reader should now be able to develop a programme of objectives along the lines that have been suggested. At this point it might be useful to summarize the stages in that development.

Procedure for writing a programme of objectives for a pupil with learning difficulties

On the basis of your existing knowledge of the child:

(1) Select a broad *subject or skill area* to be the focus of attention for the teaching programme;

(2) Write one or more *teaching goals* to describe your priority teaching intentions for each selected subject area;

(3) Write two or three *objectives* in terms of observable pupil behaviour which have already been mastered by the pupil, to represent where the programme is to *begin*;

(4) Write one or more *target* objectives to represent the *finishing point* of the programme which, if achieved by the pupil, would satisfy you that your teaching goal had been achieved.

(5) On the basis of your teaching experience and available theoretical knowledge, write a sequence of finely graded objectives which could be used as a basis for step-by-step teaching, and to *bridge the gap* between the starting and finishing points of the programme.

The reader who is new to this style of planning may initially find it a difficult and time-consuming process. A number of points might therefore be made, to offset any feelings of apprehension. First, with time and practice, thinking about and writing objectives in terms of observable pupil behaviour becomes a good deal easier, and second, classteachers should be able to call upon the help and advice of their colleagues in writing programmes of this sort. To return briefly to Peter Blakey, several meetings were held in the school at different times involving the past and present classteachers, the headteacher, a remedial adviser and an educational psychologist. If the focus of attention had been on producing a detailed programme for Peter, instead of concentrating upon various factors which were largely beyond anyone's control and consequently non-prescriptive, the classteacher might have felt better prepared and equipped to deal with the existing classroom problems, and Peter may have benefited as a result. Furthermore, this alternative orientation may well have taken less time.

It has already been stressed that the application of the objectives approach is, initially, at least a difficult procedure. The summary of steps presented above will be useful to the reader but, no doubt, issues and problems will emerge as different subject areas are analysed. In an attempt to illustrate the procedure for developing a programme, and to deal with some likely problems, the following are accounts of how three programmes were developed.

Example 1 – Arithmetic

The first decision when developing a programme concerns the need to choose a subject or skill area which represents the child's most pressing educational need. In this first example the classteacher elected to give priority to early number work. This decision was based on the teacher's existing knowledge of the child and did not involve any special assessment procedure. Next the teacher wrote, in this case, one teaching goal describing in general terms what she intended to teach within the chosen subject area:

Teaching Goal: To teach the addition of single-digit numbers.

While goals are written in terms of what the teacher intends to teach, objectives are descriptions of what the pupil will be expected to do after learning has occurred. Thus, in planning her programme, the teacher's next step was to decide what she would expect the child to do which would demonstrate that the goal had been achieved. This was the *target objective*:

States the sum of any two numbers (which total less than 10) without hesitation, and without making use of concrete materials (e.g. 'What's 4 add 3?').

The implication being that once the pupil could consistently provide immediate, correct verbal responses to verbally presented addition sums not exceeding 9, the programme would be completed and the goal achieved.

The next stage in the development of the programme was to assess the pupil's existing competence in the chosen subject area. From her knowledge of the pupil's work the teacher felt that there was a need to give some detailed attention to certain pre-number areas before getting on to the actual use of numbers. He had already done quite a bit of work on constructing sets and therefore it was decided to begin the programme with the following objectives:

(1) Constructs a set of familiar objects or toys to a given criterion (e.g. 'Make me a set of red bricks' or, 'Make me a set of cars'.);
(2) Distinguishes between equivalent and non-equivalent pairs of sets (i.e. *Q*. 'Are these sets equal or not equal?' *A*. 'They're not equal').

In making these the first two objectives in the programme, the teacher was assuming that both represented familiar ground to her pupil. In actual fact he could construct a set to *two* given criteria (i.e. when presented with bricks of various sizes and colours, responds appropriately to the instruction, 'Make me a set of big, yellow bricks'), and could 'one-to-one correspond' quite well without being able to distinguish between equivalent and non-equivalent pairs of sets consistently. It was known, therefore, that objective (1) had been thoroughly mastered although objective (2) needed further practice.

Having defined where the programme would begin and end, the last stage was to produce a sequence of steps to bridge the gap between the two. The completed programme is presented below. Notice that all the objectives are quite specific and wirtten in behavioural terms. Read the programme and see if you agree with the way in which it suggests that the skill of adding two single-digit numbers should be developed.

Teaching Goal: To teach the addition of single-digit numbers.

(1) Constructs a set of familiar objects or toys to a given criterion (e.g. 'Make me a set of red bricks' or, 'Make me a set of cars');

(2) Distinguishes between equivalent and non-equivalent pairs of sets of less than 10 by matching the members (i.e. 'Are these sets equal or not equal?');

(3) When asked to make any 2 non-equivalent sets of less than 10 objects 'equal', does so by the appropriate addition or subtraction of objects. (i.e. 'Make these sets equal');

(4) Given any 4 sets of different cardinal property (each less than 10) arranges according to their cardinal property (i.e. 'Put these sets in a line with the one with the most here, and the one with the least there');

(5) Constructs a set to any cardinal property less than 10 (e.g. 'Make me a set of 7 bricks');

(6) States the cardinal property of any presented pictured set containing less than 10 objects (i.e. 'How many things are in this set?');

(7) Writes the appropriate numeral beside any presented pictured set containing less than 10 objects (i.e. 'Write down how many things are in this set');

(8) When asked to add any 2 presented sets of objects which total less than 10, combines the sets to make 1 larger set (i.e. 'Add these sets together');

(9) States the sum of any 2 numbers, which total less than 10, by making and combining appropriate sets of objects (e.g. 'What is 4 add 3?');

(10) States the sum of any 2 numbers, which total less than 10, without hesitation and without using concrete materials (e.g. 'What is 4 add 3?').

For several reasons, this programme would not be suitable for teaching *all* children this particular skill. The objectives require the child to respond in a variety of ways, i.e. manipulating small bricks and toys, speaking and writing. As a result, it is possible that a child might have difficulties with this programme which are unrelated to the acquisition of number skills. For example, a child might have serious pencil control problems, and for him objective (7) would need modification to prevent the development of his number skills being delayed by virtue of his inability to respond in written form. Similarly, a child may have a physical handicap making the manipulation of small objects a particular problem, or an abnormality of speech may require objectives involving verbal responses to be modified. In other words, a programme of objectives written with a particular child or small group of children in mind, may not be suitable for another child who has similar competencies in number work but different strengths and weaknesses in the various sensory modes of response.

Just as one objective might be influenced by a child's abilities and disabilities to respond in different sensory modalities, sensory and physical handicaps should influence the way in which information is presented. For example, there may be a heavy reliance on the visual presentation of tasks with the child who has a suspected hearing loss, and similar reliance on aurally presented information for the child with a visual handicap. How information is presented and how the child is required to respond are described in each objective and should take account of the child's abilities and disabilities of a sensory and physical kind.

Let us look a little closer at the programme and identify those aspects with which some readers might wish to take issue. What about the terminology? This programme uses the vehicle of 'sets' to teach early number concepts and introduces the words 'add' and 'equals', deliberately avoiding the use of the words 'and' and 'makes' as alternatives. When is the best time to teach the numbers 0 and 10? In this programme they are omitted, implying that they would be taught after objective (10). When is the best time to introduce written numerals? Here, they are introduced in objective (7). In addition to these issues, objectives (1) to (4) inclusive deal with 'pre-number' work – skills and knowledge thought to be necessary for the pupil to learn successfully before working directly with cardinal numbers. Aspects of *classification* *correspondence* and *seriation* (or ordering) are represented, and readers are entitled to their view that these are over-represented, under-represented, or even presented in the wrong order. There is no right or wrong answer in most cases – it is almost impossible to write a programme in this amount of detail with which all teachers and academics would unanimously agree.

Examining this example in detail has indicated the complexity of writing appropriate detailed programmes for children with learning difficulties. Chapter 6 includes a wide range of programmes of objectives in a variety of subject areas, and discusses some of the issues involved in modifying and individualizing an existing programme. For the reader who is fresh to this approach but who wants to write and implement a programme in practice, Chapter 6 will provide a useful starting point – programmes which can be adapted to meet the reader's requirements.

Example 2 – Handwriting

Problems of handwriting may stem from poor hand–eye co-ordination or difficulties of visual discrimination, but more usually they are the product of inadequate instruction in letter formation. It is certainly true that unless adequate teaching time and supervized practice are allocated, faulty techniques are likely to develop which are extremely difficult to eradicate later. It has already been mentioned that much of the research in this area is equivocal, with important issues such as lined or unlined paper, manuscript versus cursive style, and order of teaching the letters, still largely unresolved. Experience suggests that those schools with fewest handwriting problems are those where handwriting is taught in a reasonably consistent fashion.

The programme presented here was developed with a view to providing a basis for the consistent teaching of handwriting. In this case it was not designed for an individual child but for a group of children in an infant class who seemed to be noticeably weak in this area. Most children during their early years of schooling develop the various skills necessary in order to be able to write successfully. Some, however, need more specific training if this is to happen. A programme such as the one below can provide a sound structure for giving these children regular and consistent attention in their areas of weakness.

The purpose of the programme was to take the children to a stage where they could copy manuscript writing from a blackboard. At the start of the programme all the children in the group had established consistent handedness, were able to draw and crayon, and could, to some extent, discriminate between different letter shapes. The programme was as follows:

Teaching Goal: To teach the children to copy manuscript handwriting from the blackboard.

(1) Colours within the outline of geometric shapes (e.g. 1" square, circle of diameter 1", and equilateral triangle of 1"), after demonstration and making no more than two errors:

(2) Copies accurately the following figures: circle, square, triangle, and rectangle;

(3) Identifies the letter in a series which is different when the difference is fine (e.g. n m n n n);

(4) Identified the letter in a series which is the same as a model when the difference is fine (e.g. b/d/d/b/d/d);

(5) Identified the letter in a series which is the same as a model, when the model has been removed from sight;

(6) When drawing sits with suitable posture, holding the pencil appropriately;

(7) Copies all the lower-case letters and numbers from a model directly above;

(8) Copies own name from a model directly above;

(9) Copies 5- or 6-word phrases from a model directly above;

(10) Copies 5- or 6-word phrases from a blackboard.

The programme starts, of course, in the area where the pupils already have some competence, and seeks to develop an appropriate level of skill in pencil control and discrimination of letter shapes. Then, before getting down to teaching the copying of letters, care is taken to ensure that each pupil has a satisfactory sitting posture and pencil grip. Some older children hold a pencil tightly and almost at the point, with the wrist firmly planted on the desk so that they are writing underneath the hand. This may be because they have been expected to write before their hand–eye co-ordination was sufficiently mature, or because they have not been taught an appropriate posture and grip.

The copying of actual letters commences in objective (7). Before work on this objective starts a couple of very important issues need to be resolved. First of all, it is necessary to decide upon a handwriting *model* that is to be used. Learning to write neatly and with ease is a skill which, for most children, takes a number of years to develop. For some children with learning difficulties, the process is likely to take even longer. It can be assumed, therefore, that most children will learn to write under the guidance of a number of different teachers, and it seems reasonable to argue that their task would be easier if *all* their teachers corrected faults to a particular handwriting model. It is not the intention to eliminate individual styles of writing, but rather to ensure that all children are presented with consistent instruction on how to form letters over the period of time it takes to master the skill. This, then, is an important component of teaching towards objective (7) in the programme: defining a consistent writing model, including agreed starting and finishing points for each letter. Frequently, children make errors in forming letters which are the result of starting a letter at the wrong point.

The second issue to be resolved concerns the order of teaching the letters. Although there is no clear evidence supporting any one order of presentation, there are some factors which can be taken into consideration. For example, vowels are used frequently and, therefore, might be taught early on. Also, children may be able to make useful generalizations by learning groups of letters (i.e. o/c/a/g/p) which are characterized by a common movement (i.e. anti-clockwise), although it could be argued that some such groups (i.e. h/m/n) should be separated because they are letters which are frequently confused.

Once all the letters and numbers in objective (7) have been mastered the rest of the sequence is graded until the child is able to copy phrases from a blackboard, and has, therefore, completed the programme. Planning a programme of handwriting instruction in this amount of detail, and then providing regular and consistent practice, will no doubt lead most children to write in a satisfactory manner. The step-size of the programme is geared to the needs of a group of children, but individuals within the group who might have difficulty at particular stages can be provided with such individual attention as may be required. Explanation and examples of how this might be accomplished are given in Chapter 6.

Example 3 – Reading

The third example concerns the teaching of reading. The programme was designed for a child who had already had some unfortunate experiences with the written word and had so far failed to begin reading successfully. Consequently, he had developed a certain lack of confidence about his capacity to learn to read.

Classroom assessment of the child had determined that he was reasonably competent in visual and auditory discrimination tasks involving the use of words, and if taught three words of his own choice could usually read at least two of them twenty four hours later. This 'try it and see' procedure for determining reading readiness, recommended by Durrell (1956), is, incidentally, a useful addition to the professional judgement of the teacher as to a child's readiness for learning to read.

Certainly in this case, all the indications were that the pupil was at a stage of 'readiness' to read and yet a number of attempts to teach him had proved abortive.

It was decided therefore, that a carefully structured programme could be used to teach the child in a step-by-step manner that would, hopefully, provide him with lots of success and a resultant improvement in general confidence. It was decided that the first priority was to build a suitable sight vocabulary as a basis for subsequent attention to word-attack procedures. The initial target was to provide the child with a sight vocabulary of 50 words.

The programme that was developed is an example of a slightly more flexible use of the objectives approach. Each objective refers to an unstated target word and can therefore be used repeatedly with new words that are to be learnt. However, the programme can only be said to have been completed when the goal of 50 sight words has been achieved. Notice that the objectives are still written in terms of observable behaviour and the step-size is extremely small in order to minimize the risk of failure.

Teaching Goal: To teach the child to read a sight vocabulary of 50 words.

(1) Picks out the target word when it is presented orally with a list of slightly dissimilar words (e.g. 'Put up your hand when I say "*man*". Mat, mad, man, map');

(2) Given a model, underlines the target word in a list of slightly dissimilar words (e.g. man/mat, man, map, mad);

(3) Presented with a list of printed words, underlines the target word when asked verbally to do so (e.g. 'Underline man');

(4) Presented with the printed target word and given oral options, gives the appropriate verbal response (e.g. 'Does it say ship or man?');

(5) Reads aloud the target word from a flashcard.

Target words preferably should not be taught in complete isolation (i.e. 'house'). There should usually be some *'qualifying expansion'* (such as *'my* house' or *'the* house') so that definite articles, possessive pronouns, and so on, which out of context have no meaning, need not be taught in isolation.

This sequence can be used to teach words from any source and therefore can be used with any normal reading scheme. However, a useful source of words for building an initial sight vocabulary is to ask the child to choose words from his daily news that he would like to read. This way, only words that are meaningful, relevant, and useful to the child will be taught, and also the child will incidentally develop an understanding of the purpose of the written word. It is certainly true that presenting material which is of little or no interest, about places and things of which the child has no experience, and which uses language neither understood nor used by the child, may precipitate failure and help nurture the very converse of an enjoyment of reading.

In using the programme initially, new words were introduced very gradually in order to ensure success and, of course, words already learnt were constantly revised. Words learnt were kept in a personalized *'word bank'* and used by the child to build new sentences. This provided the child with the positive experience of seeing his bank of words growing from week to week.

The Programme as a Hypothesis

We have taken pains not to disguise the difficulties of writing teaching programmes as sequences of objectives. It is a difficult process for the reader to whom the approach is unfamiliar, as it involves thinking and planning in terms of observable pupil behaviour. It is difficult also because the state of knowledge about *how* children learn and develop complex intellectual skills is incomplete. It is therefore impossible to produce a finely graded programme which would gain the unqualified and unanimous approval of all teachers and academics. The best we can do is to write a programme based on whatever practical and theoretical knowledge is available, try it out, and be prepared to modify it in the light of the experience. In other words, we are speculating that a particular programme will suit a particular child. This seems to be a necessary but eminently sensible compromise. Because we do not know all the answers, we must do the best we can on the information available. What else is there to do?

A *hypothesis* is an assumption in default of knowledge. In the absence of a *complete* knowledge of the child or the way in which he learns, we are *assuming* that the programme of objectives will provide the most efficient way of reaching our teaching goal. This is a difficult but important idea to grasp, and it is worth spending some time explaining how and why the teaching programme should be seen as a hypothesis. It is, of course, a scientific term, but it should be stressed that it is merely the idea that we are borrowing, and there are no undertones of turning the classroom into a laboratory.

Throughout this chapter we have been looking at some of the issues involved in writing a programme of objectives for an individual child. It should by now be clear that at virtually every decision point, we cannot be 100 per cent certain that what we are planning will be entirely suitable for the child. Always we have to concede that there might be a better way. For example, we are speculating that the step-size will be appropriate on the basis of previous experiences of teaching the child. Often, too, we are only speculating that objective (a) will help the pupil acquire objective (b). Writing programmes of objectives, therefore, can perhaps best be described as informed speculation. Throughout the planning of a teaching programme, we have some information upon which to base our decisions, but not enough to be certain. Our programmes are therefore hypotheses. We are hypothesizing that, on the basis of available information, the programme represents the most effective and efficient way of teaching a particular pupil a particular skill.

The hypothesis, once formulated, should be tested. In other words, implementing the programme can be seen as finding out whether your speculation about step-size, the order of objectives and so on, in fact leads the pupil successfully through the steps to the target objective. The most important implication of thinking in these terms concerns what happens if the child does not learn successfully.

It might be tempting at this stage to revert back to thinking in terms of 'child-centred' explanations for the failure, such as low IQ, brain damage, or other equally non-prescriptive factors like social history. This would be to redirect your attention to aspects of the problem over which you have little or no control, and is tantamount to giving up before you are beaten. The only available alternative strategy is to go back to your hypothesis – the programme – and see where *you*, the teacher, went wrong. Look carefully at those aspects of the programme which seem to be the source of particular difficulty for the child and consider carefully whether, by changing your teaching methods or modifying the programme in some way, greater progress can be made. Chapter 7 considers in some detail how the objectives approach lends itself to this kind of hypothesis-testing teaching. Suffice it to say here that it is crucial to think of the question of children who continue to fail despite this kind of detailed planning in terms of where the teacher, rather than the pupil, is going wrong.

It is difficult to think along these lines. Faced with trying to meet the needs of a class of thirty or more children, and having maybe spent hours planning and preparing an individual programme for one child, it is of course easier to rationalize the breakdown in terms of the pupil's own shortcomings. How much more difficult is it to go back to the drawing board, think again, plan again and try again? At least this kind of orientation holds out some hope for the child with learning difficulties, and does not involve the premature surrender of probably the only person who can help him.

Summary

Writing a carefully sequenced programme of objectives can help the teacher accomplish a most difficult task – that of presenting work at an appropriate level for the pupil with learning difficulties. It has to be stressed that this form of detailed planning is not easy, particularly since teaching experience and theoretical evidence may not provide a clear indication of the order in which objectives should be arranged. Special care should be taken to match step-size to the learning needs of the pupil. Finally, the programme has to be seen as a hypothesis that will need to be tested in the classroom.

Recommended Further Reading

Davis, R. H., Alexander, L. T., and Yelon, S. L. (1974). *Learning System Design*. New York: McGraw-Hill.
Gives lots of theoretical background to designing educational programmes using objectives.
Gagne, R. M. (1970). *The Conditions of Learning*. New York: Hold, Rinehart and Winston. An important book explaining in detail the notion of learning hierarchies. This has important implications for developing sequences of objectives.
Resnick, L. B., Wang, M. C., and Kaplan, J. (1973). Task analysis in curriculum design: A hierarchically sequenced introductory mathematics curriculum *Journal of Applied Behaviour Analysis*, **6**, 3, 679–709.
A detailed account of how some sequences of objectives were developed and evaluated.

Siegal, E. (1972). Task analysis and effective teaching, *Journal of Learning Disabilities*, **5**, 10, 519–532.
   Provides examples of task analysis and useful criteria for designing other sequences are outlined.
Siegal, E., and Siegal, R. (1975). Ten guidelines for writing instructional sequences, *Journal of Learning Disabilities*, **8**, 4, 15–21.
   Some useful tips on sequencing objectives.
Smith, E. E. P. (1976). *A Technology of Reading and Writing. Vol. 1, Learning to Read and Write: A Task Analysis*. New York: Academic Press.
   The first in a series of four volumes. Presents a detailed analysis of how children learn to read and write from the viewpoint of behavioural analysis.

CHAPTER 5

Teaching to Objectives

Chapter Goal: *To describe some of the issues involved in the classroom implementation of a programme of objectives.*

Having produced a programme of objectives the teacher next has to consider how it can most effectively be implemented in the classroom. This chapter examines some of the issues involved, and in so doing explains many of the practical advantages that can be gained from such an approach.

Let us take another example in order to consider the many issues involved in teaching to objectives. It concerns the case of David, aged six, whose severest difficulties seemed to lie in the are of language development. It has already been suggested that' sequencing objectives in this subject area can pose particular problems.

David's classteacher discussed the problem in some detail with the educational psychologist. They decided that he was relatively competent in terms of comprehension (i.e. *receptive* language) since he could follow quite complex instructions and seemed to have a reasonably wide receptive vocabulary. As a result they decided that his priority area of concern was in the use of language and that their initial teaching goal would be:

To develop the use of some basic sentence structures.

Together, classteacher and psychologist worked to produce an appropriate programme of objectives based on an assessment of David's existing capabilities, on agreed targets and on their combined practical and theoretical knowledge. This was their programme:

(1)   Uses an identity statement of the form 'This is a tree' in response to the
       question 'What is this?';   (P)
*(2)   Uses the negation of objective (1) (i.e. 'This is *not* a tree');   (–)
(3)   Uses the identity statement 'The dog is black' in response to the question
       'What colour is the dog?';   (P)
*(4)   Uses the negation of objective (3) (i.e. 'The dog is *not* black');   (–)
(5)   Uses an action statement of the form 'The boy is running' in response to the
       question 'What is the boy doing?';   (P)

*(6) Uses the negation of objective (5) (i.e. 'The boy is *not* running');   (–)
(7) Uses plural identity and action statements in response to appropriate questions (e.g.
'These are trees'
'These dogs are black'
'These boys are running');   (F)
(8) Uses the past tense of regular verbs in the form 'Jimmy *has climbed* the tree' (i.e. play, wash, jump, walk, dress, paint, count);   (F)
(9) Uses the future tense of these verbs in the sentence form 'Jimmy *is* going to draw'.   (F)

(* Objectives (2), (4), and (6) involve negations of the form 'The boy *is not* running'. It was felt that this might eventually be abbreviated to the form 'The boy *isn't* running').

As was stated earlier, working towards specific objectives in language work is completely compatible with the language-across-the-curriculum theme of the Bullock Report. In this case we are talking about a child for whom the 'linguistically stimulating environment' approach, much loved by many primary school teachers, had failed to produce any significant progress.

The reader may question various aspects of this language programme. For example, although the order of objectives seems reasonably logical, is there any substantial supportive evidence? What about prepositions, questioning words, polars, superlatives, comparatives, and irregular verbs? Rather than a grammatical analysis, why not a functional analysis or an enrichment approach? Quite simply, there is no theoretically satisfactory solution to these questions. The teacher, recognizing a need in the pupil, has pooled her practical experience with the theoretical knowledge of the psychologist, in this case leaning heavily on the ideas of Bereiter and Engelmann (1966), and, taking the pupil's existing competencies into account, has made explicit her teaching intentions.

How did the teacher go about implementing the programme? First of all she made a detailed assessment of David's capabilities in terms of the programme she had developed. This immediately presented the problem of what to do with the other children in the class while she gave her concentrated attention to David. The psychologist had suggested that it would be better if this assessment could be carried out under normal classroom conditions in order that the child would respond naturally. Furthermore, all subsequent teaching of the programme would have to be carried out within the room. By careful organization, including the help of a classroom assistant, the teacher managed to find opportunities to check David's capabilities on the programme.

Assessment was made more difficult by David's rather immature speech and consequently the teacher felt the necessity to assess each objective a number of times over a few days, using different examples of subject content. The completed results indicated that David was competent in objectives (1), (3), and (5), had some difficulty in (2), (4), and (6), and could not give the required responses in (7), (8), and (9). These results are summarized on the programme by the use of letters in brackets, after each objective. The letter 'P' represents a 'pass', 'F' a 'fail', and 'no letter' some stage in between, i.e. some success without complete mastery.

The classteacher felt encouraged by the results of her assessment. Her intuitive feeling that this was the area in which David needed attention had clearly been confirmed. On the basis of this information it was decided that work should commence on objective (2), dealing with the use of statements such as 'This is *not* a tree'. Although it appeared that David could sometimes use this structure successfully, the teacher decided that it was necessary to work on to bring it to a level of complete mastery before going on to the other two negation statements. Objectives (7), (8), and (9) were to be left until much later.

Now the teacher, having decided upon an appropriate and clearly stated objective, needed to consider issues of method and materials. How and when was the chosen objective to be taught? It was of some help when two other children in the class were found to be rather weak in the same area of language. Assessment of their capabilities revealed some variations from David, and indeed, from each other, but these differences were not so great as to make their individual needs incompatible. Consequently, it was decided that each morning, for about ten minutes, these children would take part in small-group work led by the classroom assistant. She was given a detailed lesson plan to which she was to work and it was decided that the use of a glove puppet would be helpful in gaining the children's interest. The group sessions, therefore, consisted of questions and answers between the puppet and the three children in an attempt to improve their use of the sentence structures detailed in the objectives. Pictures and objects were introduced as a basis for the dialogue.

It was felt that this work, while it was reasonably appropriate for all three children in the group in the sense that it gave them lots of opportunity to practise the sentence structures they were learning, was not sufficient on its own. As a result, individual material was produced. Because of the nature of the objectives being dealt with, it was decided to make use of teaching machines for this purpose. In this case a language master was found to be appropriate. For each objective along the sequence, lots of language master cards were prepared with attractive pictures and appropriate questions recorded on the master track. The pupil would listen to these on his own and then record his responses on the pupil track of the same card. At the end of each session, these could be checked by the teacher. This turned out to be an excellent system of recording how well the pupil was doing. So much so, that after a while it was decided to provide the pupil with a record card on which the number of correct responses could be written down. David seemed particularly to enjoy checking and comparing his own performance from day to day.

In addition to the group and language master work, the classteacher tried to keep David's current language objectives in mind during the day. It was helpful to know precisely what the class assistant was working on during the morning group sessions because this meant that the classteacher could help with the programme by providing brief, but frequent, opportunities in the classroom for David to practise the different sentence structures. When there was a group or class discussion, for example, she would occasionally find time to ask David a question that required a response drawn from the programme. She found that she could do this several times a day in a wide variety of class activities without spending a lot of time working in a one-to-one situation with David. In fact, while the programme was being used the classteacher probably spent no more time with him than usual – but the time available was arguably used more effectively because she knew precisely what she was trying to teach.

Over a period of weeks David gradually mastered objectives (2), (4), and (6). The classteacher kept a careful note of his progress and she made it clear to him that he was getting on very well. Record keeping is dealt with in greater detail later in this chapter, and David's programme (Figure 2) is used to illustrate some of the issues raised and discussed. Subsequent work dealt with objectives (7), (8), and (9), although only one of these was dealt with at a time and care was also taken regularly to revise the earlier objectives.

Eventually the programme was completed. A great deal of hard work had gone in to it but its clear success was there for all to see. Interestingly enough David's progress during this period was not confined to language development. He appeared to gain in confidence and, particularly during the latter part of the programme, made a start on learning to read. The psychologist suggested that David's feeling of achievement might well have generalized to other subject areas and that his improved use of sentence structure might also be helping him to deal more successfully with written language.

The Teaching Model

This happy account of the language programme used to help David can be analysed to produce a simple structure which will be useful in discussing the classroom implementation of a programme of objectives. In doing this, it must be stressed that it is not the intention to produce a primer of teaching techniques but rather to describe a basic teaching model that should help teachers to focus upon controllable factors that will help to overcome learning difficulties, and demonstrate how this is facilitated by the existence of a programme of graded objectives. The teaching model is shown in Figure 1.

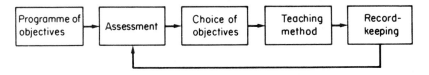

Figure 1   A basic teaching model

The model is dependent upon the existence of the programme of objectives. We saw how in David's case this was used by the classteacher as a basis for detailed assessment. The assessment led to a decision about the choice of objectives. Only then, with a clear object in mind, were questions of teaching method, resources, and organization considered. Finally, record was kept of David's progress. He was able to use a record card to monitor his own achievement from day to day and the classteacher kept a further record of David's progress along the sequence of objectives. The significance of the one feedback loop on the model is perhaps obvious from the account of David. Simply, the record-keeping, once established, formed a basis for continual assessment. As one objective was completed this information provided a basis for choosing the next task to be dealt with.

Hopefully, this analysis will seem fairly logical to the reader. It has to be stated, however, that many teachers, while accepting the principles, find it very difficult to work in this way. 'Certainly that's how we'd like to teach, but we haven't got the time!', comes the reply. Too many pressures, large classes, dinner registers, behaviour problems, mixed ability groups, and so on, are all reasons given why this teaching model, and the careful planning it assumes, might be a 'good idea in theory' but 'a non-starter in practice'. It has to be accepted that it would be difficult, if not impossible, to plan all instruction for all pupils, in this amount of detail. But remember, that is *not* what is being suggested. This type of careful planning is being presented as essential if slow-learning children are to learn successfully in the important basic subject areas.

As the process of implementing the programme of objectives is analysed through the use of the teaching model an attempt will be made to indicate how certain recent developments in the field of educational psychology can be utilized. The danger in doing this is that ideas and strategies that are perfectly feasible in a clinical situation are generalized to the classroom without paying sufficient attention to possible practical and organizational difficulties. A criticism occasionally made of educational psychologists is that suggestions they make may be perfectly legitimate in theory but that teachers have other priorities and responsibilities which may make translation of theory into practice difficult. Within this context the only adequate reply to that issue is that all the examples and suggestions presented here are based upon observation of actual classroom practice.

The rest of this chapter examines in more detail the four elements of the teaching model concerned in the implementation of the programme – assessment, choosing objectives, teaching method, and record-keeping.

Assessment

Once a programme of objectives has been devised the next step is to make a more accurate assessment of the child's existing attainments. It is already known that a few of the steps have been achieved by the pupil since this was part of the rationale used for deciding where the programme should start. What form, therefore, will this 'more accurate assessment' take?

If we return to the case study of Peter Blakey, it will be recalled that some assessment was carried out by a variety of different people. Much of this involved the use of educational and psychological tests. Peter's classteacher had used the Burt Word Recognition Test, the remedial teacher used the EPVT, and the educational psychologist administered the WISC. Unfortunately, none of the results seemed to provide much information useful in deciding what to do with Peter. Why was this?

There is considerable confusion in the minds of many teachers as to the purpose and value of tests. Perhaps we can clarify the issue. All the tests referred to above can be defined as *norm-referenced tests*. That is to say, they are all tests consisting of a series of tasks which have been previously standardized on a large number of randomly selected children of various ages. The tester can, therefore, compare an individual child's performance on the tasks with the performance of the standardization sample, using the norms provided. So the use of a norm-referenced test can be an excellent way of determining where an individual pupil stands in relation to other pupils in a group who are given the same test. Teachers will often use such tests to get a score that indicates how well each pupil is doing compared with the rest of the class.

Norm-referenced tests are therefore extremely useful in situations where it is necessary to make comparisons between children. For example, intelligence tests such as the WISC and the Stanford–Binet are very useful to an educational psychologist who needs to identify those children who are most likely to require long-term intensive help and might, therefore, benefit from placement in a special school.

The problem is that this is all that norm-referenced tests are designed to do and sometimes attempts will be made to use them for other purposes. In the case of Peter, for example, the tests used gave a good indication of his capabilities in various subjects compared to other children. Efforts to drag out from the same data information that will help the teacher decide what and how to teach the child are unlikely to be successful. What information can be yielded is simply not precise enough for this purpose. The results of a Burt Test give some idea of a child's reading level but little or no indication of what elements of the reading process the pupil has already mastered. Similarly, a test such as the English Picture Vocabulary Test may indicate a general weakness in receptive language but without generating any specific indication of what the teacher needs to do with the child.

The development of this apparent misuse of norm-referenced tests can perhaps be explained. An experienced teacher administering such a test will inevitably, as he observes the child's attempts, note a good deal of useful information. So, for example, the teacher giving a child a simple word recognition test may determine particular areas of weakness in phonics that could be useful in planning a word-attack programme. The value of this type of observation cannot be denied but this is not the purpose for which the test was designed and, indeed, it will not be particularly effective when it is used in this way.

A similar point can be made in connection with the use of the WISC. It will be recalled that this test provides both a verbal and a performance scale IQ. Teachers may have seen reports in which discrepancies between these scores have been analysed by psychologists to suggest possible emphasis in future teaching. Thus, for example, the psychologist in Peter's case may have noted the relative weakness in his verbal score and used this information to recommend to the classteacher that an emphasis on language development might be useful. This seems a perfectly legitimate suggestion to make, but again it can be seen that the teacher is still left with the problem of determining which aspects of language are in need of attention.

A further disadvantage is that by their nature many norm-referenced tests are complex and may be difficult, or impossible, for teachers to use within their everyday classroom organization. Some tests require the tester to have successfully completed a special training course, whilst others are unavailable for teacher use. It has to be said that issues such as these tend to lead teachers into the view that assessment is something outside their responsibility, being the sole prerogative of the 'expert', the remedial adviser or educational psychologist.

To sum up the argument so far, norm-referenced tests, which by their definition are designed to compare children's performance in particular subjects, are very useful when such comparisons are necessary, such as in decisions about placement, but their use as a means of planning teaching programmes is largely inappropriate. The information that they can provide us with is simply not precise enough for this purpose.

Another of the tests used in Peter's case does provide information that has more direct classroom implications. The Jackson Phonic Skills Test does not provide a comparison score but instead is intended to provide a means for gathering detailed information of the child's phonic attainments with a view to developing a remedial programme. This is an example of a *criterion-referenced test*. This type of test consists of a series of tasks which have *not* been standardized, but which are designed to tell the teacher what a child can and cannot do in any given subject area. The purpose of a criterion-referenced test is to compare the individual child, not to a group of other children, but against some fixed standard of performance.

The criterion-referenced approach to assessment is totally compatible with the use of sequences of objectives. Each objective can provide the fixed standard of performance against which the child can be compared and information gathered in this way will have direct implications for classroom practice. Furthermore, this form of assessment is meaningful to the teacher, since it does not involve the use of technical jargon, can be administered by the classteacher and, most important, can be used within the setting of a normal calssroom. Earlier in this chapter there was a brief description of a teacher using a sequence of language objectives for assessment purposes within the classroom. Each objective, containing an observable behaviour, can be tested by simply structuring a situation so that the teacher can observe the pupil's existing level of competence. It will be recalled that this was given as one of the important reasons for always including a behaviour when writing objectives – in order that the teacher should have a simple means of checking to see if learning has occurred.

Criterion-referenced assessment is nothing more than a procedure for determining what a child can and cannot do in a particular topic or subject area. A vital aspect of any successful classroom activity is an assessment of what each pupil can do in relation to the subject being taught. A teacher's inaccuracies in this area may lead to a child being frustrated and, perhaps, eventually distractable. If we ask a child to attempt a task for which he is not prepared, we should not be surprised if he fails. An eminent psychologist, David Ausubel, wrote in 1968:

If I had to reduce all of educational psychology to just one principle, I would say this: The most important single factor influencing learning is what the learner already knows. Ascertain this and teach him accordingly.

It will be necessary to give further attention to the programme of objectives in order to make accurate assessment possible. In doing this the purpose is to make each objective as unambiguous as possible, so that different teachers assessing a child along a given sequence should find little difficulty in agreeing upon his levels of achievement. There are some guidelines for making objectives unambiguous. Each objective should state *three* things:

(1) What is the child expected to do?
(2) Under what conditions is he expected to do it?
(3) How good is he required to be at it?

Reference back to the examples presented so far in this book will reveal that whilst they all include the first element, a clear description of the desired behaviour, they do not answer the other two check questions. Consequently, they are in most cases rather ambiguous and would make assessment difficult in the sense of knowing how to structure the testing situation and deciding whether an appropriate performance level had been achieved.

Let us take an example from David's language programme. Objective (1) reads:

Uses an identity statement of the form 'This is a tree' in response to the question 'What is this?'

What might you do in order to decide whether or not this objective has been achieved? Would you require the pupil to respond properly once only, or would you expect him to use the appropriate sentence structure several times before recording that it had been mastered? Would you go further and require him to use it several times on each of several consecutive days? Would you require him to use the identity statement with a variety of objects and pictures, rather than restricting the item to a tree? Would you require him to respond to your spoken question, or would you have him record his responses on a language master? You would need to make these decisions about the conditions under which the behaviour should occur and the standard of performance required, before you were able to decide whether the objective had been achieved. Look at the following objectives:

(1) Shown pictures of 10 familiar objects, uses identity statements of the form 'This is a ...' in response to the question 'What is this?', making no errors or omissions on 2 consecutive days;
(2) Presented with 10 language master cards, with a picture of a familiar object and the spoken words 'What is this?' on each, records identity statements of the form 'This is a ...' on the pupil tracks, making no more than 2 errors on 3 consecutive days.

In both these examples, we not only know what the pupil is expected to do, but under what conditions and how good the performance should be. These more specific objectives should therefore present the classteacher with fewer problems of assessment.

Examine the following objectives, which are to do with the language associated with early number work, and consider their degrees of ambiguity. To those readers who have not previously used such precise objectives, this may well be a rather difficult exercise. Each objective will need to be examined carefully and it will be useful to refer back to the three check questions.

(1) When asked the question: 'What things do you know that are round?', gives the name of at least 4 circular or spherical objects;

(2) Presented with several pairs of bricks, states that they are the 'same' or 'different' in terms of size;

(3) Identifies each of 3 shapes which are square, rectangular, and triangular without error or omission;

(4) Says the words 'many' and 'few' appropriately in comparing sets in 10 trials making no more than 2 errors or omissions.

(5) Presented with yellow, blue, red, and green bricks, points to an appropriate brick when asked the question: 'Point to the ... brick', in each of 10 trials when each colour is used at least twice.

The first and last objectives are adequate, since information is contained in each which relates to the three check questions.

The second objective indicates what the child is expected to do and under what conditions he is expected to do it, but does not explain how good the performance needs to be, i.e. is one correct response sufficient, or should there be a consistency of performance over a number of trials?

The third objective provides clear details about the standard of performance required, but is ambiguous about what the child is expected to do and under what conditions he is expected to do it, i.e. does the child 'identify' by pointing when asked 'Which is the triangle?' or does he 'identify' by saying 'This is the triangle, this is the square and this is the rectangle' in response to the question 'What are these shapes called?'. These are different skills, and that a child has mastered one does not mean that he has acquired the other.

The fourth objective is acceptable in terms of both the behaviour and standard of performance required. What are not made clear are the conditions under which the behaviour is to occur, i.e. it does not stipulate that the sets should necessarily contain a different number of members and, most important, does not state whether there is an upper limit to the number of members each set might contain. This latter point is crucial in determining the difficulty level of the objective.

Given objectives as detailed as this, problems of assessment should be largely eliminated. It is merely a matter of the teacher arranging the situation defined in the conditions of the objective, observing the pupil's response and comparing with the stated performance standard. Although occasionally there may be a need to remove the pupil from the classroom for assessment purposes, by and large it should be carried out as part of the day-to-day work of the class.

To sum up, therefore, *classroom assessment should*:

(1) Be carried out by the classteacher, whenever possible within the classroom;
(2) Use criterion-referenced techniques, measuring the child's performance against a set standard as a basis for planning appropriate work; and
(3) Make use of a carefully worked out sequence of objectives in which important conditions and performance criteria have been defined.

Choice of Objectives

The information gathered from assessment is for one purpose, to decide the next step that the child should take. It is necessary, therefore, for the teacher to study carefully the results of the assessment: Which objectives have been mastered, which are only partly achieved and, finally, which are the steps still not covered? Given this information the teacher chooses an appropriate next step for the pupil to take and then ensures that it is made explicit to both the pupil and the teaching staff concerned.

The business of stating a clear objective before dealing with questions of teaching method is a crucial principle and yet, it has to be said, it is a novel one to many teachers. Often in classroom practice, objectives are only stated in a vague fashion, while in the field of special and remedial education they are frequently not stated at all. Rather the emphasis is invariably on issues of method and materials, leaving unanswered the fundamental question of *what* is it we require the child to learn (Ainscow and Tweddle, 1977). Sadly, it is very common to see slow-learning pupils working on classroom activities which seem to have no clear purpose other than that of keeping the children busy. In all educational planning, particularly with slow-learning children, objectives must come first and they should be made explicit. Put simply, the crucial question is: How can teaching be effective if it is not aimed towards some clear, predetermined target?

The essential art of successfully teaching slow-learning children is the setting of work at an appropriate level. If the programme of objectives has been worked out with appropriate order and step-size, the choosing of an appropriate objective on the basis of detailed assessment should present few problems. Usually a child will be working on an objective from a sequence which is preceded only by objectives which are already mastered. Presumably, without such a sequence the teacher must be constantly analysing skill areas off the top of his head in order to decide what the pupil should work on next. This form of almost random presentation of steps can be a major source of difficulty to a child who already finds learning difficult. The aim should be carefully to arrange learning steps in such a way that the pupil will experience success most of the time. Charles (1976) refers to this arrangement rather appropriately as 'success structuring', and argues that pupils who have experienced the frustration of prolonged failure lose the motivation to succeed. He supports the cliché 'success breeds success'. Thus, if a child experiences successful learning as a result of the constant presentation of appropriate steps his general learning attitude will improve, and he will learn at a faster rate.

A note should be made of the date on which work commences on a new objective. This is a useful way of ensuring that a pupil does not 'stick' for an extended period at one point along the programme. The purpose of sequencing objectives carefully is to ensure progress, however gradual, and it may be an indication of weakness in the order or step-size if the same objective is being worked on for too long a period. It can also be helpful as an early warning system to make a note of the date by which results should begin to be evident.

Once an objective has been chosen it is useful to take the time to discuss it with the pupil. Tell him what it is he is aiming for, what methods he will need to follow and by when he should be successful. There is considerable evidence that this approach can greatly improve pupil motivation (Mager and McCann, quoted in De Cecco and Crawford, 1974). In addition to new objectives that are presented, the pupil will also continue practice on certain steps previously mastered. This again can usefully be explained to the child.

To summarize, the important points in *choosing an objective* are that:

(1) Objectives must be made explicit before considering questions of teaching method;
(2) Objectives should be chosen at an appropriate level to ensure success and progress; and
(3) The child should be made aware of his objectives.

Teaching Method

Once appropriate objectives have been set for the pupil the teacher is in a strong position to consider methods of instruction and materials to be used. Often the teacher's greatest skill and experience lies in decision-making in this area. It is where decisions regarding method are made without clarity of objectives that errors occur and pupil failure results. If we do not know where the pupil is going how can we choose a suitable method for getting him there?

It is not the intention here to detail examples of the ways and means by which particular objectives should be achieved. Teachers will have their own ideas about materials and methods. Styles of teaching will inevitably vary but what can be stated is that *all* methods and materials will be more effective when used in conjunction with an appropriate and precise objective.

Using clear objectives need not in any way limit the freedom of the teacher to use *any* approach he feels relevant and effective in achieving a particular objective. Projects, audio-visual aids, drama, creative writing, dance, art, music, and visits can, and should to some extent, be structured to help pupils achieve their objectives. Thus, in a well-organized classroom, with a creative teacher, basic objectives can be dealt with through learning experiences that have additional, broader, enrichment purposes. The important difference, evident on closer examination, is that these activities, experiences, and materials will be being used in a far more purposeful way than is often the case.

One of a host of practical advantages inherent in the statement of objectives in terms of pupil behaviour is the fact that praise and attention can be used with greater accuracy, and consequently to greater effect. This statement probably needs some explanation. Young children particularly *need* adult attention and are usually eager to be praised and approved of by the teacher. Some prefer loud expressive demonstrations of approval, and others prefer subtle and quiet attention. As children vary in the *kind* of attention they enjoy, so too do they differ in the *extent* to which they appear to need it. Whilst some pupils work hard for long periods of time, apparently without encouragement and with minimal contact with an adult, others crave attention and will do almost anything to get it.

All children – even the very young and handicapped – *learn* how to get whatever adult attention they need. Some *learn* that doing their work quietly and well usually leads to the teacher being very pleased. Others *learn* that wandering aimlessly around the classroom (which they might find easier than doing their work well) usually leads to the teacher 'getting them started' – on a one-to-one basis. This learning process has been explained by Skinner (1953) in what has since become known as Reinforcement Theory, which states that a *behaviour which is immediately followed by a desirable consequence is more likely to recur*. Hence, if wandering aimlessly around the classroom is followed by a short period of individual instruction and the pupil finds this pleasurable, he is likely to wander aimlessly around the classroom again in order to get some more individual instruction.

Although each child is different in terms of how much attention he needs and what kind of attention he finds most pleasurable, demonstrations of approval, attention, and praise are undoubtedly the teacher's most potent asset. Why? Quite simply because *she* can decide what her pupils have to do in order to gain her approval. By praising and paying attention to pupils for getting on with their work and making progress, you are increasing the likelihood of these same pupils working hard in the future. Cosy private lessons, for example, should be given to pupils while they are 'on-task' and directly after they have made some progress – not for getting stuck or being 'off-task'. Obviously you still need to help the child who is having difficulties, but *when* you do this is one of the variables which is within your control. Most children with learning difficulties like the teacher to sit with them and help them. It is suggested therefore that the time you choose should be when the child is working and 'on-task'. You will then be rewarding desirable, rather than undesirable behaviour.

There is a real danger that advising teachers to praise progress and pay attention to pupils when they are getting on with their work will sound rather like telling a motorist to release the hand brake before setting off. Is it not rather obvious? Mordock (1975) reported that 'approximately 80 per cent of the typical teacher's behaviour toward her children is negatively orientated'. Four-fifths of a typical teacher's time in the classroom is spent criticizing, moaning, reprimanding, nagging, complaining, and scolding? Well, this was in America, and teachers in the UK are a good deal more positive. Or are they? Regrettably the study, to our knowledge, has not been replicated in this country. Nearly all teachers claim that *of course* they praise good behaviour, work, and effort, but *it is undeniable that we could all make far greater use of praise than we do*. It is particularly important that the pupil with learning difficulties be consistently praised for effort and progress. His progress may be slow and his peers may be a good deal more able, but it is crucial that whatever steps forward are made are recognized and rewarded.

How does the existence of a programme of objectives help the teacher to use praise and attention more accurately? It is known that they are most effective if they occur *immediately* after desirable behaviour. The teacher is in a better position to administer this kind of 'instant' praise if she knows precisely what she wants to see the pupil do. Moreover, if the pupil knows clearly what the teacher requires of him, he is better able to direct his own efforts in the knowledge that these will be duly rewarded. And finally, if the programme is being properly implemented the task which the pupil is set is more likely to bring success within his reach – hence there is no need to surpass his peers or resort to aimless wanderings to win the teacher's attention.

These ideas are developed in more detail in Chapter 7, but it might help to summarize the important points made briefly here. Teacher attention and praise:

(1) Should follow desirable (and not undesirable) behaviour;
(2) Must be of an appropriate kind for each child;
(3) Should occur as soon as possible after the desired behaviour;
(4) Can be used more accurately if clear objectives have been stated.

In dealing with slow-learning children particular care has to be taken when introducing new learning steps. Often such pupils will be content to spend many hours practising skills already acquired in the happy confidence that they are unlikely to run into problems. Pupils will no doubt be recalled who prefer to do page after page of simple addition or subtraction sums, taking great delight in the rows of neat red ticks. It is where steps into the unknown are taken that such children become hesitant and display symptoms of low confidence. At this time it is most valuable for the teacher to have a close rapport with his pupil. A close relationship within which the pupil feels confident and secure can be very supportive when important new learning steps are being taken.

It is important that the teacher so organizes the class that at the point when new learning is being introduced a period of uninterrupted attention can be given. This can present problems, but it must be seen as a matter of priorities. A teacher can only spend so much time with each pupil and the time when this will be most valuable to the child with learning difficulties is when a new learning step is being taken. Ideally it is wise if new learning can be introduced in the early part of the day when the child is likely to be more alert.

Once a new step has been introduced and established, the child's need for the teacher's attention will be reduced and he can be provided with independent activities in order that he can further practise his new-found skill. At this stage help need only be provided occasionally and self-regulating, individualized materials are valuable. A good example is the SRA reading kits in which the pupil works independently on workcards, marking his completed work and recording his own progress. Materials prepared for machines such as tape recorder, language master and synchrofax are also valuable in providing individual practice on newly established objectives. It is also worth stressing that practice will be most efficient in small regular doses, rather than spending long periods on the same activity with a resultant loss of interest.

Since it is a potentially difficult learning situation that is being dealt with, it will usually be necessary to apply different teaching approaches to the achievement of a single objective. Where a method has proved unsuccessful, alternatives will be tried. It is important to be systematic in doing this by keeping dated records of the various methods tried. Examination of this type of data may indicate tendencies which could enable more successful strategies to be applied with the child on subsequent objectives.

The importance of allowing sufficient time for the pupil to practise until he has reached a mastery of the set objective has already been emphasized. This will necessitate a form of classroom organization that allows the child to work individually, at least for a part of each day. The essential rationale of teaching with objectives is that children should move at their own pace, step-by-step through the sequence, not proceeding to the next step until mastery of the former is achieved. One of the most persistent problems associated with teaching children with learning problems is their apparent difficulty in retaining skills and ideas. How often can teachers be heard to say 'He seems to learn it alright one day, but by the next he has completely forgotten'? A useful approach in combating this problem is the idea of *overlearning*, which is defined as the continued practice of a task beyond the point of mastery. In other words, once a pupil has mastered a particular skill, he is less likely to forget it if he is allowed to practise it beyond mastery.

There are lots of everyday examples of overlearning at work. It is quite common for people to learn to drive a car, pass a driving test and then, through lack of practice, forget how to drive. If after passing the test, a person drives regularly for a year or two and then stops driving, the skill is likely to be retained for a longer period. No doubt readers can think of other skills which they have not practised for a long period but which they have not forgotten. Perhaps riding a bicycle or swimming. These are skills which have been overlearnt or practised beyond the point of mastery. Within the context of teaching to objectives, skills learnt are less likely to be lost if regular opportunities are provided for pupils to practise objectives which have already been achieved and performed to a satisfactory standard.

The idea of overlearning has another important advantage. Skills which are learnt beyond the point of mastery are more likely to be generalized to other different situations. Readers may remember, for example, when learning mathematics at school, that adding and subtracting fractions was taught before problems which involve those computational skills were tackled. You may recall that solving problems became easier with an increasing mastery of the computational principles involved. To go back to the example of driving a car. The experienced car driver is more likely to be able to drive a lorry than someone who has barely mastered the skill in a car. Similarly, an arithmetic programme might require a child to count bricks in a box. But ideally, we want the pupil to be able to count milk bottles on a step, coins in a purse, and so on. We now know, therefore, that providing opportunities for overlearning brick counting will help the skill to be generalized to other settings. It should be stressed, however, that teachers should actively seek to provide practice opportunities in alternative contexts and not rely entirely on overlearning techniques.

To sum up, when *teaching to objectives* the following points are important:

(1) Clearly stated objectives need not restrict the teacher's choice of materials and methods, but will make all of these more effective;
(2) Objectives facilitate the more efficient use of reinforcement theory in improving academic skills;
(3) New learning steps should be introduced with great care and time must be allowed for mastery to be achieved before proceeding to a new objective; and
(4) Overlearning aids in retention and generalization.

Record-Keeping

A simple but efficient system of record-keeping is an essential component of an effective teaching programme. It is necessary to note the pupil's progress in attempting to master each objective of the sequence in order that appropriate work can continue to be presented. In keeping a record the teacher is seeking to determine if the pupil can now do something he could not do before instruction began. This is the crucial question, the answer to which indicates to the teacher the extent to which learning has occurred.

Record-keeping is an issue of debate in many schools. Some teachers argue that they have no need to record pupil progress since they are able to keep the relevant information in their heads. In schools where record-keeping is used it may be left to individual teachers to develop their own system. Often records are vague, involving long hours of writing by the teacher, frequently away from the classroom and the events being recorded. It is difficult to decide how much prescriptive value such records provide. The vital question each teacher should ask himself is: 'Do these records help me teach more effectively?'. If the answer is no, there seems little point in continuing with what can be a time-consuming pursuit.

Thus, having spent a great deal of time designing and implementing a teaching programme for the slow-learning pupil, we are seeking a form of recording which is realistic for classroom use and yet provides precise information about the child's progress. In detail such a system should meet *all* of the following criteria:

(1) It should clearly indicate the pupil's competence in each objective of the programme;
(2) It should be possible to record in the classroom at the time when an activity is being observed;
(3) It should provide feedback to the teacher regarding choice of objectives and teaching methods;
(4) It should be meaningful to other professionals wishing to work with the pupil; and, most important,

Name: David   **Date commenced:** 25th September

Teaching goal: To develop the use of some basic sentence structures

Objective	Working on	Mastered	Checked	Comments
1. Uses an identity statement of the form "This is a tree" in response to the question "What is this?"		25th Sept. (assessed)	10th Oct.	
2. Uses the negation of objective (1), i.e. "This is not a tree".	25th Sept	10th Oct.		Lang. Mast. cards introduced 2nd Oct. David is responding v. well.
3. Uses the identity statement "The dog is black" in response to the question "What colour is the dog?"		25th Sept (assessed)	10th Oct.	
4. Uses the negation of objective (3), i.e. "The dog is not black".	12th Oct.	18th Oct.		Lang. Mast. cards used – prefers this to group puppet sessions.
5. Uses an action statement of the form "The boy is running" in response to the question "What is the boy doing?"		25th Sept. (assessed)	19th Oct.	
6. Uses the negation of objective (5), i.e. "The boy is not running".	19th Oct.			Expect rapid progress (i.e. 26th Oct.).

Figure 2   Example of classroom record-keeping

(5) It must provide the teacher with information to help decide what the pupil should work on next.

The designing of a system to meet all of these criteria may seem a tall order, but this is not the case. The addition of a series of headed columns to the programme of objectives provides a form of record-keeping which meets all of the above requirements. The table overleaf shows how this system was operated with David's language programme. There are three columns to be filled in as the pupil progresses:

(1) *Working on.* The date when work on the objective commences is recorded here. This is used to identify points of long-term difficulty.
(2) *Mastered.* This column is dated when the pupil has mastered the objective and, once it has been filled in, indicates that the child can be introduced to the next objective in the sequence.
(3) *Checked.* It is important that a mastery of the objective be maintained, so it is suggested that at some optimum point, perhaps one or two months later, depending upon circumstances, the teacher checks that the pupil can still perform the objective.

These three columns are seen to be an essential minimum. It is crucial that the date is noted when work on an objective is commenced, when it is mastered and when it is checked. Readers might like to add further columns. It has been suggested for example that a note should be made, at the time work is commenced on an objective, of when you would expect to see evidence of achievement. You might prefer two 'check' columns, and you might incorporate space for 'comments' as in the example provided (Figure 2).

As can be seen, such a system, once established, is relatively easy to maintain. The record sheet can be kept with the pupil's books and entries made when progress is observed in the classroom. It is important that dates rather than ticks be used to indicate progress. Only by recording *when* things happen can the teacher ensure that prolonged exposure to difficulty is avoided. Furthermore, dates in the 'mastered' column will serve to remind the teacher of the need to check back on objectives previously acquired.

Further reference must be made at this point to the significance of the feedback loop in the teaching model of Figure 1. It connects 'Record-keeping' to 'Assessment' because the recording of progress in the way that has been described *is*, in fact, an accurate system of on-going assessment. Each time an objective is recorded as being mastered this provides a certain indication that it is time to introduce the child to the next step in the sequence. Obviously, as was said earlier, practice will continue on the mastered objective even while the new step is being taken. Assessment in a one-to-one situation is only necessary when the child is being newly placed on the programme or, perhaps, where a specific area of long-term difficulty is encountered.

This form of record-keeping can be very encouraging for the teacher. In normal circumstances it is almost impossible to detect progress with slow-learning children but recording in this way is a tangible sign of teacher effectiveness and, as such, can be a source of motivation for the teacher. Perhaps even more important, the system can be made meaningful to the pupil. A chart on which the child colours in steps taken along the sequence can easily be designed. For younger children this may take the form of an illustration, such as a picture of balloons in which each balloon represents one objective. When they are all coloured-in the programme has been completed. Charles (1976) recommends that pupils should be encouraged to chart their own progress and quotes evidence that children as young as three and a half may be able to manage their own recording.

A final point can be made concerning records of this type. Information gathered in this way should be meaningful to other adults who may come into contact with the child. It contains no jargon and no subjective opinion or value judgements. Consequently, in addition to their use within the classroom, the records can be made available to the child's parents as a means of explaining what is being attempted and as a meaningful basis for encouraging parental support.

To sum up, *record-keeping* should:

(1) Be realistic in terms of day-to-day classroom use;
(2) Provide a basis for on-going assessment and continued presentation of appropriate work; and
(3) Wherever possible, be kept by the pupil.

Summary

The classroom implementation of a programme of objectives is explained by a teaching model. Careful assessment leads to the choice of appropriate objectives which are then taught in a creative but systematic manner. This approach should lead the slow-learning child to progress successfully at his own pace. The objectives also provide a basis for efficient record-keeping and continual assessment.

Recommended Further Reading

Charles, C. M. (1976). *Individualising Instruction*. Saint Louis: C. V. Mosby.
Includes descriptions of classroom practice involving the use of objectives. Full of theoretically sound, practical suggestions, including assessment and record-keeping.

De Cecco, J. P., and Crawford, W. R. (1974). *The Psychology of Learning and Instruction*, 2nd Edn. Englewood Cliffs: Prentice-Hall.
A theoretical text-book providing a comprehensive account of the psychological implications of using objectives in teaching. For the teacher who wishes to dig deeper into the subject.

Herman, T. M. (1977). *Creating Learning Environments. The Behavioural Approach to Education*. Boston: Allyn and Bacon.
The hard-line behaviourist view.

Lerner, J. W. (1976). *Children with Learning Disabilities*, 2nd Edn. Boston: Houghton Mifflin.
Examines different approaches, including the use of objectives. Contains an excellent account of the various approaches and strategies that can be used in teaching basic subjects to children with learning difficulties.

Meacham, M. L., and Wiesen, A. E. (1974). *Changing Classroom Behaviour*, 2nd Edn. New York: Intext.
The theory and practice of using reinforcement in teaching.

60

Neisworth, J. T., and Smith, R. M. (1973). *Modifying Retarded Behaviour*. Boston: Houghton Mifflin.

Describes with lots of examples the use of reinforcement theory in the classroom to improve academic attainments in slow-learning children.

Smith, R. M. (1974). *Clinical Teaching: Methods of Instruction for the Retarded*. New York: McGraw Hill.

An excellent book which describes a plan for using objectives in the classroom and provides a great deal of information which will help in writing programmes in basic subject areas.

CHAPTER 6

Objectives for Basic Subjects

Chapter Goal: *To provide a wide range of examples of sequences of objectives in basic educational subjects.*

The nuts and bolts of writing, and utilizing teaching programmes using objectives have been presented in earlier chapters. Enough information has been provided, in fact, to enable the reader to write and implement a programme. However, it is one thing to read about, and understand, a logically presented set of classroom techniques and ideas. It is something else to do it; and there is no wholly satisfactory alternative to this experience. Inevitably, the newcomer to this approach will make mistakes, but what is learned through the experience of trying out this approach is not easily acquired from alternative sources such as textbooks and teachers' courses.

The main purpose of this chapter is to try to make the reader's first attempts to plan with, and teach to, objectives a little easier. Our experience of working with teachers, planning programmes in schools and workshops, has consistently indicated that it is easier to adapt and modify an existing programme than it is to start from scratch. Obviously, the extent to which this statement is true varies enormously from programme to programme, and from teacher to teacher. Presented with an existing programme, a teacher might find so many aspects in need of radical modification that there would be little or no saving in time. Nevertheless, in general terms, it is probably true to say that modifying an 'approximately suitable programme' is easier, and less time-consuming, than beginning with a *tabula rasa*. This chapter, therefore, presents over 30 examples of programmes in a variety of subject areas, many of which, in slightly modified form, will hopefully be useful to teachers in planning appropriate activities for children with learning difficulties. Obviously two or three times this number could be provided without any hope of catering for all classroom needs, but it is hoped that the material that follows will help the reader to relate his own teaching requirements to the guidelines presented in earlier chapters.

Where do these programmes come from? They have all actually been used in some kind of educational setting, and their forms have been influenced, to a greater or lesser degree, by all those people who have used them. Most of the programmes are based on curriculum material generated in the project school which is described in Chapter 9. All of the staff at that school have contributed to the development of the material by using the programmes on a daily basis in their classrooms over an extended period, and have provided invaluable practical suggestions for their improvement. A great deal of the material has also been used in a variety of other educational settings, including special schools and units, primary schools, in-service courses and teachers' workshops, and in each case the teachers, speech therapists and other professionals involved have been encouraged to make modifications to suit their own requirements and the needs of the children in their care. The programmes therefore reflect the theoretical orientations and practical experiences of a large number of people with whom, at some time, the authors have had a professional contact.

Adapting a Programme

The programmes that follow are classified in six broad subject areas for ease of reference. These areas are arithmetic, gross motor development, handwriting, language development, reading and spelling, and self-help skills. At the end of each section of programmes there is a list of recommended books and articles which the authors have found useful in producing this, and similar material. Each programme consists of a title, a teaching goal, a sequence of objectives and, in most cases, some brief explanatory notes.

All of the programmes, as they are presented here, need careful scrutiny and some modification before being used in the classroom. If the reader feels that one of these exactly suits the needs of a particular child, each objective should at least be extended to include details of the standard, or level, of performance required. In most cases there will probably be additional, more fundamental, amendments needed. Furthermore, the procedure set out in Chapter 4 for writing a programme carries important in-service training benefits in that it requires considerable thought, discussion, and probably some background reading. These benefits are lost if a programme is just thoughtlessly 'lifted' and used in the classroom without careful scrutiny.

Below is a list of the main points to check if the reader wishes to use one of these programmes with a particular child. We will assume that the subject area selected reflects the child's priority educational need, and that one of the teaching goals is appropriate for the pupil in question.

(1) *Has the pupil already mastered the first one or two objectives?* If not, there is a need for a downward extension to include earlier skills required for entry on to the programme.

(2) *Should the programme be extended upwards?* This is not as critical as (1) because new goals and objectives can be formulated on completion of this programme. Nevertheless, readers may wish to add further items if the pupil has already mastered a number of objectives.

(3) *Do you agree with the orientation taken in the programme and the sequence or order of objectives?* Careful consideration should be given to the sequence. Does your teaching experience and theoretical knowledge of the subject area

lead you to challenge, or disagree with, the order of objectives? Perhaps you feel that an important step has been missed out, or that one or two of the objectives are not essential.

(4) *Does the pupil have any sensory or physical handicap?* If so, some of the objectives may need modification in terms of the sensory modality of the response and the presentation of the task.

(5) *Is the step-size appropriate?* Does your existing impression of the child's rate of learning suggest that a finer breakdown will be required in certain parts of the programme? On the other hand, perhaps the step-size is already too small and some objectives can be omitted.

(6) *What standard of performance is to be required for each objective?* Make sure that each objective is unambiguous – especially if the programme is to be used by more than one adult. This, at least, will mean extending most objectives to include a description of the required standard of performance.

List of Programmes

Arithmetic:

(1) Language of Size and Quantity
(2) Correspondence
(3) Numbers
(4) Addition and Subtraction to 10
(5) Money
(6) Time

Gross Motor Development

(1) Body Parts
(2) Mobility
(3) Balance
(4) Left and Right
(5) Ball Skills

Handwriting

(1) Pencil Control
(2) Visual Discrimination
(3) Posture and Pencil Grip
(4) Copying a Letter
(5) Copying Words and Phrases

Language Development

(1) Attention and Co-operation
(2) Early Receptive Language
(3) Early Expressive Language
(4) Language of Shopping
(5) Opposites, Comparatives, and Superlatives
(6) Describing Relationships

Reading and Spelling

(1) Discriminating Words (Auditory)
(2) Discriminating Words (Visual)
(3) Language Experience
(4) Early Reading Book
(5) Reading with Understanding
(6) Phonics
(7) Spelling

Self-help Skills

(1) Cleanliness
(2) Dressing
(3) Feeding
(4) Toileting

ARITHMETIC 1   LANGUAGE OF SIZE AND QUANTITY

Goal: To teach some important vocabulary concerned with size and quantity.

The importance of language in the development of an understanding of numbers cannot be over-estimated. Very often young children have difficulty because of their limited understanding of key terminology necessary in grouping and comparing groups of objects. Time spent on ensuring mastery of these terms, through structured play and more formal presentation, will undoubtedly provide the slow-learning child with an excellent basis for learning number concepts. The list, of course, should not be regarded as exhaustive.

(1)   Given 2 familiar objects, states that they are *same* or *different* in size;

(2)   Given 2 familiar objects of different size, states which is *big* and which is *little*;

(3)   Given 2 objects of different length, says which is *shorter* and which is *longer*;

(4)   Given 2 objects of different thickness, says which is *thick* and which is *thin*;

(5)   Given 3 similar objects which differ in size, identifies the *biggest* and *littlest*;

(6)   Uses the words *all* and *some* in dealing with a group of familiar objects;

(7)   Uses the words *many* and *few* in describing a pile of familiar objects.

ARITHMETIC 2   CORRESPONDENCE

Goal: To teach skills of comparing sets of objects.

When the child is able to classify groups of objects and therefore to construct sets, he needs to learn how to compare pairs of sets by use of one-to-one correspondence. This will later provide the basis for learning addition and subtraction. In dealing with correspondence we come up against the issue of conservation and reversibility. Conservation is the understanding that the number of objects within a set remains the same even if the objects are re-arranged, while reversibility is the idea that it is possible to restore the objects in a set to their original positions, again without changing the cardinal property. Both concepts require the child to understand that sets do not change in number when their members are spatially re-arranged. These ideas are dealt with in the following programme by the use of two types of pairs of sets: *identical sets*, which have the same number of members in identical spatial arrangements, and *equivalent sets*, which also have the same number of members but with different spatial arrangements.

(1)   Uses the term *set* in describing a collection of objects;
(2)   Constructs a set of familiar objects or toys to a given criteria (e.g. 'Make me a *set* of red bricks');
(3)   Matches 2 presented identical sets containing less than 10 objects by connecting the members with lines (e.g. '*Match* the things in this set to the things in that set');
(4)   Matches 2 presented equivalent sets containing less than 10 objects by connecting the members with lines (e.g. '*Match* the things in this set to the things in that set');
(5)   Distinguishes between identical and non-identical pairs of sets containing less than 10 objects by matching the members (e.g. 'Are these sets *equal* or *not equal*?');
(6)   Distinguishes between equivalent and non-equivalent pairs of sets containing less than 10 objects by matching the members (e.g. 'Are these sets *equal* or *not equal*?');
(7)   Given non-equivalent sets, applies the terms *more than* and *less than* appropriately;
(8)   When asked to make the sets *equal*, does so by supplying additional member(s) to 1 of 2 non-equivalent sets.

ARITHMETIC 3   NUMBERS

Goal: To teach the numbers up to 10.

The child who has had sufficient experience in grouping objects and comparing such groups can be introduced to the notion of numbers by the following programme.

(1)   Points to a set between 1 and 9 when given an oral instruction (e.g. 'Point to a set of 2');

(2)   States cardinal property of sets between 1 and 9 after counting the members;

(3)   Constructs a set between 1 and 9 when given the cardinal property (e.g. 'Make me a set of 8 pencils');

(4)   Copies numerals 1 to 9 from a model;

(5)   Writes numerals 1 to 9 from dictation;

(6)   States the cardinal property of a presented set with no members (i.e. *nought*);

(7)   States the cardinal property of a presented set with 10 members;

(8)   Writes numerals 0–10 in order, from memory.

ARITHMETIC 4   ADDITION AND SUBTRACTION TO 10

Goal: To teach addition and subtraction of numbers up to 10.

In introducing simple computation it has been found useful to deal with addition and subtraction at the same time. Care must be taken to standardize use of terms and it should be noted that important steps are taken first of all using concrete materials, such as cuisenaire rods, and then later without the use of such aids.

(1)   In combining 2 sets of objects to form a larger set, uses the terms *add* and *equals* appropriately;

(2)   Adds sets of 1 to 9 objects orally (totals up to 10);

(3)   Uses the term *take away* when removing objects from a set;

(4)   Subtracts orally from sets of 1 to 9 objects (leaving remainders greater than 1);

(5)   Writes symbols + and = when given their verbal labels;

(6)   Adds sets, using numerals up to 10, in written form and using concrete materials;

(7)   Adds sets, using numerals up to 10, in written form, but without using concrete materials;

(8)   Given the verbal label 'take away' writes the symbol − ;

(9)   Subtracts from sets 1 to 9, using concrete materials and recording the sum in written form;

(10)   Subtracts from sets 1 to 9, without using concrete materials, and records the sum in written form.

ARITHMETIC 5   MONEY

Goal: To teach manipulation of money up to totals of £1.

It is probably advisable to delay the formal teaching of money until the slow-learning child is reasonably conversant with the computation of numbers. Most children will have had contact with coins outside school, and it can be useful to have some coins as an aid to the learning of addition and subtraction, but the problems of dealing with groups of different coins are likely to be more confidently approached when the child has a reasonable competence level in dealing with numbers. The following programme assumes such a level and is intended as a basis for structuring a variety of activities involving the manipulation of money, including classroom shop play.

(1)   States all the numbers up to, and including, 100;

(2)   Counts by 5s and by 10s up to 100;

(3)   Gives instant correct responses for addition and subtraction bonds up to 20;

(4)   When presented with single coins of any denomination, writes down their value, including the 'p' symbol;

(5)   States that 100p = £1;

(6)   Given sufficient coins, makes up any required amount up to £1;

(7)   Given 3 items costing various amounts but with total value less than £1, works out total cost;

(8)   Given totals up to £1, gives appropriate change.

ARITHMETIC 6   TIME

Goal: To teach understanding and use of time.

As with money, telling the time is best delayed until the slow-learning child has achieved certain readiness skills. To appreciate fully the meaning of 'twenty minutes past ten', the child needs to understand the numbers used, the word 'past', that 60 minutes make an hour, that 24 hours make a day and, perhaps most important, he needs to know approximately how long a minute, 20 minutes, an hour and so on, last. The following programme therefore assumes that the child has a reasonable competence in the manipulation of numbers and has had experience to help develop an awareness of the meaning of time.

(1)   States all the numbers up to, and including, 60;

(2)   Counts by 5s up to 60;

(3)   States that the short hand of a clock indicates hours and the long hand minutes;

(4)   Reads aloud times by the hour from a clock;

(5)   Reads aloud times by minutes from a clock;

(6)   States that 60 minutes equals 1 hour;

(7)   Reads aloud times by hours and minutes from a clock;

(8)   Presented with various times on a clock, states whether the minute hand is *to* or *past* the hour;

(9)   Reads aloud times by half and quarter hours;

(10)   Given times and told that they are before or after midday, states whether they are a.m. or p.m.

Recommended Further Reading

Ausubel, D. P., and Robinson, F. G. (1969) *School Learning*. New York: Holt, Rinehart, & Winston.

Pages 85 to 96 analyse important issues in the teaching of arithmetic.

Bryant, P. (1974). *Perception and Understanding in Young Children*. London: Methuen.

Discusses in detail issues of conservation and reversibility and argues that young children may seem inadequate in these areas as a result of their using inappropriate strategies for comparing groups of objects.

Kolstoe, O. P. (1976). *Teaching Educable Mentally Retarded Children*. New York: Holt, Rinehart, & Winston.

Has a useful chapter on arithmetic.

Lerner, J. W. (1976). *Children with Learning Disabilities*, 2nd Edn. Boston: Houghton Mifflin.

Includes suggestions on arithmetic.

Lovell, K. (1961). *The Growth of Basic Mathematical and Scientific Concepts in Children*. London: University of London Press.

An important book.

Resnick, L. B., Wang, M. C., and Kaplan, J. (1973). 'Task Analysis in curriculum design: A hierarchically sequenced introductory mathematics curriculum', *Journal of Applied Behaviour Analysis*, **6**, 4, 679–709.

Provides detailed information for teachers wishing to develop programmes of objectives to do with early number. Well worth getting hold of.

Smith, R. M. (1974). *Clinical Teaching: Methods of Instruction for the Retarded*. New York: McGraw-Hill.

Chapter 9 is essential reading on arithmetic.

Williams, A. A. (1970). *Basic Subjects for the Slow Learner*. London: Methuen.

Contains useful and well-regarded chapters on teaching number to slow learners.

GROSS MOTOR DEVELOPMENT 1   BODY PARTS

Goal: To teach the vocabulary and movement of body parts.

Teachers in primary schools are unlikely to cite gross motor development as being a particular child's most pressing educational need except in very unusual circumstances. It is obviously far more likely that an academic skill would be chosen as the focus of a detailed individual programme. This is not to say, however, that activities of this kind would not be incorporated in the normal school curriculum. In an unmodified form, therefore, this programme is likely to be more useful to the special school teacher working with maybe physically or mentally handicapped children.

(1)   Moves body parts when they are touched;

(2)   Moves body parts when they are pointed at;

(3)   Points to main body parts when given verbal instructions (i.e. 'Point to your ... head, hair, eyes, nose, mouth, ears, neck, shoulders, arms, hands, fingers, thumb, legs, knee, foot, toe, ankle');

(4)   Names the body parts in objective (3) when touched (i.e. 'What's this called?');

(5)   Mirror imitates movements using arms and legs;

(6)   Mirror imitates positions of arms and legs from a diagram.

GROSS MOTOR DEVELOPMENT 2   MOBILITY

Goal: To teach basic mobility skills and related vocabulary.

The notes for Gross Motor Development 1 are also applicable to this programme. It is worth adding, however, that activities of this kind provide an excellent opportunity for language work. This programme, for example, incorporates concepts of spatial relationships (such as over, between, up etc.) so that language can be acquired through experience, and shows how objectives might be used to teach skills from different subject areas during the same activity. The words printed in italics therefore represent an integral part of that objective.

(1) Walks along obstacle course and goes under, over, and between suitable objects (*over, under, between*);
(2) Walks up and down stairs using alternate feet (*up, down*);
(3) Climbs up and down domestic step-ladders;
(4) Runs, changing direction 3 times to go round step-ladders;
(5) Hops 8 times on either foot;
(6) Jumps forward using both feet together, and without falling on landing (*forward*);
(7) Jumps backwards using both feet together, and without falling on landing (*backward*);
(8) Jumps over skipping rope held at each end by other people (minimum ht 12");
(9) Skips independently using a rope.

GROSS MOTOR DEVELOPMENT 3 BALANCE

Goal: To improve balancing skills.

This programme does not, but could, include aspects of language. It is entirely to do with improving balance, and again would only be used with an individual child in a normal primary school under exceptional circumstances.

(1) Stands on tip-toes for a couple of seconds;
(2) Balances on either foot for 4 seconds;
(3) Walks between 2 chalk lines on the floor which are 12" apart and 6' long;
(4) Walks along a PE bench, wide side up;
(5) Walks backwards along the wide side of a PE bench;
(6) Walks along the narrow edge of a PE bench;
(7) Walks backwards along the narrow edge of a PE bench;
(8) Walks along the narrow edge of a PE bench, stepping over an obstacle (i.e. a rope) held 6" over the bench;
(9) Walks along the narrow edge of a PE bench going under an obstacle.

GROSS MOTOR DEVELOPMENT 4   LEFT AND RIGHT

Goal: To teach the use of left and right.

The ability to understand and use the words 'left' and 'right' is an important one. They are words which are used frequently both inside and outside the classroom. Furthermore, many children in special and normal schools have difficulty with left-right discrimination. This programme might therefore be used extensively, as it stands or in a slightly modified form, in various educational settings.

(1) Points to own left and right feet when asked to do so;

(2) Points to own left and right hands, arms, legs, eyes, and ears when asked to do so;

(3) Describes own body parts as being left or right;

(4) States that an object is to the left or right of own body;

(5) Moves to the right or left when given instructions to do so;

(6) Describes other person's body parts as being their left or right when the other person is standing by the side;

(7) Describes other person's body parts as being their left or right when the other person is facing;

(8) States that an object is to the left or right of somebody else facing.

GROSS MOTOR DEVELOPMENT 5   BALL SKILLS

Goal: To teach the throwing and catching of a small ball.

The development of adequacy in recreational skills such as throwing, bouncing, and catching a ball is important in promoting social acceptability. The child who is unable to take part in playground activities because of weakness in these skills is clearly at a disadvantage. This programme can be used to locate particular areas of weakness that can be dealt with during the PE lessons.

(1)   Tosses a large ball using both hands;
(2)   Throws a small ball underarm using one hand;
(3)   Throws a small ball overarm using one hand;
(4)   Catches a large ball using both arms;
(5)   Catches a bean-bag using both hands;
(6)   Catches a small ball using both hands;
(7)   Catches a small ball with one hand;
(8)   Bounces and catches a small ball;
(9)   Bounces a small ball off the wall and catches it.

Recommended Further Reading

Cratty, B. J. (1970). *Perceptual and Motor Development in Infants and Children.* New York: Macmillan.
Reviews the relationship between movement skills and learning problems.
Kephart, N. C. (1971). *The Slow Learner in the Classroom,* 2nd Edn. Columbus: Merrill.
In this much quoted book, Kephart relates problems of learning to the development of motor patterns. Some of the ideas in the book must be regarded as being rather speculative, but nevertheless the suggested activities have some merit.
Lerner, J. W. (1976). *Children with Learning Disabilities,* 2nd Edn. Boston: Houghton Mifflin.
Chapter 8 looks at various theories of perceptual-motor development and will be of particular use to teachers in a special school.
Wedell, K. (1973). *Learning and Perceptuo-Motor Disabilities in Children.* London: Wiley.
Reviews the research on the perceptual and motor development of children.

HANDWRITING 1   PENCIL CONTROL

Goal: To develop and improve pencil control.

A programme of pencil practice activities suitable for children with inadequate pencil control to begin formal handwriting.

(1) Makes vertical, horizontal, and circular marks on large surface using any implement;

(2) Makes vertical, horizontal, and circular marks on paper using a pencil;

(3) Using 2-dimensional letter shapes of the dimensions $3\frac{1}{2}$" (letter size) × $\frac{1}{2}$" (road width), draws a line from × to □ without touching or breaking the sides more than once.

i.e.

(4) Ditto for objective (3) with dimensions 1" (letter size) × $\frac{1}{4}$" (road width);

(5) Copies circle, square, rectangle, and triangle accurately from a model.

HANDWRITING 2   VISUAL DISCRIMINATION

Goal: To teach the skills of visual discrimination required to copy handwriting.

Before being able to copy handwriting accurately, children clearly need to be able to discriminate visually between letters. The activities in this programme are designed to develop the necessary skills of visual discrimination and would probably, with most children, be used alongside the pencil control programme. Objective (1) is intended to teach the pupil to use the words *same* and *different* appropriately as this is essential vocabulary for subsequent objectives in the programme.

(1)   Given pairs of either grossly dissimilar, or identical, familiar objects, states that they are *same* or *different*;

(2)   Points to the letter in a series which is different, when the difference is gross, e.g. p p t p p;

(3)   Points to the letter in a series which is the same as a presented model, when the others are grossly different,
e.g. a {t a t t t;

(4)   Points to the letter in a series which is different, when the difference is fine, i.e. n m n n n;

(5)   Points to the letter in a series which is the same as a presented model, when the others are only slightly dissimilar,
e.g. n {h h h n h;

(6)   Points to the letter in a series which is the same as a presented model, when the others are grossly different, but when the model is withdrawn before the series is presented (i.e. from memory);

(7)   Points to the letter in a series which is the same as a presented model, when the others are only slightly dissimilar, but when the model is widhdrawn before the series is presented (i.e. from memory).

HANDWRITING 3   POSTURE AND PENCIL GRIP

Goal: To teach the correct sitting posture and pencil grip.

This programme is intended for children who have particular difficulty with posture and/or grip, and should not be imposed on pupils whose style differs slightly from that described in the objectives but who nevertheless write comfortably. It is important that pupils are not permitted to overlearn grossly inappropriate posture and grip, and teachers should therefore ensure that these difficulties are resolved before beginning formal handwriting instruction.

(1)   Sits so that the desk top is level with the lower ribs;

(2)   Sits so that the thighs are horizontal, and feet are placed flat on the floor;

(3)   Sits so that the forearms are pivoting on the desk edge and the body is leaning slightly forward;

(4)   Sits so that the eyes are about 10" from the paper;

(5)   Holds the pencil lightly between the thumb, index finger, and middle finger;

(6)   Holds the pencil with almost an inch showing beneath the thumb;

(7)   Holds the pencil at an angle of about 45° to the paper, and pointing roughly along the line of the forearm.

HANDWRITING 4   COPYING A LETTER

Goal: To teach the copying of a single letter (h).

This detailed programme is intended for pupils who are having extreme difficulties with certain letters. Very few children should need such small step-size with more than a few letters. Nevertheless, although this programme deals only with 'h', the format can be adapted to fit any letter. The important point to remember is that each objective should ensure that the pupil successfully completes the letter. That is to say, the letter components are not taught separately and later joined together (i.e. 'l' then 'n' then 'h'). Instead, the pupil is required to complete a half-formed letter (i.e. making 'h' out of 'l'). The programme assumes that pencil control, posture, and pencil grip are adequate, and that the pupil can visually discriminate between similar letters.

(1)   Copies a row of 'h' from 'l' after demonstration, simultaneously saying 'Up, round, and down',

                    h   h   l   l   l   l

          i.e.   Demonstration

(2)   Copies a row of 'h' from 'l' from a model without demonstration, simultaneously saying :'Up, round, and down',

          i.e.   h   l   l   l   l   l

(3)   Writes a row of 'h' from 'l' from memory (i.e. with the model removed before writing is commenced), simultaneously saying, 'Up, round, and down',

          i.e.   l   l   l   l   l   l

(4)   Copies a row of 'h' from a model without demonstration, simultaneously saying, 'Down, up, round, and down',

          i.e.   h   h   h   h   h   h

(5)   Writes a row of 'h' from memory (i.e. with the model removed before writing is commenced), simultaneously saying: 'Down, up, round, and down',

HANDWRITING 5   COPYING WORDS AND PHRASES

Goal: To teach early copy writing.

This is a programme of informal instruction which, with most children, would be used in conjunction with the preceding programme. In other words, the pupil would be engaged in these kinds of activities while receiving more intensive and detailed instruction with individual letters of particular difficulty. Objectives (3) and (4) consist of self-chosen words and can obviously be extended to incorporate more words and phrases, according to the needs of the individual child.

(1)   Copies first name from a model placed directly above;

(2)   Copies surname from a model placed directly above;

(3)   Copies the names of the following familiar objects from a model placed directly above:

Date   *Date*

1. _____   _____   6. _____   _____

2. _____   _____   7. _____   _____

3. _____   _____   8. _____   _____

4. _____   _____   9. _____   _____

5. _____   _____   10. _____   _____

(4)   Copies the following 4–6-word phrases from a model placed anywhere:

Date

1. _____   _____

2. _____   _____

3. _____   _____

4. _____   _____

5. _____   _____

6. _____   _____

7. _____   _____

8. _____   _____

Recommended Further Reading

Dept. of Educ. and Science (1975). *A Language for Life* (The Bullock Report). London: HMSO.
There is a copy of the Bullock Report in most schools. Paragraphs 11.50–11.55 in particular are well worth reading.

Enstrom, E. A. (1968). 'Left-handedness: A course for disability in writing', *Journal of Learning Disabilities*, **1**, 7, 410–414.
An advanced paper which suggests that left-handed pupils should sit together during handwriting practice.

Jones, C. H. (1968). *From Left to Right*. Nuneaton: Autobates L.S. Ltd.
A programme that has been found to be useful in teaching handwriting to ESN(M) children.

Lerner, J. W. (1976). *Children with Learning Disabilities*, 2nd Edn. Boston: Houghton Mifflin.
Pages 253–260 examine important issues in the teaching of handwriting and provide examples of teaching method.

Presland, J. (1970). 'Applied psychology and backwardness in handwriting', *Association of Educational Psychologists Journal*, **2**, (7) Supplement.
A comprehensive and readable discussion of a wide range of practical issues to do with the teaching of handwriting.

Wedell, K. (1973). *Learning and Perceptuo-Motor Disabilities in Children*. London: Wiley.
An authoritative and comprehensive book which includes some useful sections on the teaching of handwriting.

LANGUAGE 1   ATTENTION AND CO-OPERATION

Goal: To teach the pupil to follow the four simple commands 'come here', 'Sit down', 'Hands down', and 'look at me'.

It is extremely unlikely that this programme would be appropriate for any child in a normal school. It represents the very beginnings of receptive language, and could be used extensively with young, mentally handicapped children. The purpose of the programme is simply to teach the pupil to respond appropriately to the four basic commands which are taken from Williams (1973). It is therefore the starting point for further language work in that only when the child is attending can he be taught anything else.

The step-size of this programme is extremely small. Each command is taught in three stages – if necessary at first using physical guidance and then gesture to ensure that the child responds appropriately. This idea is called *prompting* and is discussed further in Chapter 7.

(1)   Responds appropriately to the verbal command 'Come here' when given physical guidance to do so;

(2)   Responds appropriately to the verbal command 'Come here' when given gestured guidance to do so;

(3)   Responds appropriately to the verbal command 'Come here' *without physical or gestured guidance*;

(4)   Responds appropriately to the verbal command 'Come here. ... Sit down' when given physical guidance to do so;

(5)   Responds appropriately to the verbal command 'Come here. ... Sit down' when given gestured guidance to do so;

(6)   Responds appropriately to the verbal command 'Come here' *without physical or gestured guidance*;

(7)   Responds appropriately to the verbal command 'Come here ... Sit down. ... Hands down' when given physical guidance to do so;

(8)   Responds appropriately to the verbal command 'Come here. ... Sit down ... Hands down' when given gestured guidance;

(9)   Responds appropriately to the verbal command 'Come here ... Sit down ... Hands down' *without physical or gestured guidance*;

(10)   Responds appropriately to the verbal command 'Come here ... Sit down ... Hands down. ... Look at me' when given physical guidance;

(11)   Responds appropriately to the verbal command 'Come here ... Sit down. ... Hands down. ... Look at me' when given gestured guidance;

(12)   Responds appropriately to the verbal command 'Come here ... Sit down ... Hands down ... Look at me' *without physical or gestured guidance*.

LANGUAGE 2   EARLY RECEPTIVE LANGUAGE

Goal: To develop an understanding of basic vocabulary.

This programme follows on from Language 1 in so far as it is concerned with receptive language. In each objective the pupil is required to give a motor response to a verbal question or instruction. He is not required to speak – merely to demonstrate his understanding of what is said to him by acting appropriately.

(1)   Points to the following body parts on the command: 'Show me your ...',

	Date			*Date*
i. _ _ _ _ _ _	_ _ _ _	iv. _ _ _ _ _ _	_ _ _ _
ii. _ _ _ _ _ _	_ _ _ _	v. _ _ _ _ _ _	_ _ _ _
iii. _ _ _ _ _ _	_ _ _ _	vi. _ _ _ _ _ _	_ _ _ _

(2)   When shown a set of everyday objects and toys, points to the following on the command: 'Show me the ...',

	Date			*Date*
i. _ _ _ _ _ _	_ _ _ _	iv. _ _ _ _ _ _	_ _ _ _
ii. _ _ _ _ _ _	_ _ _ _	v. _ _ _ _ _ _	_ _ _ _
iii. _ _ _ _ _ _	_ _ _ _	vi. _ _ _ _ _ _	_ _ _ _

(3)   When shown a set of pictures of everyday objects and toys, points to the following on the command: 'Show me the ...',

	Date			*Date*
i. _ _ _ _ _ _	_ _ _ _	v. _ _ _ _ _	_ _ _ _
ii. _ _ _ _ _ _	_ _ _ _	vi. _ _ _ _ _	_ _ _ _
iii. _ _ _ _ _ _	_ _ _ _	vii. _ _ _ _ _	_ _ _ _
iv. _ _ _ _ _ _	_ _ _ _	viii. _ _ _ _ _	_ _ _ _

(4)   Carries out the following one-component verbal instruction *without gestural or facial cue* (i.e. 'Clap your hands', 'Fetch the scissors'),

	Date			*Date*
i. _ _ _ _ _ _	_ _ _ _	ii. _ _ _ _ _ _	_ _ _ _
iii. _ _ _ _ _ _	_ _ _ _	iv. _ _ _ _ _ _	_ _ _ _
v. _ _ _ _ _ _	_ _ _ _	vi. _ _ _ _ _ _	_ _ _ _

(5)   Carries out the following two-component instruction (without cue) i.e. 'Take out your book and find me a picture of a dog'.

		Date
i. _ _ _ _ _ _ _ _ _ _ _ _ _	_ _ _ _
ii. _ _ _ _ _ _ _ _ _ _ _ _ _	_ _ _ _
iii. _ _ _ _ _ _ _ _ _ _ _ _ _	_ _ _ _
iv. _ _ _ _ _ _ _ _ _ _ _ _ _	_ _ _ _
v. _ _ _ _ _ _ _ _ _ _ _ _ _	_ _ _ _
vi. _ _ _ _ _ _ _ _ _ _ _ _ _	_ _ _ _

LANGUAGE 3   EARLY EXPRESSIVE LANGUAGE

Goal: To develop the use of basic expressive vocabulary and simple sentences.

Unlike Language 1 and 2 this programme deals with the early *use* of language, or expressive language, as it is usually called. Readers wishing to adapt and use this programme should try to distinguish between language and speech, i.e. between *what* the pupil is saying (language) and *how* he is saying it (speech/articulation). It is often the case that a child who has a severe speech problem has normal language. If in doubt you should consult a speech therapist. The words given in brackets are felt by most teachers to represent acceptable abreviations.

(1)   Imitates the names of the following self-chosen objects and pictures,

	Date		*Date*		*Date*
i.	_ _ _ _ _ _	ii.	_ _ _ _ _	iii.	_ _ _ _ _ _
iv.	_ _ _ _ _ _	v.	_ _ _ _ _	vi.	_ _ _ _ _
vii.	_ _ _ _ _ _	viii.	_ _ _ _ _	ix	_ _ _ _ _
x.	_ _ _ _ _ _	xi.	_ _ _ _ _	xii.	_ _ _ _

(2)   Names the objects in objective (1) on the question 'What's this?' (i.e. A '*ball*').

(3)   Uses a sentence of the form '*It is (It's) a ball*' in response to the question 'What's this?' with all the objects named in objective (1);

(4)   Using the objects in objective (1) uses a sentence including a negative of the form '*It is not (isn't) a ball*', in response to the question 'Is this a ball?';

(5)   Uses the following self-chosen adjectives in a sentence of the form: 'It is (It's) black' in response to the question 'What's the dog like?'

	Date		*Date*		*Date*
i.	_ _ _ _ _	ii.	_ _ _ _ _	iii.	_ _ _ _ _
iv.	_ _ _ _ _	v.	_ _ _ _ _	vi.	_ _ _ _ _
vii.	_ _ _ _ _	viii.	_ _ _ _ _	ix.	_ _ _ _ _

(6)   Uses the adjectives in objective (5) in a sentence of the form '*The dog is (dog's) black*' in response to the question 'What's the dog like?';

(7)   Uses the adjectives in objective (5) and a negative in a sentence of the form '*This dog is not (isn't) black*', in response to the question 'Which dogs are black?';

(8)   Uses 6 self-chosen verbs in a sentence of the form '*The boy is (boy's) running*' in response to the question 'What's the boy doing?';

(9)   Uses the verbs in objective (8) in a sentence including a negative of the form '*This boy is not (isn't) running*' in response to the question: 'Which boys are running?'.

LANGUAGE 4   LANGUAGE OF SHOPPING

Goal: To teach a basic vocabulary associated with bakers, grocers, and butchers.

This programme might be suitable for either group or class work. It represents a language enrichment approach. That is to say we pick a topic (e.g. shopping) and teach its associated vocabulary (i.e. the 25 words printed in italics). This is a popular approach, easily applied to a wide range of topics, in areas of high social disadvantage where a relatively high proportion of children may have retarded language development. It lends itself to the whole spectrum of teaching methods, and project work associated with these objectives could include number, art, handwriting, and so on.

(1) States 2 things that can be bought at the *bakers* (*bread* and *cakes*);
(2) States 2 ingredients of bread (*yeast* and *flour*);
(3) States that *meat* can be bought at the *butchers*;
(4) Gives the names of 4 different meats (*pork, bacon, beef,* and *lamb*);
(5) States what animals provide pork, bacon, beef, and lamb (*pig, cow,* and *sheep*);
(6) States 2 things that can be bought at the *grocers* (*vegetables* and *fruit*);
(7) Gives the names of at least 4 vegtables (*potatoes, peas, cabbages,* and *carrots*);
(8) *Gives the names of at least 4 fruits (tomatoes, apples, oranges,* and *bananas*).

LANGUAGE 5   OPPOSITES, COMPARATIVES, AND SUPERLATIVES

Goal: To teach the comparatives and superlatives of 'long' and 'short'.

Many children find commonly used opposites, comparatives, and superlatives (like big, bigger, and biggest) difficult to understand and even more difficult to use. They are words which are used frequently in the classroom, and may need to be systematically taught. This programme deals only with the comparatives and superlatives associated with 'long' and 'short', and has a small step-size. However, it can be used, with appropriate word changes and different materials, to teach a wide range of comparatives and superlatives, i.e. soft–hard; hot–cold; old–young; wet–dry; thick–thin; big–small; smooth–rough.

(1)   Given 2 rods of different lengths, points to the appropriate rod when asked 'Which is the *short* rod?';   •

(2)   Given 2 rods of different lengths, points to the appropriate rod when asked 'Which is the *long* rod?';

(3)   Given several rods of different lengths, points to the appropriate rod when asked 'Which rods are *shorter* than this one?;

(4)   Given several rods of different lengths, points to the appropriate rod when asked 'Which rods are *longer* than this one?;

(5)   Given several rods of different lengths, points to the appropriate rod when asked 'Which is the *shortest* rod?';

(6)   Given several rods of different lengths, points to the appropriate rod when asked 'Which is the *longest* rod?';

(7)   Uses the words *short*, *shorter*, and *shortest* in describing rods of different lengths.

(8)   Uses the words *long*, *longer*, and *longest* in describing rods of different lengths.

LANGUAGE 6   DESCRIBING RELATIONSHIPS

Goal :   To teach some specific language skills for describing relationships between objects and people.

This programme, perhaps better than the others, illustrates some of the difficulties of sequencing objectives in language in so far as it is inevitable that the order will not hold true for all children. Its main purpose is to teach children to relationize and articulate relationships between objects and people. Obviously it is intended for older, linguistically more competent children and the relatively sophisticated language skills embedded in these objectives can be extended even further by the introduction of abstract ideas and concepts.

(1)   Uses the word *only* appropriately to describe how one object or person differs from the other members of a set,
i.e. 'This is the only brick which is red'
'Mark is the only boy with brown shoes';

(2)   Uses the words *all*, *some*, and *none* appropriately to describe the characteristics of a set of people or objects,
i.e. 'All of the boys like football'
'Some of the girls are wearing blue skirts'
'None of the bricks are green';

(3)   Uses '*AND-statements*' to describe the dual attributes of a set of people or objects
i.e. 'These bricks are big and red'
'These children are in class 7 and have brown hair';

(4)   Uses '*OR-statements*' to describe a set of people or objects,
i.e. 'These bricks are blue or red'
'These children were naughty in class or were late for school';

(5)   States whether pairs of objects are the *same*, *similar*, or *different*;

(6)   States how similar objects differ by describing or discriminating characteristics,
i.e. Q. 'How is a pen different from a pencil?' A. 'A pencil is made of wood and a pen is not'
Q. 'How is a plate different from a saucer?' A. 'You stand a cup on a saucer but not on a plate';

(7)   States how different objects are alike by describing a common characteristic,
i.e. Q. 'How is a pen like a pencil?' A. 'Both are used for writing'
Q. 'How is a plate like a saucer?' A. 'They are both crockery'.

Recommended Further Reading

Bereiter, C., and Engelmann, S. (1966). *Teaching Disadvantaged Children in the Pre-School*. Engelwood Cliffs; Prentice Hall.
A highly structured approach which emphasizes the 'Language of instruction' and forms the basis of the Distar Lang. Programme (SRA).

Gahagan, D. M., and Gahagan, G. A. (1970). *Talk Reform*. London: Routledge and Kegan Paul.
Some useful suggestions for teaching method in this account of language project carried out in East London infant schools.

Kirk, S. A., and Kirk, W. D. (1971). *Psycholinguistic Learning Disabilities*. Illinois: University of Illinois Press.
An approach which is very different to the one advocated within these pages. Kirk and co-workers have also produced the Illinois Test of Psycholinguistic Abilities (1968).

Shiack, G. M. (1974). *Teach Them to Speak*. London: Ward Lock.
Descriptions of 200 language lessons suitable for use with 4- to 7-year-olds with difficulties in language.

Tough, J. (1976). *Listening to Children Talking*. London: Ward Lock.
This book is based on the Schools Council Project 'Communication Skills in Early Childhood'.

Williams, C. (1973). *A Language Development Programme*. Lea Hospital, Bromsgrove: IMS.
A language programme for young, mentally handicapped children which advocates the use of behaviour modification techniques.

READING 1   DISCRIMINATING WORDS (AUDITORY)

Goal: To teach the auditory discrimination of similar sounding words.

It is important that the child who is about to learn to read has developed an ability to discriminate between similar sounding words. Teachers must, of course, be on the look-out for children who have a hearing loss and in such cases arrange an audiometric examination. This programme can be used to develop efficient discrimination of simple consonant-vowel-consonant words of the type normally found in early reading books. It should be used at the same time as providing instruction in visual discrimination.

(1)   Discriminates between 2 spoken words which differ grossly, by saying *same* or *different*,
e.g. cat–horse, ball–ball, hat–piano;

(2)   Discriminates between 2 spoken words which differ by initial consonants only, by saying *same* or *different*,
e.g. bat–cat, red–bed, tin–tin;

(3)   Discriminates between 2 spoken words which differ by final consonants only, by saying *same* or *different*,
e.g. tub–tug, pen–pen, sad–sat;

(4)   Discriminates between 2 spoken words which differ by medial vowels only, by saying *same* or *different*,
e.g. bag–big, tan–ten, not–not;

(5)   Recognizes a sound in a series of words, where the given sound is an initial consonant,
e.g. 'Raise your hand when you hear a word that starts with b – sat, mat, bat';

(6)   Recognizes a sound in a series of words, where the given sound is a final consonant;

(7)   Recognizes a sound in a series of words, where the given sound is a medial vowel;

(8)   Given a sound, provides words that begin with that sound,
e.g. 'Tell me words that begin with t';

(9)   Given a series of rhyming words, supplies new words,
e.g. 'cat, bat, sat, _____, _____'.

READING 2   DISCRIMINATING WORDS (VISUAL)

Goal: To teach the visual discrimination of similar looking words.

Ability to distinguish between individual letters and individual words is again crucial to success in learning to read. As with hearing, teachers must look out for children with visual abnormalities. It should be noted that, unlike many commercial reading readiness schemes, this programme focuses on the discrimination of letters and words rather than on pictures and geometric shapes. There is no evidence to support the view that skill in these latter tasks helps the child in learning to read.

(1)   Points to the letter in a series which is different when the difference is gross;

(2)   Points to the letter in a series which is the same as a presented model, when the others are grossly different;

(3)   Points to the letter in a series which is different when the difference is fine;

(4)   Points to the letter in a series which is the same as a presented model, when the others in the list are only slightly dissimilar;

(5)   Points to a word in a series which is different when the difference is gross;

(6)   Points to a word in a series which is the same as a presented model, when the others are grossly different;

(7)   Points to a word in a series which is different when the difference is fine;

(8)   Points to a word in a series which is the same as a presented model, when the others are only slightly dissimilar.

READING 3   LANGUAGE EXPERIENCE

Goal: To develop a sight vocabulary of words chosen by the pupil.

Although no one system of teaching reading will succeed with all children, the language-experience approach (Carrillo, 1972) is very useful, particularly with children who have poor language development. The approach demands that reading is made a meaningful process and that children develop an understanding of its purpose. They need to learn that the spoken word can be written and that the written word can be read. There is a need, therefore, to establish a close relationship between instruction in reading, writing, and spelling. The language-experience approach, probably better than any other, helps to develop an appreciation of purpose by having the child (i) talk about a subject of his choice, (ii) either write about it or watch the teacher write what he says, and then, (iii) read it. The following simple programme ensures the necessary sequence – experience/language/writing/reading. The child dictates to the teacher a simply story or account of some personal experience and then:

(1)   Copies the sentence from a model directly above;
(2)   Presented with the sentence and a related picture drawn by himself, reads aloud the sentence;
(3)   Reads aloud the sentence without being able to see the picture;
(4)   Reads each word of the sentence when presented in isolation on flash cards;
(5)   Writes the sentence from dictation, spelling each word correctly.

READING 4   EARLY READING BOOK

Goal: To teach the reading of a simple reading book.

When the young, slow-learning child is put on to the first reading scheme, it is important that care be taken to ensure success. This programme can be used with an early reader from any of the normal classroom schemes. It is essential that all the objectives should be complete *before* the child moves on to the next book in the series. It has been found to be useful not to let the child have the actual reading book until he has mastered objectives (1) to (4). Thus, by the time he is given the book, he is able to read it without any difficulty.

(1) Given words from the book, uses them in appropriate, spoken sentences, i.e. 'Give me a sentence with _____ in it';

(2) Presented with the sentences from the book on cards with related illustrations, reads aloud the sentences;

(3) Presented with the sentences from the book on cards in isolation, reads aloud the sentences;

(4) Reads aloud the words from individually presented flash cards;

(5) Reads aloud the book fluently, without error or omission;

(6) Answers oral questions about the factual content of the book;

(7) Writes the words from the book from dictation, spelling them correctly.

READING 5   READING WITH UNDERSTANDING

Goal: To teach reading with understanding.

Once the child has made a start in reading and goes on to more complex written material, it is important to monitor carefully his understanding of what he reads. Skill in reading comprehension will aid the pupil to predict the probable next word in a sentence. This sequence of objectives can be applied to books from any reading scheme or individual library books. Objective (2) is an excellent procedure for determining the appropriateness of the level of language in the book for a particular child.

(1)   States appropriate meanings for important vocabulary in the book;
(2)   Given sections of the book read aloud to him, but with every tenth word omitted, guesses appropriately the missing words;
(3)   Reads aloud important new words from the book when presented in isolation;
(4)   Reads the book fluently;
(5)   Writes the words in objective (3) from dictation, spelling them correctly;
(6)   Answers oral questions about facts, events, and details in the story;
(7)   Relates the sequence of events in the story;
(8)   States the main idea of the book.

READING 6   PHONICS

Goal: To teach some phonic skills.

The importance of phonics in early reading is a matter of dispute amongst teachers. It cannot be denied that *some* knowledge of phonics is necessary if the child is to have available efficient word attack strategies. Thus, for example, where a child predicts the likely word in a sentence by using context cues, a knowledge of letter sounds and certain basic phonic rules may help him to determine the exact word. No doubt, some readers will question the suggested order in this sequence of objectives.

(1) Presented with consonant-vowel combination, e.g. ba_, adds suitable consonants to make new words;

(2) Presented with initial and final consonants, e.g. d_g, adds suitable vowels to make new words;

(3) Presented with vowel-consonant combinations, e.g. _in, adds suitable consonants to make new words;

(4) Reads aloud isolated words with common, initial digraphs, i.e. sh_ wh_ qu_ ch_

(5) Reads aloud isolated words with common, initial consonant blends, i.e. bl_, br_, sc_, cl_, cr_, sm_, fl_, dr_, sn_, gl_, fr_, sp_, pl_, gr_, st_, sl_, pr_, sw_, tw_, tr_;

(6) Reads aloud isolated words with common, final consonant blends, i.e. _ck, _ct, _ft, _mp, _nd, _ng, _nt;

(7) Reads aloud isolated words with common, vowel digraphs, i.e. _oo_, _ee_, _ea_, _ai_, _oa_.

READING 7   SPELLING

Goal: To teach the spelling of a target word.

In some of the earlier reading programmes, spelling of new words has been indicated by one of the later objectives in the sequence. Obviously the child's spelling level will be some way behind his reading level. This programme can be used to teach an important word (i.e. address) with which the child is having particular and long-term difficulty. *Objective (4) should be followed by four more objectives in which a further letter is deleted at each step. Thus, the number of objectives in a sequence of this kind will depend upon the number of letters in the target word.

(1)   Uses the target word in an appropriate oral sentence;

(2)   Reads aloud the target word from a flash card;

(3)   After looking at the word and then removing it from sight, fills in the missing final letter of the word, i.e. schoo_;

*(4)   After looking at the word and then removing it from sight, fills in the missing final two letters of the word, i.e. scho__;

(7)   After looking at the word and then removing it from sight, writes the whole word, i.e. _____;

(8)   Writes the word from dictation, spelling it correctly.

Recommended Further Reading

Carrillo, L. W. (1972). 'The language-experience approach to the teaching of reading' in Melnik, A. and Merritt, J. (1972). *Reading: Today and Tomorrow*, London: University of London Press.

One of a number of important articles in this book.

Dean, J., and Nichols, R. (1974). *Framework for Reading*. London: Evans.

A useful reference book on teaching methods. Includes some interesting tick-lists.

Dept. of Educ. and Science (1975). *A Language for Life* (The Bullock Report). London, HMSO.

Essential reading for anybody concerned with the teaching of reading.

Pflaum, S. W. (1974). *The Development of Language and Reading in the Young Child*. Ohio: Bell and Howell.

A very useful reference book, relating research evidence to classroom practice.

Reid, J. F. (1972). *Reading: Problems and Practices*. London: Ward Lock.

A selection of articles about reading difficulties.

Smith, E. P. (1977). *A Technology of Reading and Writing. Volume 3: The Adaptive Classroom*. New York: Academic Press.

Excellent examples of how research findings can be applied to classroom practice.

Smith, F. (1973). *Psycholinguistics and Reading*. New York: Holt, Rhinehart, & Winston.

An important book which includes a particularly thought-provoking chapter on the use of phonics.

SELF-HELP SKILLS 1   CLEANLINESS

Goal: To teach basic cleanliness skills.

The four programmes in this subject area are likely to be most useful in nursery, infant, and special schools of various kinds. They can be used with groups of children as well as individuals. Self-help skills usually occupy a prominent place in the curriculum with young, mentally handicapped children, and it is conceivable that for such children step-size may need to be reduced even further.

(1)   Co-operates when being washed;
(2)   Washes hands without help;
(3)   Washes and dries hands independently;
(4)   Washes face (but has to have ears and neck washed);
(5)   Washes face, ears, and neck satisfactorily;
(6)   Washes and dries face, ears, and neck satisfactorily and independently;
(7)   Combines hot and cold water to an appropriate temperature;
(8)   Brushes teeth given a brush with toothpaste on it;
(9)   Uses a toothbrush and tube of toothpaste satisfactorily and independently.

SELF-HELP SKILLS 2   DRESSING

Goal: To teach basic dressing skills.

(1) Helps actively to undress;
(2) Helps actively to dress;
(3) Takes off the following articles of clothing excluding difficult fastenings: – socks pants jumper coat;
(4) Puts on the following articles of clothing excluding difficult fastenings: – socks pants jumper coat;
(5) a. Undoes zip fastening,
    b. Does up zip fastening;
(6) a. Undoes button fastening,
    b. Does up button fastening;
(7) a. Undoes lace fastening.
    b. Does up lace fastening.

SELF-HELP SKILLS 3   FEEDING

Goal: To teach the appropriate use of spoon, knife, and fork.

(1)   Feeds self with spoon but spills a lot;
(2)   Feeds self with spoon only occasionally spilling;
(3)   Uses fork appropriately when feeding;
(4)   Feeds self with spoon and fork together;
(5)   Uses spoon to sugar and stir tea or coffee;
(6)   Uses knife to spread jam or butter;
(7)   Uses knife to cut bread or meat;
(8)   Feeds self with knife and fork together.

SELF-HELP SKILLS 4   TOILETING

Goal: To teach the independent and appropriate use of the toilet.

(1)   Indicates to the teacher when wet or soiled;
(2)   Sits on the toilet willingly for a few minutes;
(3)   Uses the toilet when put on it;
(4)   Indicates to the teacher the need for the toilet (with occasional accidents);
(5)   Takes down pants and uses the toilet when taken;
(6)   Cleans him/herself satisfactorily after using the toilet;
(7)   Pulls up pants and tucks in shirt after using the toilet;
(8)   Flushes the toilet after use;
(9)   Indicates the need for the toilet with infrequent accident and completes the whole task in the presence of the teacher;
(10)   Indicates the need for the toilet without accident, and completes the whole task independently.

Recommended Further Reading

Azrin, N. H., and Foxx, R. M. (1978). *Toilet Training the Retarded*. Champaign, Ill.: Research Press.

A comprehensive tome including all the work of Azrin *et al.* in the treatment of eneuresis.

Baker, B. L., Brightman, E. J., Heipetz, L. J., and Murphy, D. M. (1978). *Steps to Independence: Basic and Intermediate Self-Help Skills*, (2 vols). Barnstaple: Chelfham Pub.

Comprehensive volumes on teaching self-help skills to mentally handicapped children.

CHAPTER 7

Hypothesis-testing Teaching

Chapter Goal: *To describe how the objectives approach can be developed as a basis for hypothesis-testing in special schools and units.*

There is a growing commitment to the view that handicapped children should be educated in normal school whenever practicable (DES, 1978). This development in special education is borne out of an increasing awareness of the dangers and disadvantages of segregated special schools, which are discussed in detail in Chapter 9. It is perhaps most significant that handicapped children *are* being educated in normal schools more and more throughout the country, and there can be no doubt that the trend will continue. We have been particularly conscious of this development in writing this book in so far as it is intended for teachers who teach children with problems in learning – wherever they may be. Teachers in normal schools will probably find the techniques and ideas so far described useful in planning appropriate programmes of work for the child or children in their class who have such difficulties. The first six chapters in fact were written with the normal school classteacher in mind.

The reintegration of handicapped children into normal schools of course can only go so far. There will always be those who need more intensive help than can be provided in the normal classroom, and for such children there will continue to be some form of segregated or partially segregated provision. The emphasis in this chapter, therefore, is shifted in so far as it is intended to be of particular relevance to the 'specialist' – the person whose job is primarily to do with pupils who have learning problems which cannot be dealt with in the normal classroom. We have in mind special school teachers and those who teach in special classes or units in normal schools particularly, but advisers, psychologists, and specialists helping individual children on a referral basis might also find it helpful. This shift in emphasis is manifested most obviously in two ways: (i) The approach outlined in earlier chapters is taken further to incorporate more sophisticated and advanced ideas and techniques, and, (ii) Many of the situations and suggestions described require small teaching groups and flexible time-tabling arrangements. Nevertheless, the normal school classteacher should find a great deal of interest in this chapter, and a number of ideas which are entirely applicable in the normal classroom.

It was once said that some 'special' schools and units are special only because 'the classes are smaller and the children have to travel long distances to get there'. It suits our purpose here to be appropriately outraged by this suggestion, and we will therefore proceed on the assumption that they are special schools because sophisticated teaching methods and techniques are used in them. In other words, we will assume that the small, flexible teaching groups are a means to an end, and not an end in themselves. The procedures described here require a lot of thought, a good deal of special knowledge, careful planning and record-keeping, and a willingness on the part of the teacher to work hard both inside and outside the classroom. In fact, it is the kind of system which should be operated in a special school or unit if it is 'special' in more than name only.

A crucial aspect of the objectives approach is that it focuses attention on aspects of a learning problem which are within the teacher's control, and this is a consistent feature of previous chapters. The *only* thing which the teacher has complete control over is her own behaviour, and consequently the emphasis is on what *she can do in the classroom*. Variables such as social history, brain damage and IQ are either largely, or completely, *outside* the teacher's control, therefore give us no specific indication of how the problem might be overcome, and are deemphasized accordingly. To take the approach further we need a means of systematically manipulating the variables under her direct influence. There follows a detailed description of a procedure which is intended to meet this end.

This procedure might be used with a pupil who, despite detailed planning and carefully prepared teaching sessions, is making particularly slow progress on a programme. However, it need not necessarily be seen as a first aid kit to be used only when things are going wrong. It is a natural extension of the ideas presented in earlier chapters and is therefore an integral part of the objectives approach. The procedure has five stages and *might be discontinued at any of these beyond the first*.

1. *What is the problem?* We begin with the assumption that a learning problem must be defined before it can be resolved, and discuss methods of problem-definition.

2. *Would any other teaching methods or materials work better?* Given a clear definition of the problem, a framework is presented within which aspects of classroom organization, materials, and teaching methods can be manipulated with the aim of optimizing learning conditions for the pupil.

3. *Have preceding objectives in the sequence been mastered?* If the problem persists, the programme records are checked to ensure that all objectives which precede the 'problem' objective are *recorded* as mastered.

4. *Are the pupil's programme records correct?* If all objectives which precede the 'problem' objective are recorded as mastered, these are checked with the pupil to ensure that they are still intact.

5. *Modifying the programme.* Finally, *if* all objectives which precede the 'problem' objective can still be performed to the required standard, it is assumed that the programme needs to be modified in some way, and we discuss some of the issues involved in further detail.

It is suggested that this procedure provides a framework within which variables directly within the teacher's control can be manipulated to the pupil's best advantage. The remainder of this chapter is devoted to a detailed discussion of each stage of this procedure.

There are two important points to be made at this stage. First of all, readers will recall that Chapter 4 was concerned solely with writing clear programmes in terms of observable pupil behaviour. In Chapter 5, however, in the section on assessment, guidelines are presented for writing complete and unambiguous objectives. These describe not only what the pupil is expected to do, but also the conditions under which he is expected to do it and how good his performance is expected to be. Without details of all three components, namely the behaviour, the conditions, and the performance levels, ambiguities and anomalies will arise, and accurate assessment in particular becomes impossible. *It is therefore assumed throughout this chapter that the programmes being used consist of complete objectives.*

Secondly, attention is drawn elsewhere to the idea of considering a teaching programme as a hypothesis in the sense that it is an assumption in default of knowledge. We can rarely be certain that a programme, no matter how carefully it has been written, represents the most efficient means of teaching a particular pupil a certain skill. We can merely speculate on the basis of whatever theoretical and practical knowledge is available. The hypothesis, once formulated, should be tested. Consequently, implementing the programme can be seen as a means of finding out whether your speculations about step-size, the order of objectives and so on, in fact lead the pupil successfully through the steps to the target objective. It must be emphasized that even though the programme has been used in the classroom and the pupil has not reached the target, we are *not* yet ready to abandon the hypothesis. There are a number of checks to be made and ideas to try out before resorting to any wholesale modification of the programme itself.

STAGE 1: WHAT IS THE PROBLEM?

A problem that has not been defined cannot be resolved – except by accident. Lamenting 'insoluble' classroom problems in terms of hackneyed clichés such as 'In all my years of teaching I have never known a slower child ... I just cannot get through to him ... He doesn't seem to be able to remember anything ... It's as if he has a complete blockage, etc.' will generate no detailed practical solution. Probably the only thing that such statements might achieve is to destroy the morale of all those who deal with the pupil in question. In order to know *in detail* what to do about a problem, you need to know *in detail* what the problem is.

Before describing an objectives approach to problem definition it might be interesting to look again at Peter Blakey, whose problems were considered in Chapters 1 and 2. A number of outside agencies were consulted, and readers may have noted that only *specific* questions were answered *specifically*. For example, the medical officer was asked whether Peter had a hearing loss, the psychologist was asked about school placement, and the speech therapist was asked about his suitability for regular speech therapy. Each of these questions was answered unambiguously. For the rest, however, advice given to the school tended to be general and rather vague. One of the main reasons for this failure to provide detailed practical support was the absence of any precise problem definition. In fact, the advice given was as precise as the questions asked.

Let us take an example to show how this difficulty might be overcome using familiar techniques and ideas. A four-year-old boy was admitted to a special nursery because of his poor expressive language. The teacher adapted Language Programme (3) from Chapter 6 as a basis for short, daily teaching sessions to be given by herself and her nursery assistant. The programme used was a follows:

Goal: To develop the use of a basic expressive vocabulary and simple sentences.

1. Imitates the names of each of the following objects or pictures on 3 consecutive days: car, bike, boat, door, chair, fire, ball, book, Mummy, Daddy, Stephen, doll, house, bed, dog, cup, hat, tree, sweet, cat, bat, sock, shoe, head, leg, hand, foot, clock, spoon, fork;
2. Names each of the objects or pictures in objective (1) on the question 'What is this?' on 3 consecutive days;
3. Uses a sentence of the form 'It is a ball' in response to the question 'What is this?' with all objects or pictures named in objective (1) on 3 consecutive days.

An assessment showed that the boy could imitate 6 out of the 32 words in objective (1), and name 4 of these in objective (2). After eight or nine weeks, objective (1) had been completely mastered, and he could name 28 out of 32 objects in objective (2). During this period the child appeared to enjoy the work and his mother, who was helping with a five-minute practice session each evening, was delighted with his progress. Work had also been started on objective (3) but with virtually no success. Almost three weeks had gone by and the child was clearly having considerable difficulties in extending his verbalizations beyond one-word responses.

Here the problem is defined quite clearly. The boy was able to imitate several (32) words and produce single-word responses to simple questions (28). Progress in both these skills was encouraging. The problem is: How do we extend 'cup' to 'It is a cup' or even 'It's a cup'? The problem is still there, of course, but we now know exactly what it is, and we can go about working out a solution. Quite simply, without clear problem definition, detailed practical solutions are unattainable, and certainly the procedure which follows is impossible.

Problem definition to this degree of specificity is often a considerable advance on existing classroom practice. However, many of the suggestions described later in this chapter require even more detail. With difficult problems it is often necessary to record *every* classroom activity which is related to the programme. This need not be as tiresome and laborious as it may sound. A standard form (see Figure 3) can be developed and duplicated for this purpose which requires only a brief entry after each session. The entries in this example are related to the four-year-old's language programme, and take only *one* minute to make. Over a period of time a *very* accurate picture of progress is built up, and areas of difficulty are pinpointed quickly and accurately. The nature of the information recorded in 'Description of Activity' will vary from programme to programme as will be seen more clearly later, and it should also be stressed that this kind of recording would normally supplement *and not replace* the usual programme records.

Date	Time	Objective	Description of activity	Quality of performance
2.10.78	11.10–11.30	1	*Pract*: 'car', 'bike', 'house' (Picts) *Taught*: 'bed', 'chair', 'sock' (Picts)	'Sock' poor
3.10.78	9.30–9.35	1	*Pract*: 'bed', 'chair', 'sock'	'Sock' still poor
4.10.78	11.10–11.20	1	*Pract*: 'car', 'bike', 'house', 'bed' 'chair', 'Mummy', 'Daddy', 'sock'	'Sock' better

Figure 3   Supplementary record-keeping

STAGE 2: WOULD ANY OTHER CLASSROOM ORGANIZATION OR TEACHING METHOD WORK BETTER?

Having got this far in the procedure we have made a small but significant forward step. We have a clearly defined problem expressed in terms of where in a programme of objectives a pupil is faltering. What else can be done? On the simplest level advice can now be sought within a precise frame of reference. The four-year-old's teacher, for example, is looking for new methods of extending his one-word responses to short sentences. The discussion on teaching method now has a precise and meaningful basis, and advice can be sought purposefully both inside and outside the school. We have mentioned the possibility of inviting suggestions from colleagues. In addition there are likely to be people working within your local authority whose specialist interest is related to your problem. Nothing radically new is being proposed here. Teachers already exchange ideas about methods and resources in situations ranging from the informality of the staffroom to organized meetings, case conferences, and exhibitions of resources. All that has so far been suggested is that this process can be made more efficient if advice is sought for a specific purpose, and with a precise definition of the problem.

In Chapter 5 various issues were discussed in the section on teaching methods, including the use of praise and rewards, and the importance of clear and consistent instructions. In order to take these ideas further we need a simple means of classifying teaching methods variables so that they can be considered more thoughtfully and systematically. There are basically two categories of teaching method variables.

1.   What the teacher does, and the classroom conditions which she creates, *before* the pupil is required to respond

For example, the teacher needs to decide upon the time of day the pupil is to be taught, the frequency and duration of the teaching and practice sessions, where in the classroom he is to be taught, what materials are to be used and the instructions which are to be given. All of these variables may have a considerable influence on how well the pupil responds, and all are *pre-response classroom conditions*. In other words we want to create a situation which is most likely to get the best possible performance out of the pupil.

2. What happens to the pupil *after*, and as a result of, his response

For example, the child may be praised or scolded, cheered or jeered by his classmates, or ignored. He might be given accurate and immediate feedback on his performance and he might be required to record his progress on a wall chart. All of these things, over which the teacher has considerable (although incomplete) control, happen to the pupil after he has responded, i.e. *post-response classroom conditions*, and all are likely to have some influence on his performance.

This idea of thinking in terms of pre-response and post-response variables is not a new one. Behavioural psychologists, for example, use the terms '*antecedents*' and '*consequences*' to describe conditions and events which occur *before* and *after* a particular behaviour, respectively. This same idea prompted Smith (1974), in a discussion on the problems of 'motivating' the 'reluctant learner', to say: 'Children cannot be motivated. They can be stimulated and appropriately rewarded'. In other words, Smith is suggesting that the level of a child's 'internal motivation' cannot be directly influenced. We cannot send him for an operation or for special treatment which will render him more 'motivated' when he returns to school. All that the teacher can do is to 'stimulate' him by creating a situation which is likely to capture his attention and interest, and then 'reward' him for his efforts and achievements. That is to say, we can manipulate pre-response and post-response classroom variables to the pupil's best advantage. This idea can be illustrated by Figure 4.

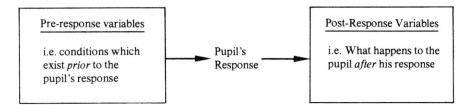

Figure 4   A classification of teaching method variables

During the next few pages we will describe a number of variables from these two categories. It is hoped that this simple classification will help the reader to consider more carefully the wide range of variables which can be manipulated at this stage in the procedure. Remember, we are at the point of having a clear problem definition, we know which objective is causing the problem and we are seeking ways of optimizing both pre-response and post-response classroom conditions in order to help the pupil overcome his difficulty.

1. Pre-response Variables

1(i)   Where is the best place to teach?

Imitating or *modelling* is an essential learning skill. Speech, for example, could not be acquired without imitation of models. In fact, a child who is particularly poor at imitation will have considerable difficulties in learning any but the most basic skills. The importance of modelling in making new learning steps, and consolidating skills which have already been acquired, has considerable implications for the teacher. She must ensure that a good model is made available for the pupil to imitate, both from an adult when a new learning step is being made, and ideally from other children in close proximity when the skill is being practised.

Take as an example the pupil who is having difficulties with handwriting. It may be that he is prone to using an unsuitable grip, perhaps grasping the pencil in the palm despite persistent efforts by the teacher to have him hold the pencil properly. It could well be that the time spent by the teacher on this problem is being wasted because the child in question spends most of each day imitating his workmate whose pencil grip is not much better than his own. A similar example might be the left-handed child who needs to learn a slightly modified grip to the right-hander so that he can see what he is writing. If a left-handed pupil models a right-handed pupil, all kinds of problems might subsequently emerge, and therefore it is advisable to have left-handed pupils sitting together for handwriting practice.

Slow-learning children are often described as having 'poor concentration' or a 'short attention span'. This may be so, but it should be emphasized that the length of time for which a child will attend, whether slow-learning or not, is usually a function of the kind of activity in which he is required to engage. In other words, with most children attention span is not fixed, but depends largely upon what the activity is, and whether it is perceived by the pupil as interesting or in some other way rewarding. Nevertheless, for whatever reasons, children with learning difficulties are usually more easily distracted. It might therefore be that the classroom can be better arranged in order to reduce extraneous distractions. This should not be interpreted as a proposal that walls should be bared and classrooms divided into small hardboard cubicles. Rather, there might be a case (wherever possible) for a part of the classroom to be set aside for individualized or small group instruction in which the general noise and distraction levels are lower than in the remainder of the classroom. Such an area, preferably away from doors and large windows, can be used when important new learning steps are being taken or in the kind of situation described above in which a pupil is having difficulties with a particular part of a programme.

The point has been made that *where* the pupil is taught may have a considerable bearing on how much is learnt, and clearly this is one pre-response variable which the teacher can quite easily manipulate. This suggestion, however, should be tempered by a word of warning. Continual rearrangements of furniture and groupings can in itself be particularly distracting. Experienced teachers will testify that major organizational changes in the classroom are usually followed by a period of high distractability as the children become accustomed to their modified environment. Changes should therefore be made infrequently and with very good reason. Furthermore, changes of working groups or seating positions that *are* necessary should be made in a standard manner which the children have been taught, and wherever possible should be made on a regular basis each school day. Changes within the class are likely to be less traumatic if they are conducted in a routine way.

1(ii)   When is the best time to teach?

The problem of children with learning difficulties seemingly being able to attend to a single activity for only limited periods has further implications for the teacher and identifies another pre-response variable which can be manipulated in the classroom. *When* children are taught can have a crucial bearing on how much learning occurs. For example, the experienced teacher would never attempt to teach a new skill or try to overcome a particularly difficult learning problem late in the school day when the pupil (and probably also the teacher) is tired. She would wait until the child is fresh and alert, and consequently more likely to attend for longer periods.

This simple principle can be developed further. Young children particularly, function better in the morning than the afternoon. Most special school teachers (and their colleagues in primary schools for that matter) tend to do most of their teaching of basic subjects in the morning, therefore, and organize less demanding, informal activities for the afternoons. Beyond this generalization, it is quite often the case that children have particular times of the day when they function best of all. It is not unusual to hear comments like 'Carol is at her best between morning break and lunch'. Before that she is presumably still waking up and after that falling back to sleep. If Carol was making no progress on her programme, the hour between morning break and lunch would be the time to tackle her most severe difficulties.

One of the ways in which home environment *can* have a direct bearing upon classroom activity is where children arrive at school from some kind of unhappy home situation. Experienced teachers will probably recall children arriving in the morning obviously in a distraught mood because of difficulties they have experienced before setting out for school. Frequently children from disadvantaged homes come to school having gone to bed very late, having had disturbed sleep because of overcrowding and, even, having had no breakfast. It is sad to relate that in the late 1970s such situations are not uncommon and teachers, particularly those working in deprived areas, are used to making allowances for them. As a rather extreme example, a Portuguese teacher recently told of her experience working in a very deprived rural district, during which it was quite common to have to deal with children who had had nothing for breakfast other than stong, crude red wine. During the early morning lessons these children had considerable difficulties in focusing their attention.

A related issue concerns whether or not 'distributed' practice is more efficient than 'massed' practice. In other words, are four ten-minute teaching or practice sessions more likely to facilitate learning than one forty-minute session? In general terms, short frequent sessions are known to be more effective than long infrequent sessions, but this is one of those 'rules' that has a number of exceptions. The development of computational skills in number work, for example, is thought to be facilitated by long rather than short sessions. Nevertheless, the important point to be made is that children with learning difficulties usually *are* easily distracted, and it is therefore probably true that they will usually learn more efficiently if teaching and practice sessions are kept short, made interesting, involve the learner's active participation, and occur frequently. This is particularly the case when young children are taking new learning steps – short regular doses invariably work best.

1(iii)   Which is the best way to present the task?

It is very easy to assume that children understand words which are, in fact, unfamiliar to them. Just how easy this is can be seen in the majority of classrooms on most days. The classteacher gives an instruction to the class which seems simple enough to her. Most of the children may follow her command, but invariably there is at least one who waits for the others to begin before he is able to commence. We once watched a group of five- to seven-year-old ESN children during PE – apparently following the teacher's commands to climb 'over' the box, 'through' the beams, 'under' the rope and so on. It was later discovered that more than half the children understood *none* of the important spatial concepts used in the lesson. They had been 'following the leader'. Great care should therefore be taken to ensure that the pupil understands precisely what is required of him. Keep the instruction as short and as simple as possible. And when a new learning step is being taken, use the *same* instruction until the skill is established.

Another important point to do with presenting a task is to emphasize accuracy at the expense of speed. It is crucial, especially in subjects like arithmetic in which the skills and ideas are hierarchical, that good habits are established. Speed is relatively unimportant and can be developed at a later stage. Teachers should therefore avoid praising pupils who complete a task quickly. Other children will assume, quite reasonably, that teacher is pleased if tasks are completed rapidly. Praise accuracy – no matter how long it takes. This point can be made to the child as a part of the instructions.

Most children who have difficulties in basic subjects find difficulty in discriminating between relevant and redundant information. Presented with a problem, they are often unable to identify the important bits of information which hold the key to the solution. For instance, it is known that good readers tackle unfamiliar words using a wide range of information contained on the page. They may know the initial letter or the word ending, or a particular consonant blend may be familiar to them. They may use the length of the word to eliminate a number of possibilities, or search for clues in any illustrations which are in the book. And they may look for clues in the text itself, in previous sentences or by reading ahead. Good readers are skilled in seeking out and using relevant information which may lead them to the correct word. Less competent readers usually have fewer skills in using context clues of this kind, and may need help in discriminating between useful and redundant information.

Finally a couple of points which are rather more obvious but no less useful. Pupils' attention can often be captured and retained merely by using attractive and varied materials. Finding the materials most likely to hold children's attention is a matter of experience – trial and error over an extended period – and requires thought and often time in finding and sometimes making a range of teaching materials. Several teachers pooling their resources is a good idea – increasing the range of materials available and, at the same time, reducing preparation time. And finally, it is sometimes possible to capitalize on the pupil's interests in order to make the task more attractive. For example, the child with retarded language development may be good at jigsaws, and so with careful planning the two might be combined, teaching to a specific language objective through the medium of doing non-verbal puzzles.

1(iv)   How much help should be provided?

We are referring here to the amount of assistance the pupil should be given to perform a task. If, for example, the child is being taught to button up his coat, should he be given physical help to complete the task or should he be left to find out the best way for himself? If he is being taught to write a letter 'b' should his hand be physically guided? How much help and support should be provided at the time of the task being performed? Is it better to allow a pupil to struggle for a long time on the assumption that 'he will never forget if he discovers for himself'? Or, at the other extreme, should the teacher provide enough help to *make sure* the task is completed successfully?

Before trying to shed some light on this important issue, we should perhaps first of all acknowledge that whatever help is provided may occur at the same time as the pupil's response. If the teacher physically guides a pupil's hand to write the letter 'b', for example, the support and the response are obviously occurring simultaneously. Why then discuss this issue under the heading of '*pre*-response variables'? Quite simply because support of this kind may occur before or at the same time, but *never* after the response. We have therefore chosen to preserve this classification because it suits our purpose here, while acknowledging this anomaly.

Deciding how much support to give the child at the time of his being asked to perform a task depends largely upon *which child* and *what the task is. There is no valid generalization which applies to all teaching situations.* However, there is considerable agreement that, during the early stages of learning (i.e. teaching basic skills to young children), it is preferable to provide whatever help is necessary for the task to be completed successfully (Ausubel, 1968). This is probably particularly true of young children with learning difficulties. There are two main reasons for this conclusion. First of all, failing to provide this amount of support may be tantamount to allowing the child to practise errors which will subsequently need unlearning. And secondly, to allow the pupil to fail to produce even an approximation of the required response is hardly likely to promote an eagerness to try again, or facilitate an enthusiasm for learning. In general terms, therefore, it is better to provide whatever help is necessary, as far as possible making sure that the task is completed successfully and avoiding errors being rehearsed.

What kind of help can be provided to ensure that the pupil completes a task successfully? This can take many forms. To take the example of the child learning to write the letter 'b', the teacher may gesture the shape in the air with her finger, she may have him trace the letter or use a template, she may say 'Down, up, and round' while he writes, or she may need physically to guide his hand to form the letter. The child learning to button up his coat might be able to complete the task if the teacher 'talks him through' the stages, gestures the required actions or physically guides his hands. Acquisition of an early sight vocabulary can be facilitated by the use of pictures paired with the words to be learnt (Corey and Shamow, 1972). Therefore, the help may involve demonstrations, verbal commentary, gestures, physical guidance (either by hand or device), or the use of illustrations.

Some general points can be made at this stage about the help which the teacher should provide at the time of presenting a task:

(1) Try to provide sufficient help to ensure that the task is completed successfully;
(2) Do *not* provide help which the pupil *does not* require to complete the task;
(3) Try to withdraw the help gradually, ensuring if possible that the pupil is successful at all times.

Providing assistance to the point of guaranteeing successful completion of a task is a technique known as *prompting* and the gradual withdrawal of prompts is called *fading*. Whilst the presented guidelines (as far as they go) are entirely valid and, hopefully, of some practical use, the technology of prompting and fading is an advanced and specialist field. To deal with these issues comprehensively, and in sufficient detail to enable the reader to use them (or to advise on their use) in the classroom, is beyond the scope of this book. However, readers wishing to pursue this area further might begin with Vargas (1977) or Meacham and Wiesen (1974).

So much for pre-response variables. We have suggested that where in the classroom the pupil is taught, when, how the task is presented, and the amount and kind of help provided, are all likely to have a considerable influence upon how much learning occurs, and are all variables which are *within* the teacher's control. There now follows a similar discussion on post-response variables.

2. Post-response Variables

Can what happens to the pupil *after* he has responded influence how much he learns? Certainly. The pupil who gets 2 out of 10 for his sums and is shouted at by his teacher for his trouble is likely to approach his next arithmetic lesson with a good deal less enthusiasm than another pupil whose performance was faultless and rewarded by a gold star. Children like praise and attention, and enjoy success, although (like adults) they differ in terms of the amount and kind they need. Although the proposals outlined earlier try to ensure that work is set at precisely the right level (thus increasing the probability of success on the pupil's part), it is important that success is explicitly recognized by the teacher and generously praised.

The use of teacher attention and praise in the classroom was discussed briefly in

Chapter 5 and some general guidelines were presented. These ideas are taken further in the next few pages, but it might be helpful first to summarize the important points from the previous discussion. It is emphasized that teacher attention and praise: (i) should follow desirable (*and not undesirable*) behaviour; (ii) must be of an appropriate kind for each child, and (iii) should occur as soon as possible after the desired behaviour.

Skinner's (1953) basic idea – that behaviour followed by some desirable or pleasurable consequence is more likely to recur – is not a complex one, and yet its implications are considerable and by no means obvious. In fact, during the past twenty-five years an advanced and sophisticated technology has been developed by Skinner and innumerable other behavioural psychologists around the world who have adopted his ideas. It must be emphasized therefore that this is a *very* specialized field with a vast literature. In the following few pages we can do no more than introduce some of these ideas and make suggestions for further reading for those who wish to pursue any point. Because this chapter is intended to be of particular interest to the specialist (as defined in the opening paragraphs), it is assumed that most readers may have some knowledge of these ideas. Many of the references are therefore from specialized journals and books, and may be of a technical nature. However, the books which are recommended at the end of the chapter are of variable difficulty. This compromise is forced upon us because, on the one hand, the field cannot possibly be comprehensively covered here but, on the other, some of these ideas are too important to omit entirely. We should perhaps also say at this stage that the number of practising local authority psychologists whose orientation is toward behavioural psychology has grown considerably in recent years, and it might be therefore that the interested reader, as well as being able to follow up the references provided, has some available local expertise.

2(i) Rewards

We have so far referred only to praise and attention, and suggested that most children find these '*rewarding*'. In fact, in behavioural psychology the word *reward* has a precise meaning – it is *an event which increases the frequency of the behaviour it follows*. It is defined, therefore, in terms of its effect on a child's behaviour. For example, if a pupil (who prefers quiet and unobtrusive attention from the teacher) is 'rewarded' each time he puts up his hand to answer a question with loud and generous praise, he may *stop* putting up his hand. What the teacher *believes* is a reward is not actually *acting* as a reward – it is not increasing the frequency with which the pupil raises his hand to answer a question. In other words a 'reward' is only a reward if it increases the frequency of the behaviour which it follows – whether or not an adult *thinks* that the event should be pleasurable to the child.

This is an important point which the reader should grasp before continuing, since the word 'reward' is subsequently used with this definition in mind. Incidentally, although we will not be discussing *punishment* here, this too is defined in terms of its effect upon behaviour. An event – even 'corporal punishment' – is only a punishment if it *decreases* the frequency of the behaviour which it follows. The important point here is to forget what seem to us (as adults) to be pleasant and unpleasant consequences for a child, and think of reward and punishment purely in terms of their effect on behaviour. Givner and Graubard (1974) and Poteet (1974) are relatively brief and introductory books about the use of reward and punishment in the classroom, which are written particularly for teachers. O'Leary and O'Leary (1977) is a veritable encyclopaedia of behaviour modification techniques in educational settings.

Before discussing different kinds of rewards and how they can most effectively be used in the classroom, we should perhaps deal with a couple of related points which seem consistently to trouble many teachers. The first concerns the confusion between rewards and *bribes*. Some teachers think that to use rewards (even praise and attention) in a planned and premeditated way to deliberately influence a pupil's behaviour is tantamount to *bribery*. This feeling of uneasiness, albeit unfounded, is to some extent understandable, but there are two important counter-arguments which should belay such fears: (a) Rewards are used constantly in the classroom anyway. Teachers reward children spontaneously, and for that matter children reward (and punish) teachers. If it is possible to use rewards more carefully in a way which will benefit the children, what reason is there for not doing so? (b) A 'bribe' is defined in the Oxford English dictionary as 'an inducement offered to persuade someone to do a dishonest or illegal service'. It is suggested that teachers should reward children for working well and making progress – these are obviously neither dishonest nor illegal practices. We are not therefore advocating bribery – rewards and bribes are completely different.

The second point which frequently concerns teachers about the use of rewards is the question of whether or not it should be necessary. 'There should be no need to offer productivity deals to eight-year-olds who don't want to do their sums' and 'Why should teachers make special arrangements to reward some children more systematically and generously than others?'. It is true of course that ideally pupils should *want* to learn. After all, acquiring new skills and knowledge is, in itself, a satisfactory experience – at least for some of us. The fact of the matter is that it is clearly not rewarding enough for *all* children. Why else would teachers complain that some pupils seem 'difficult to motivate', if the intrinsic satisfaction of gaining new knowledge kept them on-task and progressing throughout their school life? If children with learning difficulties are to learn, they must perceive a need to participate in instructional activities. Such a perceived need might be brought about by optimizing pre-response conditions but, if this is found not to be possible, the *only* available course of action is to provide some additional incentive to supplement the intrinsic satisfaction of learning. What else is there to do?

There are many possible reasons *why* some children might initially need some kind of additional reward. Experienced teachers may have taught some older children who, as a result of prolonged exposure to failure and frustration in the classroom, have been 'turned off' learning. On the other hand, there are those children who have been influenced by their families or neighbourhood peer groups, and taught that succeeding at school is unimportant. Whatever the reason (and in most cases we can do no more than speculate) there will always be children who, despite the classteacher's meticulously prepared teaching sessions, will seem apathetic or uninterested. At such times the careful and consistent use of reward in the classroom is just about all that the teacher has left.

2(ii) Types of Reward

We began (in Chapter 5 and at the beginning of this Chapter) by referring to 'praise and teacher attention'. We have now adopted the word *'reward'*, and given it a clear definition. In fact, there are a number of different kinds of reward – teacher attention and praise are usually called *'social rewards'*. Sulzer *et al.* (1977) and Stephens (1977) provide comprehensive accounts of a wide range of different types of reward, but here we are going to focus our attention on just three kinds: (a) Social Reward, (b) Knowledge of Results (Feedback), and (c) Activity Rewards. These have been selected for discussion because it is felt that they are of most practical use to the teacher of children with mild to moderate learning difficulties. For example, *primary rewards* (i.e. sweets, drinks etc.) are not dealt with in detail here because, whilst they may be useful to the teacher of mentally handicapped children, the less severely handicapped child can usually be taught satisfactorily without resorting to such tangible incentives.

Social reward

We have already emphasized the importance of constantly praising the slow learner for his efforts and achievements and made the point that, whilst all teachers use praise to some extent, there is almost certainly room for improvement in most classrooms in so far as it could be used *more* effectively. There are innumerable examples of published work showing how praise and attention can be used to improve academic performance and attention to task (e.g. McKenzie *et al.*, 1968, and Broden *et al.*, 1970, respectively). Moreover, we have presented some basic guidelines for its use in the classroom.

Social reward can take many forms. It certainly does *not* mean that the teacher should necessarily provide a constant verbal bombardment of 'That's much better', 'Well done', 'That's great', and 'Good boy' – like some kind of malfunctioning tape recorder. Remember that children vary in terms of what kind of adult attention they enjoy. Some can be rewarded by a nod, wink, smile, or even a look or a tone of voice, and others find a few minutes of 'private chat' or one-to-one instruction a powerful incentive. Very young children, on the other hand, often like close proximity and overt affection. One often hears teachers say that they 'know' their pupils. This is one thing that the skilled teacher of children with learning handicaps would certainly need to *know* about her pupils: What kind of adult attention and praise does each child like best? When trying to find out, remember that a 'reward' is only a reward if it increases the frequency of the behaviour which it follows. In other words, you try them all until you find the one which has the desired effect – i.e. increased effort and progress.

One final point should be made about the teacher's own use of praise. *It is a teaching skill which needs practice.* Without denying the existence of the occasional gifted teacher who can 'lift' children to new heights of commitment and achievement, spontaneously and naturally, most mortals like ourselves need consciously to develop skills of assessing what kind of social reward works best with individual children *and* the act of praising itself. There are times when it is not easy to appear genuinely delighted that a pupil has tied his shoe laces or written his name with only one spelling mistake.

There may be other kinds of effective social reward available within the school, beyond the teacher's own attention. For example, there might be another teacher or assistant who, for whatever reason, a child particularly likes. An arrangement can easily be made whereby a pupil takes a piece of work to show another member of staff who has been primed to be appropriately impressed. It may be that the headteacher can occasionally be used in this way, or that the work is recognized to be of merit in the school's assembly. Another important source of reward which, with some children, can be extremely effective is *other children*, for example 'Brian has worked so hard this morning that the whole class can have three minutes extra playtime'. There are a number of published studies (e.g. Evans and Oswalt, 1968) describing how a whole group or class can be rewarded in some way when a particular pupil works hard or makes some significant progress. This idea is obviously most likely to be effective with the pupil who seems heavily invested in gaining the approval of his peers.

Finally, it should be stressed that social rewards should never be replaced by any other kind of reward such as those described below. Activity rewards or visual displays of progress are intended to supplement teacher approval and praise – *not to replace it*. It is far more preferable that the child progress satisfactorily on teacher attention and praise, and have no need for any additional incentive, because social rewards have a number of important practical advantages over the rest. For example, other forms of reward tend to lose their 'power' after a while, whereas the power of social reward seems more persistent. Furthermore, social rewards can be administered immediately and naturally with no need of special arrangements which can be time-consuming and inconvenient. And most important, the effects of social reward seem to *generalize* more readily than other kinds of reward. That is to say, the pupil who is rewarded consistently for progress on a reading programme, for example, is more likely to make better progress in areas other than reading if the rewards are social.

Knowledge of results (Feedback)

Commonsense tells us that providing a pupil with details of how well he has performed and how further improvements might be achieved must be of major importance in the learning process. However, beyond a general consensus that feedback tends to facilitate learning, there is a surprising dearth of research evidence which unequivocally confirms its indispensability. There are interesting reviews of the literature on the subject in Ausubel (1968) and DeCecco and Crawford (1974). Due to a rather confused picture, therefore, it is difficult to offer detailed advice which is applicable to a wide range of teaching situations. However, some general points can be made. There is widespread agreement that feedback serves two purposes. (i) Being told that he has been successful will probably act as an effective *reward* to the child. As a central thesis of this book concerns the importance of setting work at an 'appropriate' level (i.e. ensuring high success levels and introducing new learning in small, well-planned doses), the pupil should usually respond well, and feedback therefore becomes a reliable source of reward. (ii) Feedback should provide the pupil with information which he can use to improve subsequent performances. It should help to clarify misconceptions, confirm his mastery of certain aspects of the task, and help him to focus his efforts on those aspects which require further attention. It has been shown in fact, that pupils who are provided with qualitative feedback (i.e. *why* answers are right and wrong) learn more effectively than pupils who are only provided with information describing the overall quality of performance (Bryan and Rigney, 1956, reported in Ausubel 1968).

The idea of using feedback as a reward can be further developed to include the use of visual displays of progress (Lindsley, 1974). Simple graphs and star charts can sometimes be designed to provide the pupil with visual evidence that he is progressing well. Whilst this can be straightforward in certain subject areas, if it is to be developed as an important aspect of a teaching programme, it would be advisable to seek further expertise in its use.

Activity rewards

Allowing pupils to engage in a favoured activity can be an effective reward with children of *all* ages. There are a host of activities in and around the classroom which children may find rewarding but which may never have occurred to the teacher – favours which she may distribute almost at random but which might be harnessed to elicit greater effort from her pupils. Being allowed to hold the door open for the rest of the class to leave the room for example, can be a potent reward for some young children. Distributing equipment, collecting up books and running messages are all jobs which most teachers give children and most children like doing. Used thoughtfully, these activities can increase effort and progress on a programme. Ross and O'Driscoll (1972) for example used 'free time' to improve spelling across an entire class.

The idea of using favoured activities (e.g. listening to a record) as a reward for a less favoured activity (e.g. work on a spelling programme) was first described by Premack (1959), and is usually referred to as the 'Premack Principle'. The procedure was further developed by Addison and Homme (1966) with their use of a *reward menu* (Ulrich *et al.*, 1974). This is a card upon which are depicted a number of activities which are known to be enjoyed by most children. These activities can be described in writing for children to read (or have read to them) or be represented by simple pictures or cartoons for younger children. In fact we know of one teacher who has made a 'reward booklet' with one activity depicted in picture on each page, and uses this idea with all her children as part of her routine teaching. Quite simply, for a period of hard work during which time good progress has been made, the pupil is allowed to select from the menu what he would like to do as a reward. It would seem with most children that not only does the preferred activity act as a reward, but also they like making the choice with all the necessary adult attention that this involves. Figure 5 is an example of part of a reward menu which is read out to the child who is to be rewarded.

REWARD LIST

Listening to a record at the end of the day
Class monitor for the day
Taking the register to the office
Three minutes extra playtime for the whole class
Reading comics for five minutes
Taking lost property around the school

Figure 5   Part of a reward menu

Obviously the nature of the activities displayed on the menu will depend upon the age of the children and the range of choices made available by school and class organization. Very young children obviously prefer activities like water play, finger painting and sitting by the teacher at storytime. If this idea is used over an extended period it is important to change the list of rewards available as some may lose their 'power' after a while. The important advantage of this system is that it helps to overcome the problem of matching the reward to the individual child – he is unlikely to select an activity he does not enjoy.

2(iii)   Using Rewards in the Classroom

Having discussed three kinds of rewards we will now turn our attention to their *use* in the classroom. We would remind readers of our previously stated fears that trying to simplify complex ideas paradoxically runs the risk of causing confusion. We would therefore strongly advise anyone wishing to become *deeply* involved in the classroom implementation of any of these to follow up the references and contact their local psychologist. Nevertheless, there are a number of points which are too important to omit entirely and which will hopefully be of some practical help in their presented form. Some of these have previously been mentioned but are important enough to repeat.

(1)   Social rewards (and in particular teacher attention and praise) are particularly effective if used skilfully, and only occasionally should any additional incentive be necessary. Teachers should be constantly assessing what kind of social reward works best for each child.

(2)   Special arrangements to use rewards over and above praise and attention should be reserved for those children who seem reluctant to try, are 'poorly motivated', or have a tendency to distract easily. The child who is having

difficulties *despite* obviously trying his utmost to succeed is unlikely to be helped by the addition of further incentives. In fact, this may lead to increased frustration. By the use of rewards we are seeking to create an incentive in cases where it is speculated that insufficient incentive already exists.

(3) Remember that rewards are defined in terms of their effect on the child's behaviour. If they do not effectively change the pupil's behaviour in the required direction they are *not* rewards. This requires careful and astute classroom observation.

(4) Children vary considerably in what they find rewarding, and the 'power' of particular rewards (especially activity rewards) varies over time with the same child. Reward menus are useful in overcoming this problem.

(5) If incentives are provided over and above the teacher's use of social rewards, these should *not* be seen as a substitute (or replacement) but an addition. Activity rewards and visual displays of progress should always be accompanied by praise and teacher attention.

(6) Rewards should be administered *immediately*, and after *desirable* behaviour. Care should be taken not to inadvertently reward undesirable behaviour, e.g. prolonged individual attention following a period of being off-task.

(7) While children can *learn* that good work is generally followed by pleasurable consequences, it is usually more effective if possible to tell the pupil what he is required to do and what reward he will receive for doing it.

(8) The teacher cannot praise every child every time he or she performs a desirable behaviour – it is not practicable – and in any event we want children eventually to dispense with the teacher as an essential source of reward. There must therefore be some kind of selection on the part of the teacher. It is when new learning steps are introduced, especially with the child who has difficulty persevering with unfamiliar or demanding tasks, that rewards should ideally be continuous. When the pupil gains in confidence and familiarity with the task, the frequency of rewards can gradually be reduced.

(9) We have referred to rewarding 'on-task behaviour' and making progress almost interchangably without dwelling upon any distinction which may exist. Obviously we want to see progress towards an objective and it is this which ideally we would reward. However, attention to task is essential if progress is to be made, and so this too can legitimately be rewarded.

(10) Rewards can be used in the classroom much more consistently and systematically than has been described above. A number of reward *systems* such as contingency contracting (i.e. Homme, 1976; Thorne, 1978), *token economies* (i.e. Bushell *et al.*, 1968; Miller and Schneider, 1974) and *shaping* (Johnston *et al.*, 1966) have been developed and used successfully with children with learning difficulties and are described fully in a vast *behaviour modification* literature. It should be said that this kind of systematic programme is not normally necessary with children with mild to moderate

learning difficulties and should only be undertaken under expert supervision.

Important note: Remember, the first stage of the procedure involved asking the question 'What is the problem?' and focused on achieving precise definition using the programme of objectives and the teacher's records. During this, the second stage, we are asking *'Would any other classroom organization or teaching method work better?'*, and a number of variables have been identified and discussed which might help the teacher to optimize learning conditions. These are summarized in Figure 6. In terms of the procedure, we are concerned with teaching to one objective only – the one which has been earmarked as the focal point of the problem. It should therefore be emphasized that there should be some limit to how long the teacher perseveres with the same objective. We are aiming to prevent classroom failure and it is unthinkable that the teacher might work through *all* the suggestions made here. There can be no clear-cut rules for deciding how long the teacher should continue working on the same objective. Suffice it to say that two or three weeks is a very long time in the life of a small child – especially if each day he is asked to do something which is beyond him. *It is perhaps a reasonable guideline to say that if in doubt move on to the next stage of the procedure.*

There are two categories of teaching method variables which can be manipulated to optimize learning conditions in the classroom. We have called these pre-response and post-response variables.

Pre-Response	*Post-Response*
Where is the best place to teach?	Can social rewards be used more effectively?
When is the best time to teach?	
	Is any additional incentive required?
Which is the best way to present the task?	
How much help should be provided?	

Important: The teacher should not teach to the same objective for too long without progress being made. If in doubt move to the next stage of the procedure.

Figure 6   A summary of teaching method variables

STAGE 3: HAVE ALL PRECEDING OBJECTIVES IN THE PROGRAMME BEEN MASTERED?

Having defined the problem in precise terms using the programme records, and manipulated pre- and post-response variables, trying to optimize classroom learning conditions for the pupil without success, what else can the teacher do?

Teaching children with learning difficulties would be very much easier if they all learned by progressing through sequences of objectives without deviation, mastering the first, then the second, the third, and so on, in a linear fashion to the learning target. In reality of course this is often not the case. We have stressed that the programme should be seen as a hypothesis for the very reason that we can rarely be certain that it will suit the child. Some subject areas present greater sequencing problems than others and in areas like language development (where the present state of knowledge is far from complete) pupils may 'skip' objectives and even occasionally master one objective before achieving one or more which precede it. Hence programmes can be used flexibly even to the point in some instances of working on two or more objectives in the same sequence at the same time. At this stage in the procedure we have to think again about the decision to begin work on the particular objective which is causing the problem. As a rule, the following guideline can be applied.

Have all preceding objectives been mastered? If they have then this stage in the procedure is completed and you can move on to the next. If they have not, then work on the problem objective must be suspended until this is so.

STAGE 4: ARE THE PUPIL'S RECORDS CORRECT?

We have now defined the problem, tried a range of different teaching methods without success and checked that all preceding objectives in the programme have been recorded as mastered. What next?

No matter how diligently records are kept, one can never be certain that they are entirely accurate. Children with learning difficulties frequently forget what they have learnt — hence the 'checked' column in the records. It might be that despite this precaution, objectives recorded as mastered and checked are no longer intact. If this is found to be happening frequently, it may be that the check is occurring too soon after mastery has been recorded, and as a matter of policy should be delayed. Alternatively, teachers may have as many 'check' columns as they feel able to operate and, as a matter of course, check important objectives in crucial areas of learning at three or four-weekly intervals.

For the child who is having prolonged difficulties in a particular area of the programme, it is at this stage that a systematic checking of the records should take place. It is a matter of finding out whether objectives *recorded* as mastered (which after Stage 3 should be all those preceding the problem objective) are in fact still intact.

Given that the programme consists of complete objectives, containing the three important components, this should be a matter of creating the conditions (e.g. materials, instructions etc.) and observing the pupil's behaviour, hopefully to the standard of performance described in the objectives. Most of this, with careful planning, can be done during normal class and small group activities, and of course assistants can be trained to help.

As a rule the following guidelines can be applied:

If it is found that one or more objectives, which precede the point of difficulty in the programme, are no longer intact, then obviously further practice on earlier work is required and teaching related to the problem objective should be suspended. Revision must continue until the standards of performance described in each objective are re-established. Only then can work on the objective which was the focus of the problem be resumed. If, on the other hand, this process of checking the records confirms that objectives recorded as mastered can still be performed to the required level of competence, then this stage of the procedure is completed and you can move on to the next.

STAGE 5: MODIFYING THE PROGRAMME

We began by suggesting that the teaching programme should be seen as a hypothesis – an informed speculation (based on whatever practical and theoretical knowledge is available), that the sequence of objectives represents the most efficient means of teaching a particular skill to a particular pupil. If the pupil fails to make progress or 'sticks' at some point on it, and the procedure outlined above is then used but also fails to overcome the difficulty, there is one remaining course of action – to modify the programme. Even at this point the reader will notice that there is no regression to child-centred explanations of the failure. There is no recourse to IQ figures, brain damage, social history, or any other justification for declaring the problem insoluble. Quite simply, the programme must be modified and the whole process started again.

Writing programmes of objectives was dealt with in Chapters 3 and 4. It is emphasized there that there is no easy-to-follow guide to writing definitive and unequivocal sequences. If there were, it would not be necessary to view programmes as hypothesis, and consequently no need to contemplate changing them. It is a case of doing the best we can with the information available. The same is true here, except that we now know more than we knew before. We have tried out one programme and found it to be in some way unsatisfactory. The fact remains however that the 'rules' for modifying programmes can be no more definitive than the guidelines for writing them.

There is a dearth of good teachers' books which focus directly and extensively on the question of sequencing objectives. There are some which consider the problem in detail (e.g. Holland et al., 1976) but these tend to be extremely technical. We have therefore chosen to discuss five aspects of the problem in rather more detail. These represent what we have found in practice to be the most frequently occurring issues in writing and modifying programmes.

1. Changing Conditions and Performance Levels

Let us begin by looking at an example in some depth. The following sequence is an adaptation of Arithmetic Programme 4:

Goal: To teach addition and subtraction up to 10.

(1) In combining two sets of objects to form a larger set, uses the terms *add* and *equals* appropriately on 5 consecutive days;

(2) Correctly states the answer to verbally presented addition sums (which total 10 or less) in 7 out of 8 consecutive trials *with* the aid of concrete materials;

(3) Uses the term *take away* appropriately when removing objects from a set on each of 5 consecutive days;

(4) Correctly states the answer to verbally presented subtraction sums (with numbers less than 10 and leaving a remainder greater than zero) in 7 out of 8 consecutive trials *with* the aid of concrete materials;

(5) Writes the symbols + and = when given their verbal labels (i.e. 'add' and 'equals') on each of 5 consecutive days;

(6) Presented with printed addition sums (totalling 10 or less), writes the correct answers in 7 out of 8 consecutive trials *with* the aid of concrete materials;

(7) Presented with printed addition sums (totalling 10 or less), writes the correct answer in 7 out of 8 consecutive trials *without* the aid of concrete materials;

(8) Writes the symbol − when given the verbal label (i.e. 'take away') on each of 5 consecutive trials;

(9) Presented with printed subtraction sums (using numbers less than 10 and leaving a remainder greater than zero), writes the correct answer in 7 out of 8 consecutive trials *with* the aid of concrete materials;

(10) Presented with printed subtraction sums (using numbers less than 10 and leaving a remainder greater than zero), writes the correct answer in 7 out of 8 consecutive trials *without* the use of concrete materials.

As this programme is subsequently discussed in some detail, readers are advised to read the programme two or three times before proceeding. Let us imagine that initially things went well and objectives (1) to (6) were mastered over a fairly short period. The first problem arose when it was realized that, although objectives (2), (4), and (6) could be taught to the stated standard of performance quite easily, a check some time later indicated that the skills were being forgotten almost as quickly as they were being learnt. Consequently the teacher was having to return repeatedly to these objectives to provide further practice.

We have found this to be a common problem, but it is not one which is difficult to overcome. Earlier we discussed the idea of *overlearning*, which involves practising a skill beyond the point of mastery − thus rendering it less likely to be forgotten. We can use this idea here. In objectives (2), (4), and (6) we require the pupil to make only 7 correct responses out of 8 consecutive trials on any one day, but we could increase the standard of performance required. We might, for example, require the child to make 18 out of 20 correct responses on each of 2 consecutive days. This would mean that progress from one objective to the next may *seem* slower, but the skill is much less likely to be forgotten, and the persistent need for revision would probably be eliminated. Objective (2) could therefore read:

(2) Correctly states the answers to verbally presented addition sums (which total 10 or less) in 18 out of 20 consecutive trials on each of 2 consecutive days *with* the use of concrete materials

and objectives (4) and (6) could be similarly amended.

Readers will recall that practising skills beyond the point of mastery has the additional advantage of aiding *generalization*. That is to say, in this instance, making it more likely that the pupil could, for example, add coins in a purse or bottles in a crate. Fresh objectives could therefore be added to ensure that generalization was taking place, which would have the additional benefit of providing practice in the same skill using a variety of interesting materials. Objective (2) could therefore read:

(2) Correctly states the answers to verbally presented addition sums (which total 10 or less) in 11 out of 12 consecutive trials using at least 3 of the following 6 materials: coins, bottles, sweets, buttons, and bricks

and again objectives (4) and (6) could be similarly amended.

In effect all that we are doing here is taking the objectives which are being quickly forgotten and manipulating (i) the standard of performance required of the pupil and (ii) the conditions under which the behaviour is expected to occur. In other words we are demanding that the pupil reaches a high level of mastery in the skill and/or that the skill be performed under a variety of conditions and using a variety of materials.

2. Writing Bridging Sequences

The question of *bridging sequences* can be illustrated and discussed within the context of the same arithmetic programme. Let us imagine that the same pupil, as a result of the above modifications, masters objectives (1) to (6) to the revised standard of performance and under the stated conditions, but then 'sticks' at objective (7) which, since revision, now reads:

(7) Presented with printed addition sums (totalling 10 or less), writes the correct answer in 18 out of 20 consecutive trials *without* the aid of concrete materials.

The only difference between objectives (6) and (7) is that the former permits the use of concrete materials, like bricks or counters, and the latter does not. The pupil is therefore having difficulty 'doing without' concrete aids, and it seems likely that merely increasing the standards of performance required in earlier objectives is not the best solution. The pupil is apparently heavily dependent upon her counters and needs to be *taught* to be less dependent.

Here we require a *bridging sequence* to bridge the gap between the problem objective and the previous objective which has been mastered. In a sense we are writing a new programme and the guidelines in Chapter 4 are entirely applicable. The first objective in the bridging sequence will be the original programme's objective (6) and the target objective in the bridging sequence will be the original programme's objective (7). We now need to bridge the gap with as many carefully graded steps as we think will be necessary. In practice this can be as many as six or seven new objectives but may be as few as one.

In the presented example the following bridging sequence introduces two additional steps:

(1) Presented with printed addition sums (totalling 10 or less), writes the correct answer in 18 out of 20 consecutive trials on 2 consecutive days, *using* objects to construct and combine 2 sets (a modified form of objective (6) in the original programme);

(2) Ditto (1) using concrete objects to construct but *not* combine 2 sets;

(3) Ditto (1) using concrete objects to construct *only one* set;

(4) Ditto (1) *without* using any concrete objects (a modified form of objective (7) in the original programme).

It is assumed that the pupil, asked for example to add 3 to 4, makes two sets with 3 and 4 members, joins them together and counts the members in the resultant larger set. In the second objective, therefore, we permit her to make the two sets but force her to combine them mentally, and in the third we allow only one of the sets to be constructed, ensuring that the remainder of the process is internalized. Thus we hope that the dependency on concrete aids is gradually eliminated.

Step-size should be matched to the predicted rate of learning of the pupil for whom the programme is being written. This was discussed in detail in Chapter 4 where it was emphasized that this is an immensely difficult task. We are *guessing* the optimal size of steps for a particular pupil in a particular skill or subject area, and it is not surprising that occasionally the programme needs modifying in the light of trying it out. Writing bridging sequences, like the one above, is a matter of reducing the step-size in that particular part of the programme where it is found that the pupil needs smaller steps.

3. Chaining and Backward Chaining

Despite the absence of any ready-made procedures for reducing step-size, the techniques of *chaining* and *backward chaining* are often useful in bridging sequences. It is a means of reducing step-size at a particular point in the programme by adding a number of intermediate steps between one objective (which *has* been mastered) and the next (which has *not*). It can *only* be used when the required response in the problem objective can be broken down into smaller steps which can then be performed independently.

Chaining and backward chaining are techniques which were used in Language Programme (1) and Reading Programme (7) respectively in Chapter 6. It would be helpful to refresh your memory by looking carefully at these two programmes once more. In the first we want the pupil to sit and attend, and therefore teach him to follow the commands 'come here', 'sit down', 'hands down', and then 'look at me'. Each of the four components is separate and can be performed independently. And so it is logical to break down the *total* task and build it up, gradually adding a fresh component at each step. In the spelling programme the same idea is used in reverse. The spelling of the word *school* is taught by first presenting schoo_, then scho__, sch____, and so on, removing one additional letter at each stage. (Obviously you can elect to remove blends and diagraphs instead of individual letters if you so wish.)

Both of these techniques can be used *only* if the target task can be broken down into components which can be independently performed. The following objectives can all be broken down in this way: (a) assembles a 5-piece jigsaw independently; (b) copies a square accurately from a model; and (c) puts on a long-sleeved jumper without assistance. The following objectives on the other hand do *not* consist of a number of components which can be performed independently: (a) balances on either foot for 4 seconds; (b) given 2 rods of different length, points to the appropriate rod when asked 'Which is the *shorter* rod?'.

Let us take one final example to illustrate the point. A pupil can be taught to complete a 5-piece jigsaw with the following programme which uses the idea of *backward* chaining:

(1) Given a 5-piece jigsaw with pieces A, B, C, and D already in position, completes the jigsaw successfully;
(2) Given a 5-piece jigsaw with pieces A, B, and C already in position, completes the jigsaw successfully;
(3) Given a 5-piece jigsaw, with pieces A and B already in position, completes the jigsaw successfully;
(4) Given a 5-piece jigsaw, with piece A already in position, completes the jigsaw successfully;
(5) Assembles a 5-piece jigsaw independently.

The example above could be backward chained *or* chained. The former was chosen because it has the important advantage of having the pupil *complete* the jigsaw in each step in the programme, and successful completion is an effective reward with most children. If there is a choice, therefore, it is usually preferable to *backward* chain, but a choice does not always exist. For example, the pupil cannot be taught to 'sit down' until he has 'come here', and cannot be taught to 'hands down' until he has 'sat down'.

When re-examining a programme with a view to making some change, therefore, it is useful to bear these techniques in mind. If the problem objective can be broken down into separate components which can be performed independently, it may be that the bridging sequence can consist of a chain or backward chain. Accounts of these two ideas (and how they can be used in teaching) are in most behaviourally orientated textbooks on learning problems (e.g. Neisworth and Smith, 1973; Gardner, 1977).

4. *Training Abilities v Teaching Skills*

During the 1960s *diagnostic-prescriptive* teaching became the vogue in remedial and special education in both America and the UK. This approach to dealing with children's learning difficulties depends upon identifying *underlying psychological disabilities* − malfunctions of internal processes which, it was thought, prevent the pupil from learning normally. A number of tests were produced commercially which purported to enable a psychologist to identify and measure these underlying structures. The diagnosis completed, a programme could be designed to rectify the weaknesses, thus hopefully rendering the child able to learn academic skills, such as reading and writing, more easily. The Frostig Developmental Test of Visual Perception (Frostig, 1964) and the Illinois Test of Psycholinguistic Abilities (Kirk *et al.*, 1968) are the most widely used of these tests. As well as tests, a number of teaching kits and programmes were also produced, some of which were specifically designed for use with particular diagnostic tests, e.g. Goal Language Programme (Karnes, 1972). And of course there are innumerable teachers' books which describe approaches based on these ideas, (e.g. Tansley, 1967; Kephart, 1971; Kirk and Kirk, 1971).

This approach is often referred to as '*ability training*' (Ysseldyke, 1973; Ysseldyke and Salvia, 1974) because its primary concern is not the direct teaching of literacy and numeracy skills, but the identification and training of underlying psychological abilities which supposedly enable or disable the learner. A specialized vocabulary was developed to describe these various abilities which in part at least has filtered into common use among remedial and special school teachers. For example, phrases such as visual and auditory perception, visual and auditory sequential memory, haptic-kinaesthetic and visuo-auditory integration, form constancy, and figure ground may be familiar to some readers.

Despite the obvious and instant appeal of this style of intervention, supportive evidence is scarce. For example, we would need valid and reliable tests with which to identify and measure the underlying psychological structures, but these are simply not available (Hammill and Larsen, 1978). Of the many other problems associated with the diagnostic-prescriptive model we will describe only one, and this concerns the basic question of whether or not children actually benefit from programmes based on this kind of diagnostic information in terms of their success in learning basic academic subjects. There is no convincing evidence that they do. For example, Sabatino and Dorfman (1974) designed reading programmes which emphasized either the auditory perceptual modality or the visual perceptual modality, and used them with groups of children diagnosed as having particular strengths and weaknesses in auditory and visual perception. All the groups progressed equally well − irrespective of their diagnosis or the emphasis of the programme. In other words, a programme designed for a child diagnosed as having good auditory perception but poor visual perception was just as effective if used on a child with the opposite diagnosis.

We have entered this discussion in some detail because ability training is still practised widely in remedial and special education today − at least in this country − despite considerable and freely available evidence which casts doubts on all of the major assumptions upon which it is based (Gardner, 1977). It is a distinction which must be made when writing a programme. *Objectives in a sequence should be directly related to the target skill. There is no theoretical or experimental justification for including objectives which are intended to train supposed psychological abilities.* Detailed reviews of the arguments involved in the ability training versus task analysis issue are contained in Lerner (1976) and Haring and Bateman (1977).

We have found that some experienced teachers, when writing programmes in workshop situations, persistently revert to including 'ability training objectives'. For instance, in a reading programme they might include an objective which requires a pupil *visually to discriminate* between pigs with four legs and pigs with three legs, or to select a house from a row of houses because it has no curtains at the top right-hand window. The assumption is of course that visual discrimination is an ability which needs to be trained before a child can learn to read. But what have stick pigs got to do with it? Certainly a pupil needs to be able visually to discriminate between similar *words – since this is directly related to the reading skill.*

The diagnostic-prescriptive model is dying hard, and we have found this to be a continually recurring issue when working on programmes with teachers. One final example might serve to underline the problem. Tansley (1967) speculates a wide range of underlying psychological abilities and structures, and makes suggestions as to how these might be assessed and if necessary remediated. For example, he explains that one means of assessing *visuo-kinaesthetic integration* is to blindfold the pupil, guide his hand to form a figure or letter in the air, and have him select what was drawn from a selection of printed models. If this is a skill which you feel it is important for the pupil to develop, then that is fine – although we might beg to differ with your priority judgement. However, there is no theoretical or experimental justification for including this in *any* programme of objectives which is intended to teach literacy or numeracy skills.

Remember that we want to teach skills, not train abilities. Therefore, when re-examining a programme with a view to making some changes, look carefully at the preceding objectives and make sure that they are directly related to the problem objective.

5.   Task Analysis v Developmental Charts

There are a great many commercially available '*developmental checklists*', e.g. Sheridan (1973) and Jeffree and McConkey (1976). These are lists of behavioural statements arranged in the order in which most normal children seem to acquire them. Here is an example:

(1)   Picks up small objects in a pincer grip (18–24);
(2)   Removes wrapper from a sweet (18–24);
(3)   Folds a piece of paper in half (36);
(4)   Threads beads onto a string (48);
(5)   Cuts edge off paper using scissors (60).

These items are all related to hand control and object manipulation, and the figures in brackets indicate the approximate age in months that they emerge in average children. This then *is* a programme of objectives in so far as each statement describes an observable action and the items are arranged in a step-by-step manner from the easy to the difficult. Or is it?

There is, in fact, a subtle distinction between developmental checklists and programmes of objectives of the kind advocated in this book which is currently a matter of considerable debate among advocates of the objectives approach. The main problem concerns the extent to which items in the list relate *directly* to the target item. You will remember we suggested in Chapter 4 that ideally an objective should be included in a programme on the grounds that it will help the learner acquire subsequent objectives more easily. The question is, therefore, will learning to fold paper help the pupil when he comes to tackle threading beads? And will threading beads be of benefit when he comes to use scissors? And, for that matter, will removing sweet wrappers have any positive effect on his capacity to learn *any* of these skills? The answer to all of these questions is probably 'No'. Not only could the pupil be taught to use scissors without first threading beads or taught to thread beads without first folding paper and so on, but it is likely that there will be no positive transfer from any of these items to the next. In fact, they are a collection of independent *target objectives* which are grouped together only because they all involve manipulating objects with the hands.

In order to underline this distinction, look at the following programme using backward chaining:

(1) Given a square with *one* side missing (i.e. ⊏), completes the square accurately from a model;

(2) Given a square with any *two* sides missing (i.e. ⌐), completes the square accurately from a model;

(3) Given a square with any *three* sides missing (i.e. ⁻), completes the square accurately from a model;

(4) Copies a square accurately from a model.

Here there is a *direct* relationship between the objectives in the programme and the target, and the pupil will, for example, benefit significantly from acquiring objectives (1) and (2) when he comes to tackle objective (3).

The task analysis approach has a number of advantages over developmental check lists. The first, and arguably most important, involves the distinction which has just been described. Children are liable to acquire skills in a different order to that described in a developmental checklist. A pupil may learn to use scissors *before* he can thread beads if, for example he has more opportunity to practise the former, or if he has some mild physical condition which makes scissors easier to manipulate than string and beads. Detailed lesson preparation is obviously easier if it is known that the pupil will progress through a programme in a linear manner as would be the case with the sequence on 'copying a square'. There are a number of other disadvantages associated with using commercially available checklists. First, the items are rarely sufficiently specific for teaching purposes. For example, threading beads can be as easy or as difficult as you make it, depending upon the size of the beads, the bore of the hole and the material to be threaded; there are many sweets which adults can unwrap only with difficulty; and how accurately does the pupil have to be able to fold paper? And secondly, there is a tendency for checklists to cater mainly for pre-school and handicapped children. The areas covered tend, therefore, to be self-help skills, gross- and fine-motor development, and language. Important subject areas like reading and arithmetic are usually not represented.

Whilst the task analysis approach suffers none of these disadvantages, we would not wish to write-off checklists as being worthless. They have been found to be useful for example in making an initial assessment of a child's general level of attainments with a view to identifying areas of special need. Then, once appropriate learning targets have been chosen, a task analysis approach can be used to develop a teaching programme. And in the final analysis of course − *they are better than nothing.*

In terms of re-examining a programme upon which a pupil is faltering, this is an important point to bear in mind. To take the checklist concerning hand control, because of its developmental nature it would not be surprising if a pupil became 'stuck' at any one of the five items. It would then be necessary to write a short programme of objectives with the problem objective as its target. *This would not be a bridging sequence because the preceding objective is not directly related to it.* For example, a child who has mastered (1) and (2) may get stuck on 'threading beads'. A programme designed to overcome this problem would be an entirely independent programme and might consist of four or five objectives in which progressively more difficult materials were being used. Each item would then be a 'bead-threading item' and hence there would be a *direct* relationship between each step and the target.

Summary

This chapter is intended primarily for the specialist (the special school teacher, remedial specialist, adviser or psychologist); those whose job it is to teach, or advise on the teaching of, children with learning difficulties. Many of the ideas and suggestions described require small teaching groups and flexible timetabling arrangements. Nevertheless it is equally true that the normal school classteacher should find some useful ideas which are directly applicable to the normal school.

A procedure is described (Figure 7) which may, to the newcomer to the objectives approach, sound complex and time-consuming. It should be said that with practice and regular use it becomes an internalized framework − a mental process with which to tackle the most difficult classroom learning problem. Problems are defined in terms of difficulties with particular objectives without recourse to comparisons with peers or meaningless generalities lamenting an overall lack of progress. New methods and ideas are sought with a specific objective in mind, and records are constantly reviewed and consulted to check the appropriateness of earlier decisions. In the final analysis the programme is seen as a *hypothesis* − an informed speculation that the sequence of objectives represents the most efficient means of teaching a particular skill to a particular child. If the pupil fails to reach the target of the programme and 'sticks' at some point on it, and the described procedure fails to overcome the difficulty, then the hypothesis is abandoned and the programme must be modified in some way. Even at this point there is no regression to child-centred explanations of the failure (e.g. brain damage, IQ etc.) or other variables outside the teacher's control (i.e. social history). Quite simply, the programme must be modified and the whole process started again.

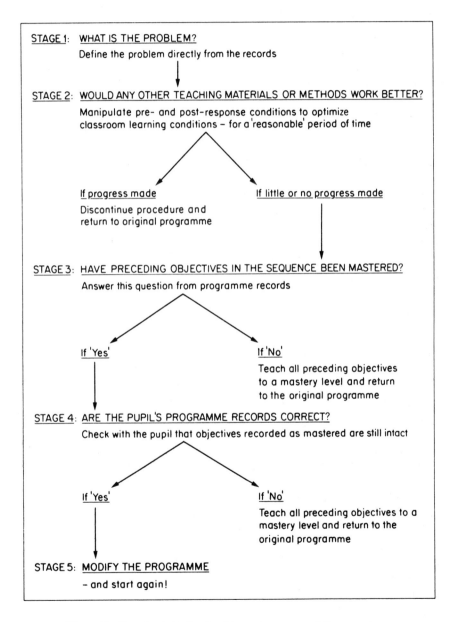

Figure 7   Hypothesis-testing teaching: a summary of the procedure

Recommended Further Reading

Gardner, W. I. (1977). *Learning and Behaviour Characteristics of Exceptional Children and Youth.* Boston: Allyn and Bacon.
A comprehensive volume describing all aspects of the behavioural approach and providing excellent source material.

Haring, N. G., and Schiefelbusch, R. L. (Eds). (1976). *Teaching Special Children.* New York: McGraw-Hill.
Relates research on applied behaviour analysis to special education. Includes interesting chapters on language teaching.

Holland, J. G., Solomon, C., Doran, J., and Frezza, D. A. (Eds). (1976). *The Analysis of Behaviour in Planning Instruction.* Reading, Mass: Addison-Wesley.
Highly technical but well worth the effort.

O'Leary, K. D., and O'Leary, S. G. (1977). *Classroom Management: The Successful Use of Behaviour Modification,* 2nd Edn. Oxford: Pergamon Press.
An extensive account of the use of behaviour modification in the classroom. Definitely *not* an introductory text.

Stephens, T. M. (1977). *Teaching Skills to Children with Learning and Behaviour Disorders.* Columbus, Ohio: Charles E. Merrill.
Uses a skill-training orientation to describe classroom strategies for dealing with academic and social learning problems.

Vargas, J. S. (1977). *Behavioural Psychology for Teachers.* New York: Harper and Row.
A readable introductory book.

Ulrich, R., Stachnik, T., and Mabry, J. (Eds). (1974). *Control of Human Behaviour, Volume 3. Behaviour Modification in Education.* Illinois: Scott, Foresman.
Contains accounts of the application of behaviour modification in a wide range of educational settings.

CHAPTER 8

Classroom Evaluation

Chapter Goal: *To discuss issues of classroom evaluation with regard to the presented approach.*

Textbooks about evaluation tend *not* to be written specifically with the teacher of the slow learner in mind. Bloom *et al.* (1971), for example, is an authoritative 900-page tome containing sections on Art, Industrial Education, Science, and the like. Most books of this kind tend to be long and technical, concerned with the evaluation of entire school systems and their curricula, and are likely to be most relevant to the student of evaluation. If this is your interest there are a great many books to choose from, for example Mehrens and Lehmann (1973), Gronlund (1976), and Anderson *et al.* (1975).

Most of this book is concerned with writing and implementing programmes of objectives for individual children in the normal school classroom. The goals of these programmes are usually limited to one or two specific skills in a particular subject area. This chapter, therefore, is intended to be introductory in so far as it assumes no previous knowledge of or experience in evaluation, and is geared particularly to evaluating such a programme. It is important to stress that the issues and techniques involved in evaluating a school's curriculum (such as the project described in Chapter 9) are not comprehensively covered here, and further reading would be necessary before such an evaluation exercise was undertaken.

To become effectively involved in classroom evaluation requires more than a knowledge of evaluation techniques. An appropriate set of attitudes is a fundamental requirement. There needs to be an explicit acknowledgement that what we do as teachers in the classroom is fallible, that there is almost certainly room for improvement, and that we have a responsibility to seek out where these improvements should be made. There needs to be a readiness to make private classroom plans and teaching methods explicit to colleagues, to share experiences and knowledge, and to pool ideas. There needs to be a willingness to ask fundamental questions about what we are doing and the way in which we are doing it – questions which may challenge long-established classroom practices and the habits and beliefs of a lifetime. Precisely what are we trying to teach these children to do that they cannot do already? How successful are we being? Is there a better way of doing it? There is a need to ask questions of this kind, actively to seek out information which will help to answer them and, perhaps most important of all, to be prepared to adapt and change in response to this information.

We do not mean by any of this, of course, that children's programmes of work should be displayed on a notice-board at the school gates alongside a Suggestion Box. Nor is it even implied that any professional person outside school need *necessarily* be involved. What *is* required is a *desire* for some kind of self-appraisal with a view to becoming more effective. It is necessary to be able to say 'This is what I am going to teach, and this is the way I intend going about it. Let's see how successful I am, and how I might improve'. Moreover, asking and trying to answer questions of this kind must be coupled with a willingness to respond, adapt and change – if change seems appropriate. And finally, this process of continually seeking out ways of teaching more effectively can be made much more productive if it is shared by colleagues. If, and only if, these attitudes prevail can classroom evaluation be effective.

Is this not much ado about nothing? Most teachers *are* adaptive, responsive, continually seeking to increase their effectiveness, and always welcoming of constructive criticism. Or are they? Bessent and Moore (1967) suggest that the typical school is 'a somewhat somnolent system reposing in a state of long-established norms ... and staunchly devoted to remaining in this condition'. Whether or not this is true of schools and teachers in general can be argued. We know of no directly relevant empirical evidence either to indict or to vindicate the teaching profession on this issue, and so it is probably wise to avoid generalizations in either direction. Nevertheless we have found a growing interest in and commitment to self-appraisal, and it is within context that the word 'evaluation' has become a part of our common vocabulary.

What is Classroom Evaluation?

Classroom evaluation was defined by Gronlund (1976) as '*a systematic process of determining the extent to which instructional* [behavioural] *objectives are achieved by pupils*'. Whilst the many published definitions vary slightly from one to another, nearly all make reference to two important aspects of evaluation. The first is that it is a 'process', and the second is that it is primarily concerned with discrepancies between teaching goals and pupil achievements (or objectives and actual learning outcomes). These two aspects of classroom evaluation are so fundamental that each is discussed in detail here.

The idea of evaluation being a process is a relatively new idea which was not widely recognized until the late 1960s. Until that time evaluators were concerned solely with the final outcome or product of the teaching programme. Evaluation came at the end, was entirely retrospective, and usually focused only on the extent to which the main goals of the programme had been achieved. A number of problems were found to be associated with this 'product mentality' to evaluation, as it became known in the literature. First of all, while this approach satisfactorily determines the extent to which the main programme goals are achieved, it invariably provides only limited insight into why a programme fails. For example, a teacher may develop a reading programme to be used with a small group of children on a withdrawal basis. It might be decided to 'evaluate' the project at the end of a term. The product approach to evaluation would simply determine what the pupils could do at the end of that period which they could not do at the beginning, with reference to the goals and objectives of the programme. If it is found that the programme's main goal has not been achieved, what happens next? Why has the programme failed? Is it worth maintaining the programme for a further term? If so, what modifications could be made that would improve its chances of success? Quite simply, no data has been collected upon which these questions can be answered.

Secondly, this approach to evaluation – by definition – yields no information which can be used *while the programme is running* as a basis for *ongoing* modifications. Throughout the implementation of a programme, the classteacher needs to make innumerable important decisions on a daily basis to do with such issues as: when and how to introduce new objectives, the length and frequency of the practice sessions on mastered objectives, and which teaching methods to use. 'Product evaluation' provides feedback on the appropriateness of all these decisions 'lumped together'. In other words, at the end of a fixed period of time, the teacher has some measure of how effective the implementation has been overall, but is provided with no useful ongoing information upon which to base her daily classroom decisions.

Evaluation then is a *process* in the sense that it is ongoing and continuous. It has to be if the information which it yields is to be of practical use to the classteacher. It is, in fact, an inseparable part of both the planning and the implementation of a programme.

The second important aspect of evaluation *involves* its primary emphasis of clarifying the discrepancies that exist between goals and practice – between the teacher's objectives and the pupil's observable achievements. Evaluation is therefore an ongoing information-gathering process which focuses upon the discrepancies between intent and actuality and methods of removing these discrepancies. The fundamental implication of this aspect of evaluation is the assumption that precise objectives which are expressed in observable terms have been previously rectified. As Gronlund (1976) says, 'Without previously determined objectives, it is patently impossible to judge the nature and extent of pupil learning'. Put like this the point is an obvious one, but of no less crucial importance. How can a programme be evaluated if its objectives were not made explicit before it began? Or, expressed in even simpler terms, how can you decide if you have achieved something if you have not yet made up your mind what you want to achieve?

Evaluating a Teaching Programme

We have so far emphasized that evaluation is a process and is primarily concerned with the discrepancy between the teacher's objectives and the pupil's observable achievements. It is an integral part of planning and implementing a programme. Central to these two ideas is the notion of 'feedback', a word used in evaluation jargon to describe information which is collected and used to help make decisions in the classroom. Feedback can take many forms and can be gathered in many ways (some of which will be described later), but without it: 'evaluation becomes a toothless vehicle for maintaining the status quo, even when change is appropriate' (Hayman and Napier, 1975).

The first step in evaluation is to decide upon the desired learning outcomes of the programme, or the specific behaviour changes required of the pupils. In other words the first step, vital to the total role of evaluation, is to write a programme of objectives. During these early planning stages a host of important decisions are taken in sequence, beginning with the selection of a broad subject area and the identification of teaching goals, and gradually becoming more specific until you have a sequence of carefully graded objectives leading to the targets of the programme.

What kind of information is used in the making of these decisions? Simply deciding upon a subject area to be the focus of the programme involves the teacher recalling the pupil's competencies in the basic skills and deciding which represents the 'priority educational need'. Relevant to this question is not only information on what the pupil can and cannot do, but value judgements about the relative importance of literacy, numeracy, handwriting, and other subject areas. From this point, and throughout the programme's development, a great many important planning decisions are made which are based upon a range of different kinds of information. For example, decisions are taken about teaching goals, target objectives, where the programme should begin, the sequence or order of objectives, and step-size. The information upon which these decisions are based includes:

(1) Existing knowledge of the pupil (preferably from written records) to include details of current competency levels and usual rate of learning;
(2) Teaching experience including information about how similar problems have been tackled previously with other pupils;
(3) Advice and information from colleagues who may have greater experience and knowledge in the particular area of the problem;
(4) Available theoretical knowledge relevant to breaking down the target into a sequence of objectives;
(5) Value judgements about the relative importance of different subject areas, and conditions and performance levels described in the objectives.

Collecting information of this kind and using it to make various planning decisions *is* an important part of the evaluation process. Chapters 3 and 4, therefore, were as much about evaluation as writing programmes – the two are inextricably interrelated.

Chapter 5 was about implementing a programme of objectives. A basic teaching model is used to help the reader conceptualize the sequence of decisions which must be made in planning and recording teaching and practice sessions. First a detailed assessment is carried out and the results recorded in order to determine exactly what the pupil can and cannot do in terms of the objectives of the programme. This information is essential for deciding what new objectives will be taught first and which objectives need further practice. Having decided *what* to teach, questions of materials, classroom organization and methods are considered. The sources of information relevant to this decision include one's own imagination and teaching experience, and advice and ideas from colleagues. During the development of a programme a number of stages are clearly identified. At each stage a decision is made and information relevant to that decision must be collected. This pattern is continued throughout the implementation of the programme – relevant information is collected (e.g. assessment data) which is then used to make a decision (i.e. what to teach next).

Chapter 7 described how the approach can be developed to incorporate more sophisticated techniques and ideas, and in so doing offered a strategy for tackling more persistent and long-term classroom learning problems. Nevertheless, the pattern persists. At each stage in the procedure information is collected which is then used to make a decision about either implementing or modifying the programme. Each decision, both in writing and implementing the programme, represents an aspect of the evaluation process. Chapters 5 and 7 therefore were as much about evaluation as implementing programmes – the two are interdependent.

The data upon which implementation decisions are based are the programme records – the dates when work on each objective is commenced, when each objective is mastered, and when each is checked. When to move on to the next new objective, when to practise mastered objectives and which need most revision, when to try out new teaching methods, and when and how to modify the programme, are all decisions which are taken on the basis of records kept during the implementation. This is the built-in and continuous check that all is going well and the early warning system should problems occur. Without this ongoing monitoring of progress, problems would not be identified the moment they arise, they could not be clearly defined, and no information would be available upon which a decision could be taken to overcome the problem. *This is the feedback without which evaluation cannot work.*

We began by saying that effective classroom evaluation is (i) a process, (ii) primarily concerned with identifying and removing discrepancies between the teacher's objectives and the pupil's observable achievements, and (iii) impossible without feedback. What we have in fact argued in this section is that Chapters 3, 4, 5, and 7 collectively were as much about evaluation as they were about writing and implementing programmes of objectives. Adopt the approach to learning problems outlined in detail earlier, and inevitably you will be involved in classroom evaluation.

A Broader View

We have consistently emphasized that classroom evaluation is primarily concerned with stating clear objectives and keeping detailed programme records. This is indeed the *central* component of the evaluation process, but by no means the only one. To leave the reader with such a narrow view of evaluation would be seriously to mislead by omission.

Most children with a problem in a particular subject have other problems as well, although perhaps not quite as severe. It would be rather unusual albeit not rare for a pupil to have very severe difficulties in one area but to be competent in all others. It is perhaps more usual for a pupil to have some difficulties in a number of subjects and particular problems in one or two. Furthermore, it is probably true to say that learning problems *tend* to be associated with poor attendance, misbehaviour in the classroom, lack of parental support, relationship difficulties with peers and so on. Whatever teaching programmes you develop and operate in the classroom, it is important that these arrangements are perceived and evaluated within the broader context of the child's educational needs. That is to say, while it is essential to be specific in terms of focusing on one or two particular aspects of the pupil's difficulties, this should not be a preoccupation at the expense of all else.

It is conceivable that a programme is written for a pupil with handwriting difficulties, and special arrangements are made for him to have an extra fifteen minutes supervized practice each day. Whilst it is obviously important that the evaluation takes account of progress made on the programme, there may be other incidental benefits which are quite independent of the development of handwriting skills. It might be that his attendance improves while the programme is running, or that his parents become involved whereas previously they were apparently uninterested. It might be that his self-confidence is boosted, or that he joins in school activities in which previously he would take no part. It might be that the frequency of classroom misconduct decreases, greater progress is made in other areas which are not the subject of the programme, or his willingness to relate to peers is improved. Any one or more of these positive developments may occur as a result of the adult attention received and progress made during the programme.

On the other hand, although it is much less likely, it is nevertheless possible that a programme may appear to have undesirable side-effects. For example, the pupil may be fearful of all the adult attention he is receiving, or resentful of being made to feel 'different' from his friends. It may be that the arrangements are *causing* peer relationship difficulties, if for instance he is being ragged in the playground. It is important that the teacher be sensitive to these issues, and does not become entirely preoccupied with the technical aspects of the objectives approach.

How can the classteacher take account of these broader aspects of programme evaluation? It might help to bear the following points in mind.

(1) It is half the battle merely to be aware that implementing a programme may influence a pupil's behaviour in a variety of ways which are apparently unrelated to the goals and objectives of the programme.

(2) An important, and often ignored, source of evaluation data is the pupil. Depending upon the age and language level of the child, try to encourage him to provide feedback on specific aspects of the programme, and emphasize that his opinion counts – as it should.

(3) Whenever possible try to collect objective data to supplement your impressions. For example, attendance can easily be monitored with reference to class registers, parental involvement can to some extent be quantified by making note of communications between home and school, and class records can be used to monitor progress in other subjects. If the child in question seems frequently to misbehave in the classroom, you could keep a diary of

serious misdemeanours (described in terms of observable pupil behaviour, of course) to see if the introduction of the programme has any effect.

None of the above suggestions is intended to be immensely time-consuming – the development and implementation of programmes remains the important feature of the approach and its evaluation. We are concerned here merely to stress that programme records (important though they are) are not the be all and end all of evaluation data, and that the class teacher should be sensitive to a wide range of possible changes in pupil behaviour.

The Question of Accountability

The idea of *accountability* assumes that the public have a right to demand that professional educators be held responsible for the results they achieve. This assumption, that schools, headteachers and classteachers, should be accountable or 'answerable' to society for what they do and how well they do it, is now probably not disputed by many. The thorny question, likely to provoke heated debate in any staffroom, concerns *how* they are held responsible. For example, Shearer (1977) argues that 'Those who are fearful of the demands for "accountability" suspect it could result in a return to a "payment by results" system'.

It can be argued that teachers *are* accountable and that satisfactory procedures already exist which safeguard all public rights and standards of education in our schools. After all, parents have the facility (and in many cases are actively encouraged through PTAs and the like) to take a full part in the life of the school, to discuss policy, programmes of work and so on. Furthermore, local authorities have procedures for monitoring standards in basic educational subjects, and local and national machinery exists to receive and deal with cases of parental and public discontent, whether the problem is to do with the individual child or an entire school. And in the final analysis, of course, the idea of accountability is built into our education system in so far as the public elect local councillors, who in turn elect and control the local education committee, to whom the Chief Education Officer is responsible, and so on right back to classteacher.

On the other hand, without denying the existence of professional hierarchies, local politics, complaints procedures, PTAs and the rest, it can also be argued that these are too often ineffective and that, in practice, teachers and schools can virtually be a law unto themselves and accountable to no-one. For example, if a child learned to read an average of three new words each week throughout his school career, he would leave school with a sight vocabulary well in excess of 1000 words. A weekly target of three new words seems ludicrously modest for a 'normal' child and yet hundreds of normal sixteen-year-olds leave our comprehensive schools each summer with a sight vocabulary of a mere fraction of this total. If our present accountability procedures worked adequately, how could such a situation exist unless condoned by the public?

It is probably true to say that accountability is more of a burning issue in America than in Britain. In recent years, for example, a number of States have passed laws making teachers and other school personnel accountable for the learning and development of their pupils. Teachers of handicapped children are typically required – by law – to prepare objectives for each course or programme they teach, and evaluation instruments (usually pupil records similar to the kind advocated in this book) for measuring and reporting on pupil progress at regular intervals. Furthermore, programmes of work usually need to be agreed by all parties concerned – including parents – before they are commenced. Little wonder it is a burning issue in many States.

This question is raised here, neither because we hold either of the polar views expressed above, nor because we would welcome the introduction of accountability laws like those which currently operate in parts of America. Rather, accountability is an important and integral part of the total role of evaluation, and some of the procedures which are associated with it are useful, operated on a voluntary basis.

How should the general principles of accountability affect the normal school classteacher who is operating a programme of objectives? Again, the available literature on this issue is extensive and varied (especially from American sources), but it is generally agreed that for accountability to become a reality, three important conditions must exist:

(1) There must be a programme of objectives, defined in behavioural terms, and including details of performance levels;
(2) The programme must be understood, as far as possible, by everybody concerned;
(3) It must be clear to everybody concerned what everybody else is 'contracted' to do in terms of producing and operating the programme (i.e. role specification).

The point should be emphasized that role specification applies to everybody – it should not be, for example, that the headteacher knows what everybody else has to do, but nobody knows what the headteacher has to do. Everyone must be accountable, and the procedure must work in all directions, independent of status or professional hierarchies.

To see how all of this might work out in practice we can return to where we began – with Peter, the subject of the case study in Chapter 1. You will remember that Peter was in the first year of a primary school's junior department. He could read only six or seven words on the Burt WRT, and was struggling with simple computation possibly, it was speculated, due to a lack of understanding of basic number concepts. It was suggested in Chapter 3 that suitable teaching goals for Peter might be:

(1) To teach an initial sight vocabulary;
(2) To teach an understanding of simple numbers.

You will remember too that Peter's mother was co-operative, and that a number of outside agencies became involved, including a remedial specialist and an educational psychologist.

If the following arrangements were agreed and made explicit to all concerned, there would be genuine accountability. The *classteacher* agrees to:

(1)   Write a suitable reading programme for Peter;
(2)   Spend ten minutes on the programme each day in the classroom;
(3)   Keep careful programme records and report progress weekly to the parent and headteacher.

The *headteacher* agrees to:

(1)   Co-ordinate the efforts of all those concerned, i.e. confirm verbally made arrangements in writing, distribute copies of programmes etc.;
(2)   Call and chair meetings whenever necessary, including the weekly 'progress meetings' with the parent and classteacher.

The *parent* agrees to:

(1)   Explain the arrangements to Peter as best she can;
(2)   Attend a short weekly progress meeting at the school;
(3)   Whenever possible, spend five minutes each day working on some aspect of the programme suggested by the classteacher.

The *psychogist* agrees to:

(1)   Help the classteacher write the programme;
(2)   Visit the school at least once every three weeks for a term on an advisory basis.

The *remedial specialist* agrees to:

(1)   Visit the school at least once during the term to advise on teaching methods and resources.

Peter agrees to:

(1)   Try his best whenever his teacher or mother is helping him with his reading.

Arrangements of this kind must be made through discussion and negotiation among all interested parties. Agreement must be unanimous, and all role specification must be common knowledge. If these conditions exist, the idea of accountability need not be seen as threatening or potentially punitive to the professional. Instead, it becomes a procedure with a number of built-in practical advantages. Planning, in terms of both writing and implementing a programme, is made easier and more efficient. There is a genuine team effort in so far as everybody knows exactly what everybody else is contracted to contribute towards the achievement of a set of commonly agreed goals and objectives. And evaluation feedback is made easier to collect and more comprehensive through regular meetings and clearly defined channels of communication.

Summary

This chapter introduces some of the important issues involved in the classroom evaluation of a programme of objectives. It is stressed that effective evaluation is (a) an on-going process which begins when the programme is being written and continues during its implementation; (b) primarily concerned with identifying and removing discrepancies which exist between the teacher's objectives and the pupil's observable achievements, and (c) impossible without feedback, which can take many forms but must include detailed programme records.

It is argued that evaluation, programme planning, and classroom implementation are interdependent, and that Chapters 3, 4, 5, and 7 incorporate effective evaluation procedures. Nevertheless, evaluation should be seen in a broad context, and the classteacher should be aware that a programme may influence a wide range of pupil behaviour in areas which are apparently unrelated to the targets of the programme.

Finally, the question of accountability is raised, and procedures are suggested which have a number of practical advantages while de-emphasizing the threatening connotations often associated with the concept.

Recommended Further Reading

Anderson, S. B., Ball, S., Murphy, R. T., and Associates (1975). *Encyclopedia of Educational Evaluation.* San Francisco: Jossey-Bass.
Contains a useful glossary of evaluation jargon.
Bloom, B. S., Hastings, J. T., and Madaus, G. F. (1971). *Handbook on Formative and Summative Evaluation of Student Learning.* New York: McGraw-Hill.
Necessary reading for the student or specialist evaluator. It is quoted and referred to in most subsequent text books on evaluation.
Gronlund, N. E. (1974). *Determining Accountability for Classroom Instruction.* New York: Macmillan.
A 60-page account of the main issues and problems involved in accountability programmes which emphasizes the importance of behavioural objectives.
Gronlund, N. E. (1976). *Measurement and Evaluation in Teaching.* New York: Macmillan.
600 pages and rather technical. Again recommended only for the student of evaluation. Focuses rather heavily on tests and testing.
Hayman, J. L., and Napier, R. N. (1975). *Evaluation in Schools: A Human Process for Renewal.* Belmont, Calif.: Wadsworth.
A highly recommended 130-page introduction to the basic principles of evaluation in schools.

CHAPTER 9

Objectives and the Special School Curriculum

Chapter Goal: *To describe how the objectives approach was used in the development of curriculum in a special school for children with learning difficulties.*

Most of the suggestions and ideas in this book concerning the use of objectives when teaching children with learning difficulties were developed as a direct result of the authors' work in a special day school for educationally subnormal (mild) children. In our respective roles as headteacher and consulting educational psychologist, we have field-tested the application of the objectives approach in this school, the population of which consists of pupils with extreme forms of learning difficulty. Because of this, the approach used had to be more systematic than could be reasonably expected when dealing with slow learners in a normal school. Thus, the approach came to be used within the much wider framework of curriculum development.

The purpose of this chapter is to describe the development of this objectives-based curriculum. Issues of practical interest concerning this project are discussed and should be of use to teachers working in a variety of educational settings. This will be of particular relevance to colleagues working in special schools and units who may also wish to apply the approach in the direction of curriculum development.

To provide a setting for the reader we will first of all describe some of the important features of the school concerned in the project. It is a day ESN(M) school, catering for 160 children in the age range 5–16 and is situated in an urban area of the West Midlands. It was opened in 1959 and has a traditional building, with eight class bases, plus specialist housecraft and handicraft facilities. In addition, a youth club wing was added in 1975 and this has made further space available for use during the school day. The building, while being of a traditional design, provides a very flexible setting with large classrooms and spacious corridor and cloakroom areas that have been converted to provide extra working and storage spaces.

During the past four years the value of the space available in the school has become more obvious with the rapid increase in staffing. The local authority, being generous and positive towards special education, has staffed the school at the level recommended by the DES in 1973 and, at the time of writing, the staff of the school consists of sixteen teachers, including the head, and four ancillary assistants. As the story of the curriculum development project in the school is told, the importance of the flexible building and excellent staffing level will be seen to be of importance.

The other important factor in the story is the pupil population of the school. The nature of the pupils in an ESN(M) school is very much governed by its geographical position. Most of the children who attend the project school, because of its situation within an industrial town, come from 'socially disadvantaged' homes – homes in which material poverty is often compounded by problems of a social, emotional, and, very often, medical nature. The emphasis within the school, therefore, while seeking to meet individual pupil needs, is to serve a relatively homogeneous population of children with a narrow range of experience. More precisely the staff recognize that a common deficit of many of the pupils is in the area of language development. Bereiter and Engelmann (1966) have said: 'There is a justification for treating cultural deprivation as synonymous with language deprivation'. A commitment to this notion is reflected in the curriculum that was developed.

An important factor which influenced the work of the school was a radical change in the admission age. When the present Head joined the staff in 1974 the peak for admissions was around 10 and 11 years of age. It was felt in the school that an earlier intervention was likely to be more successful. Very often children with extreme learning difficulties can be picked out quite early on in their infant school and if they can at that point be provided with appropriate teaching, the risk of secondary handicaps, resulting from extended exposure to failure, can be avoided. About the same time the local authority, under the guidance of its Psychological Service, began to experiment with a system for the early identification of educationally 'at risk' children. Traditionally, it has been argued that children should be given a reasonable period in normal school before referral for possible special education (Cleugh, 1968). Recently, however, there has been growing support for an earlier intervention in the lives of children liable to have educational problems. As a result, the school underwent a fairly rapid change from a situation where most children were being admitted between 8–11, to one where the usual age of admission was between 5–7. This is in line with the kind of thinking outlined in Chapter 2, in which it was argued that there was a need for an earlier, preventative approach to children with learning difficulties, rather than attempting to ameliorate problems compounded by repeated failure and frustration. An obvious progression that should result from earlier admission to the special school, is that greater numbers of such pupils will progress to a stage where they can be successfully reintegrated into mainstream education. This possibility was also to have some effect upon the work of the project school.

Special Schools – For and Against

What, then, were the circumstances that led this particular special school, typical of many such schools in our urban communities, to seek to use the objectives approach as a basis for curriculum development? Probably the overriding factor was an organizational one, concerning the very nature of a segregated special school.

In recent years there has been increasing criticism of the whole notion of educating ESN(M) children in separate educational facilities. On a philosophical level, at least, there is an increasing belief that such children might be as well, if not better, off, if they were to receive their education within a fully integrated setting. The main arguments against educating slow-learning children in special schools are that:

(1)   Parents are frequently unhappy about their child being admitted to a special school;

(2)   There is a stigma associated with special schools that can be very distressing for children, particularly at the adolescent stage;

(3)   The label 'educationally subnormal' is often associated in people's minds with mental subnormality;

(4)   There is no unequivocal evidence that slow-learning children make better progress as a result of being educated in a special school;

(5)   The curriculum of a special school must inevitably be more restricted and consequently opportunities for wider educational development are limited;

(6)   The special school child is denied the opportunity to interact with 'normal' children;

(7)   Since children often travel out of their home district to attend the special school, they lose social contact with their neighbourhood peer group;

(8)   Transfer to a special school seems almost inevitably to be a 'life sentence' since, although transfer back is theoretically possible, in practice it rarely occurs.

This summary of the main arguments against sending children to special schools is weighty and impressive. Indeed, if special schools did *not* exist we would find it difficult to make a conclusive argument for their creation. Nevertheless, they do exist and are likely to continue to do so. What, then, apart from a good staffing ratio and generally caring environment, are the advantages of segregating a slow-learning child?

Probably the greatest strength of a special school is the concentration of staff who, at the very least, have a shared commitment to working with and helping children with learning difficulties. Often, teachers in ordinary schools who have a specialist interest in working with slow-learning children, work in isolation or, at best, in minority groups within a staff whose interests are wide and diverse. Frequently, the special or remedial teacher in an ordinary school has a low status, has access to limited resources, has only a minor voice when it comes to requesting changes in school policy and organization, and has limited career opportunities in comparison with more academic colleagues. Teachers in a special school need experience none of these disadvantages. The Head and staff together are in a position to make a strong collective request for additional resources, policy and organization of the school are totally concerned with providing an appropriate environment for the slow learner, and career prospects within special schools are usually excellent. But, more than all of these, the special school has one overriding advantage – the joint commitment of the staff can be utilized to provide a powerful weapon to overcome the most severe learning problem. The education within a special school can be provided in a highly consistent and continuous fashion in order that the child's difficulties can be dealt with effectively over an extended period. Furthermore, the teacher interaction that can be on-going leads to a much higher level of professional competence and confidence amongst the staff.

Sad to relate, however, visits to some special schools lead us to realize that this advantage is not always applied. In some special schools the classes appear to be totally independent with no apparent system for formally relating the work going on in one class with that going on in the others. So, as the child moves from one teacher to the next the process of education seems to come to a halt and then restart, often without any attention being paid to what has gone before. The advantage of getting teachers to share their expertise within the special school is lost when no formal or semi-formal procedure is available for discussion and comparison of ideas and experiences. It has to be said that it is in such a situation, where the major strength of a special school is largely ignored, that the arguments *against* segregation are most compelling.

Curriculum Development – an Organizational Format

Returning to the situation in the project school, the plan was to maximize this major advantage of a special school – the continuity and consistency of teaching that can be provided. The problem was to find a strategy to make this theoretical aim work in practice. Furthermore, we were seeking a system that could fully utilize the excellent staffing level within the school, despite the limitations of a formal classroom arrangement that had tended to dictate a primary school, class-classteacher form of organization. What was required was a system that could fit into this traditional setting in a way that would allow maximum involvement of all staff with the children.

The first important decision that was made was an organizational one. It was decided that in order to improve the team work of the staff there must be some forum for discussion – a formalized procedure whereby Head and staff could debate and make decisions about issues regarding the running of the school. This may seem obvious, but it is surprising how often special school teachers are heard to complain about the lack of communication within their schools. It is essential that clear information on day-to-day issues is available to *all* members of the staff. The efficient and calm running of a special school is vital if a suitably stable working atmosphere is to be maintained. Very often children with learning difficulties have great difficulty in adjusting to changes of routine and certainly last-minute, apparently unplanned, changes can completely throw such pupils and destroy the working atmosphere within a class. Therefore, consistent organization, based on a clear procedure for decision-making, is essential.

It was decided that school should commence each morning with a fifteen-minute staff meeting. This was to be a time when organizational matters could be sorted out and all the staff made aware of important changes. It was also seen as a forum at which organizational procedures and approaches to individual children could be discussed and, where necessary, modified. The implementation of these meetings was a simple but effective step towards developing greater consistency, and can be fully recommended to colleagues in other schools.

Very soon it became apparent that while many of the day-to-day issues could be dealt with in the morning meetings, there existed a great many more complex matters about which there was a need for prolonged staff discussion. These were to do with actual classroom practice. It became obvious that the most crucial area that needed long and detailed attention was the curriculum of the school. Clearly, fifteen minutes each morning, however valuable, was not sufficient even to scratch the surface of this enormous issue. It was decided, therefore, that there was a need for regular after-school meetings.

Thus the organizational format for curriculum development within the school was created – a series of on-going, after-school discussions which all staff were encouraged to attend and to contribute to by debate. Initially the meetings were very tentative. Matters of common concern (e.g. visual perception, auditory discrimination, organization of reading resources, etc.) were dealt with as they came up. No overall plan existed and no clear long-term goal was set.

Gradually certain guiding rules emerged from the meetings. First of all, in fairness to staff with family responsibilities, the programme of meetings was planned well ahead and time limits set for each meeting. Secondly, a reasonably clear brief was set for each meeting and, whenever possible, members of staff were presented with a discussion document to help structure and stimulate the argument. Individuals, or groups of staff, with a particular interest usually took on the task of preparing the discussion documents. Finally, at every meeting there was some attempt to reach a conclusion and, as soon as possible afterwards, each member of staff was provided with a written summary of the decisions made. The intention was that these basic guidelines would make the meetings purposeful, enjoyable and, most important, decision-orientated in order that practical classroom developments would result.

It must be stressed at this point that for a long time the meetings, whilst often being interesting, did not lead to any massive classroom changes. Some of the issues discussed, on reflection, were of marginal importance and the decisions made were relatively uninformed. Nevertheless, an organizational pattern was set and it was a pattern that was to be maintained over a period of years, and ultimately was to lead to important classroom developments.

This form of school-based curriculum development within a special school, which should in the long run lead to greater consistency and continuity of teaching, has two important side effects:

(1) It provides a powerful system of in-service training within the school. Collectively the staff of the school can decide upon their own in-service needs and then, together, they seek to pool their ideas, experience, and expertise to meet these needs. The questions asked are specific to the school and the answers provided are relevant, meaningful, and realistic. If possible, outside expertise, such as educational psychologists, speech therapists, advisers and inspectors should be called in to provide additional inputs.

(2) The discussion, being relevant and meaningful, leads to a greater

understanding of the curriculum decisions that are taken. Furthermore, each member of staff clearly has a say in the decision-making process. Together these factors lead to a greater commitment amongst staff to the decisions made and, consequently, the chances of implementation at classroom level are much better. Too often schools have beautifully written curriculum documents but, perhaps because of a lack of staff involvement at the development stage, there is no apparent evidence of direct implementation.

To sum up so far, in order to maximize the major benefit of a special school, the collective strength of staff expertise used in a consistent and continuous manner, an organizational procedure relying heavily on discussion meetings and consensus decision-making was implemented, and this formed a basis for school-based curriculum development and in-service training. The next stage was to try to provide some structure for development and clear goals at which to aim. The danger is that teachers will happily meet to discuss their problems but, without some clear plan, never reach a stage of decision. Furthermore, the development of an entire curriculum for a school with an age range 5–16 is a daunting prospect. If a conceptual framework is not provided there is a strong possibility that the complexity of the issues involved will mitigate against the work ever being taken to a level where practical implications are evident.

A Curriculum Model

A strong influence on the thinking within the school was Bloom's (1975) notion of mastery learning, previously described in Chapter 2. It will be recalled that in mastery learning the emphasis is switched from a consideration of ability and other factors which imply a limited learning potential, to aptitude, which suggests that all children will learn successfully provided the teacher optimizes classroom conditions to match the pupil's needs.

In these terms we can move away from thinking of the ESN(M) child as having poor ability or low IQ to thinking of him as a child with different aptitude for learning. This simply means that, although he may learn a particular task at a much slower rate than other children, provided the teacher presents appropriate learning tasks matched to the learner's understanding, interests, and experience, he will make educational progress. It must be stressed, of course, that a pupil's aptitude may vary from subject to subject or even within a subject. Thus, you may have a pupil slow to learn arithmetic who makes average progress in reading, or a child who takes a long time to master one aspect of arithmetic but then moves quickly through some later stages. It is perhaps more accurate to talk of 'slow-learning behaviour' rather than to label a child who, in certain situations, may learn quite quickly, as 'a slow-learner'.

In attempting to apply mastery learning thinking in developing a curriculum for a special school, if we are realistic it is necessary to recognize that for a child who learns at a very slow rate it may take an enormous period of time to achieve total mastery of any given topic. So it is necessary to consider carefully whether the time and effort to achieve this is justified in terms of the overall educational needs of the pupil. Brennan (1974) suggests that for slow learners 'the areas where learning must be for thoroughness or mastery should be reduced to an essential minimum.'

As far as developing a special school curriculum is concerned, what rationale can be used in deciding which skills the children will need to master? Indeed, why have mastery learning at all? As parents we do not hesitate to teach basic skills of physical safety to a mastery level at a very early age. For example, we would not expect to have to justify continuing with instruction in a skill such as crossing the road until an acceptable level of competence is achieved. The difference seems to be that in schools we often fail to identify those areas of skill and knowledge that we consider to be *essential* for our pupils to master. Consequently, in the absence of such a decision, the teacher may leave a crucial topic only partially achieved by some of her pupils. Every teacher has a responsibility to make decisions about areas of mastery learning for her pupils. Her decision need not be regarded as final since she may wish to modify it in the light of her pupils' progress. As Bloom (1975) says, 'not all school subjects need strive for mastery learning, and perhaps not all students should strive for mastery learning in all subjects'.

In trying to apply the mastery learning idea to the development of curriculum in the project school the ideas of Brennan (1974) were useful. In his book *Shaping the Education of Slow Learners*, he makes the important point that techniques of modern curriculum development and design have not been widely applied to curriculum for slow learners. He traces the historical development of approaches to the education of slow learners and identifies two basic orientations that appear to exist. The first of these is based upon assumptions about limited capabilities and stresses basic minimum learning that may realistically be achieved; because the pupil can learn only a minimum amount, the teacher spends a lot of time teaching basic subjects. He suggests that this approach is usually 'arid, repetitive, lacking in excitement and transfer outside the school situation'. The second orientation attempts to see slow learners in terms of their future needs and thus tends towards curriculum approaches based upon relevant projects or centres of interest. Brennan argues that whilst this may generate interest it frequently fails 'to transfer it back to the school as a motivator of more routine learning in the basic subjects'. No doubt, readers with a wide knowledge of special schools will be able to think of examples of schools where the general orientation fits closely to these two definitions.

The approach to curriculum planning for slow learners that is recommended by Brennan is to combine aspects of both the above orientations by thinking about curriculum in terms of two distinct areas: one in which learning with thoroughness or mastery is essential, and the other where learning to familiarity or awareness is more appropriate. This approach is a development of the ideas of Tansley and Gulliford (1960) who also proposed a curriculum consisting of two parts – a core of language and number and a periphery of additional useful knowledge about the environment, creative abilities and practical interests – and is consistent with the application of mastery learning outlined above. Brennan goes on to suggest that the teacher should treat neither area as being permanently superior to the other, allowing the relationship between the two to vary according to pupil needs, and that interaction between the two should be cultivated 'in order to motivate and reinforce learning, generate transfer of learning, and balance thoroughness and breadth in the curriculum'. This concern for balance in the curriculum is very important and should be the concern of all teachers working with slow learners, particularly in special schools where there is a distinct danger of providing a very limited and, indeed, limiting educational programme.

The obvious practical problem in attempting to implement Brennan's approach is in deciding how to divide subject matter into the two broad areas. Ideally this should be done individually for each pupil, taking into account existing levels of attainment and future needs, but, initially at least, in a special school with a relatively homogeneous population it is more realistic to think in terms of the needs of the pupils as a whole and then later to use the produced plan as a basis for assessing individual pupils and planning appropriate programmes.

In order to apply Brennan's curriculum approach within the school as a basis for structuring the staff discussions a simple model was designed. Figure 8 attempts to illustrate the two major dimensions of the model and serves as a basis for discussing their relationship. It may also be used as a reference point for groups of teachers wishing to develop a curriculum along similar lines.

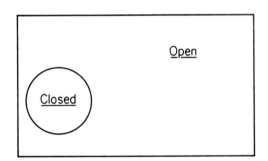

Figure 8   Diagram of a two-part curriculum model

One aspect of the model was referred to as the *Closed Curriculum*. This title indicated an area of skills and knowledge that was to be regarded as essential learning for all the children in the school; essential that is, in terms of two possible long-term goals – integration into mainstream education or assimilation into adult society at school-leaving age. In other words, the Closed Curriculum was seen as an attempt to predict those skills and knowledge areas necessary for the child's subsequent classroom success and, in the long run, essential to his success and happiness in post-school life. Vital to the definition of the Closed Curriculum was that all skills and knowledge should be learned to a mastery level.

The other aspect of the model was labelled *Open Curriculum*. This was viewed as being open-ended, with content being modified as a result of the on-going assessment of each pupil's attainments, needs, and interests. Also within the definition of this aspect of the curriculum was the question of developing appropriate values, attitudes, and interests.

From the outset, the two distinct areas were seen as being very much interrelated, with many aspects of the Open Curriculum being seen as vehicles for the application and elaboration of skills and knowledge defined in the Closed Curriculum. Furthermore, while the distinction was clearly made at the stage of staff discussion and decision-making it was always emphasized that teachers should not take the segregated curriculum form and apply it rigidly when making classroom decisions regarding methods and organization. Later on in this chapter we will consider the relationship between the two aspects of the curriculum in greater detail.

The use of the terms 'Closed' and 'Open' has no definitive significance outside the school, and we have no desire to see them put to use in other schools. It was merely useful for discussion purposes to provide some verbal shorthand. Certainly the terms have been useful and have become meaningful to the staff of the school – 'Closed' suggesting a distinct agreed section of minimum essentials that the staff were committed to teach to a mastery level, and 'Open' indicating a far broader and more changeable section in which achievement would inevitably vary according to individual pupil differences. Outside of their use within the school's curriculum discussions no other specific meaning or connotation is implied, or should be inferred, by their use.

Aims, Goals, and Objectives

Having created an organizational system and a theoretical framework for curriculum development, the next stage was to convert this into practical classroom terms. Figure 9 will help to explain how this was accomplished. It is an approach to curriculum planning which develops from the general to the specific.

Figure 9   The relationship between content areas, goals, and objectives

Usually curriculum planning begins with a statement of rather philosophical, long-term aims. Within this context we would prefer to abbreviate debate of the issue, not because it is considered to be of relegated importance, but for reasons of space and a belief that there is an adequate basis of agreement among most educators of children with learning difficulties. It is often argued that, at this level of curriculum development, special education does not exist since within a democratic society the general aims of our educational system must be the same for all children. To extend this discussion to the many and complex issues involved in the 'aims of education' is certainly beyond our brief. However, for those who wish to pursue this matter, a useful starting point is Tansley and Gulliford's (1960) much-quoted aims, concerning the development of personal and social adequacy.

The three levels of curriculum development represented in Figure 9 should now be familiar and meaningful to the reader who has digested the earlier chapters of this book. The format for curriculum development follows the same sequence as in developing an individual teaching programme and represents a series of decisions that have to be made by the members of staff involved in the development:

(1) *Content areas* – What broad areas are to be taught? This can be defined in terms of traditional school subjects or as projects or centres of interest;
(2) *Teaching goals* – What are the priorities within this particular content area? Written down as broad statements of the teachers' intentions;
(3) *Objectives* – What will the pupils have to do that will indicate that the teaching goal has been achieved? Clear statements of observable pupil behaviour.

Returning to Figure 9, we can now see the significance of the wedge shape. Because they are so general and long-term, there will only be a few content areas. However, within an educational programme there will be numerous goals and from these will be generated an even greater number of objectives.

Curriculum Objectives – Some Theoretical Issues

Before going on to consider in more detail how this style of curriculum planning was used in the project school it is necessary to stop and draw the reader's attention to certain theoretical issues related to the use of objectives in the field of curriculum. We have already seen how objectives can be used in planning individualized teaching programmes for children with learning difficulties and how this can provide a number of important practical advantages. These same advantages are implicit when using objectives in curriculum development but there are a number of other implications which we cannot ignore.

During the 1960s, with the development of programmed learning, there was considerable interest and argument about the use of explicit learning objectives. The aim was to develop objectives that were *behavioural* – that is, objectives that focus on the pupil's observable performance at the end of an educational activity and which confirm that learning has occurred. This type of objective came to be known by a variety of names, including behavioural objective, performance objective, and instructional objective, although the format is the same, and has been used for planning in a wide range of fields, including psychology, the training of aircraft pilots, commercial management, and curriculum development. An important feature of a behavioural objective, in whatever field it is used, is that it should make clear to those involved in an activity precisely what is going on and where it should lead. As we have already explained, this type of clear thinking is vital to a teacher who is planning work for children who have had long experience of learning failure.

Perhaps the most important advantage in using behavioural objectives in the field of special education is that, as we have seen, when they are carefully sequenced to provide an analysis of a learning task, they provide the teacher with a basis for planning suitable teaching procedures to meet the needs of individual pupils. In so doing, we are moving towards the goal of many special education teachers – individualized instruction. We have also seen that behavioural objectives are beneficial in performance assessment, monitoring progress, and teaching method evaluation.

However, in discussing the use of behavioural objectives within the context of curriculum development it is necessary to consider certain issues which continue to be a matter of dispute. In so doing we will highlight some of the difficulties and possible pitfalls in using this particular style of curriculum planning.

The literature on behavioural objectives contains widely differing views as to their value. Many of the arguments involved are highly theoretical. Readers who wish to pursue these issues in greater detail would be advised to read Popham (1972) and MacDonald-Ross (1975) in order to consider examples of the two polar views. For our purposes, concerned as we are with practicalities, we will leave most of the arguments for theoreticians and consider only those questions which are of relevance to the classroom teacher.

One of the main issues concerns the ambiguity of behavioural objectives. The suggestion is made that no matter how careful a teacher is in defining her objectives in behavioural terms, other teachers may still not clearly understand their precise meaning. In practical terms, this seems to be an unrealistic argument. Objectives written in terms of behaviour that can be observed and measured are the least likely to be ambiguous. Rather, they will provide a good basis for team teaching and continuity of approach where more than one member of staff is dealing with a pupil.

A related issue is that of specificity of objectives, since many would argue that where an objective is felt to be ambiguous it is necessary to specify the learning behaviour in clearer terms. Teachers then face the problem of lists of objectives that are too long to be of practical use. The question is, how specific should we make our objectives? No completely satisfactory answer can be given since the degree of specificity should be related to the practical needs of a given situation. Thus, for example, an objective written at the level of specificity of the one that follows may lead to some disagreement as to what is intended:

Copies a circle neatly when asked to do so.

To clarify the issue, greater detail about the desired performance might be added:

Copies a circle of radius 3" so that any diameter does not exceed $3^1/_2$" or be less than $2^1/_2$".

Further detail could also be given about the quality of the drawing. So the objective could get longer and longer. In general terms, however, a useful guide is to ensure that the objectives are specific enough to be meaningful and usable for both teacher and pupil (Tyler, quoted in Hayman and Napier, 1975).

A further issue, related to the ambiguity-specificity question, concerns the *generalizability* of learnt behaviour. That is to say, a behavioural objective demands that the important conditions, under which the observable action takes place, should be clearly stated. If, therefore, a child demonstrates an understanding of the word 'different' in a situation described in the objective, can the teacher be sure that he can generalize the concept to other contexts? For example, a child may identify a brick as 'different' on the basis of colour, but could he understand and use the word appropriately with materials which differ on another dimension, that is, shape or size? Clearly, we cannot generate sufficient objectives to cover every situation in which the word 'different' might be used. At the same time, to have the pupil use the word successfully in only one context should not be taken as evidence that the concept 'different' can be generalized to other contexts.

There is a feeling among some teachers that using behavioural objectives to plan lessons may not always be appropriate. In some lessons we may wish to present situations where the child must discover solutions and where there may be a number of acceptable answers possible. For example, in a lesson where a picture of a seaside scene is being used to stimulate the children's self-expression the teacher is seeking to get each pupil to make an individual statement and, in such a situation, all relevant responses are appropriate. It is also argued that children may benefit incidentally and in an unplanned-for manner during a particular lesson. Many teachers like to be flexible in their approach, taking advantage of situations that spontaneously arise to make useful educational points. The use of behavioural objectives need not exclude any of these possibilities. It is not suggested that teachers stick rigidly to predetermined learning paths. Behavioural objectives can and should be used flexibly. Furthermore, they should be constantly reassessed and if necessary modified to meet the changing circumstances of the pupils. Objectives should serve the teacher, rather than the teacher serve the objectives.

Certain subject areas are more readily described in behavioural terms than others. Important areas, such as creativity and the development of personal values and attitudes, present particular difficulties when the teacher attempts to define her objectives in precise and observable child behaviours. Furthermore, in some lessons we are concerned that our pupils should take part in an experience rather than master a specific level of achievement. In such a case the means are more important than the ends. For example, young children are often encouraged to take part in dressing-up, not in order to achieve competence in some aspect of the activity but simply because it is felt to be a useful experience in its own right.

To sum up, there clearly are problems associated with using behavioural objectives. Additional problems, concerning sequencing, have already been described in the earlier chapters. Nevertheless, none of the problems need be insurmountable. As the story of the curriculum development in the project school is further described we will seek to show how these problems and weaknesses can be approached.

Relating Objectives to the Curriculum Model

It has been suggested that some content areas do not lend themselves readily to the behavioural objectives format. For example, to predict observable behaviour at the end of a learning activity is to suggest that all children must exhibit homogeneous behaviour in order to demonstrate that the learning target has been attained. Implicit in many creative activities is an intention to elicit a wide variety of totally individual responses. As a result of this, behavioural objectives were not adopted exclusively throughout the Closed *and* Open Curriculum.

It is noticeable that the 'hard-line' approach of insisting that *all* curriculum material be expressed in behavioural terms has been abandoned by many influential advocates of the approach. Even Popham, one of the most famous supporters of their use, who during the 1960s is said to have distributed car-stickers to his students which read 'Help stamp out non-behavioural objectives!' has mellowed to the extent that they now read 'Help stamp out *some* non-behavioural objectives!' (Popham, 1975).

If behavioural objectives offer so many advantages why should they not be used to express all curriculum material? Some of the reasons have already been given. Chiefly it is a matter of cost-effectiveness and recognizing that there are limits to the amount of preparation and record-keeping that the most conscientious teacher can undertake. Behavioural objectives offer a means of systematic and effective teaching – but they are time-consuming. It was decided therefore that the Closed Curriculum should be expressed exclusively in terms of behavioural objectives for two main reasons:

(1)   The subject matter lends itself more readily to this style of presentation;
(2)   In order to have children master the essential skills and knowledge included in the Closed Curriculum, teachers' planning and instructional sequences must be as systematic and effective as possible.

As far as the Open Curriculum was concerned there were certain aspects that could appropriately be expressed in behavioural terms. Behavioural objectives were preferred as a format for skills and knowledge which are clearly hierarchical (i.e. where the learning of one idea is dependent upon knowledge of another) or which, by their nature, are manifested by homogeneous behaviour. However, it had to be recognized that many aspects of the Open Curriculum were far more appropriately stated in non-behavioural terms. Here, Eisner's (1975) notion of *expressive objectives* was found to be useful. This he defined as an objective that 'does not specify the behaviour the student is to acquire after having engaged in one or more learning activities'. He continues, 'An expressive objective describes an educational encounter: It identifies a situation in which children are to work, a problem with which they are to cope, a task with which they are to engage, but it does not specify what from the encounter, situation, problem or task they are to learn'.

Most of the remainder of this chapter is concerned with the details of the development and implementation of the Closed Curriculum in the project school. This emphasis is not because the Open Curriculum is regarded as being unimportant but because it is felt that it is within the vital areas of the Closed Curriculum that learning failure is most significant, and where the objectives approach is most beneficial. Certainly, if a child does not master these essential areas of skills and knowledge he will lack prerequisites for further self-development and, incidentally, will have quite likely failed to develop a suitably confident attitude to learning of any kind. It is not implied that teachers should allocate large proportions of each school day to the Closed Curriculum. Rather it is hoped that the structure provided will lead to more efficient teaching and learning of the Closed Curriculum objectives, thus leaving more time for the stimulation and enrichment of the wider aspects of the Open Curriculum.

Developing the Closed Curriculum

The Closed Curriculum has been developed over a period of four years and, of course, is still subject to further modifications. Only those skills and areas of knowledge felt by the staff to be essential for the children to master were included. It was developed in the form of two overlapping sections – junior and senior – and we can look at their development separately, to some extent.

The *junior section* was developed with children of the age range 5–11 years in mind. In the light of the trend towards much earlier admission of pupils to the school and the resultant new goal of possible reintegration of some of these children into ordinary schools, the emphasis was on basic educational subjects necessary if the child is to take a full part in later educational activities. Six Content Areas – Arithmetic, Gross Motor Development, Handwriting, Language, Reading, and Social Competence – were eventually agreed. Other areas were considered and, in some cases, even adopted.for a time, but were eventually omitted. At one stage, for example, there was a Visual Perception section, based largely upon the Frostig Developmental Test of Visual Perception (Frostig, 1964). Eventually it was agreed that there was insufficient evidence to support the claim that children trained in 'form constancy' and 'figure ground' skills are better able to learn to read and write as a result. Many of these visual perception objectives were therefore abandoned, although others, where appropriate, were incorporated into different Content Areas. For example, hand–eye co-ordination skills are demonstrably important in learning to write, so these objectives were included in Handwriting, and an ability to discriminate visually between similar letters and words was found to be most appropriately placed in the Reading section.

Another Content Area considered but eventually rejected, was 'Cognitive Style'. There is some evidence which suggests that learning failure is certainly associated with, and may even be caused by, a pupil not knowing how to learn or, in other words, having a 'faulty cognitive style' (Stott, 1974). Some believe that an appropriate cognitive style can be taught by training attention span, 'impulse control', persistence and so on. However, the evidence is by no means unequivocal, and it was eventually agreed that for the stated population, distractability is usually caused by educational failure, rather than failure being caused by distractability. Cognitive Style was therefore abandoned as an independent Content Area on the assumption that if appropriate tasks are presented in an interesting and meaningful way, ensuring educational success, distractability will decrease, and attention skills and persistence will improve.

Special mention should be made of the emphasis on the teaching of language in the Closed Curriculum. The relationship between language development and success in school is now fairly widely recognized; the consistent connection between retarded language development and failure in school has been witnessed by most teachers who have worked in a heavily industrialized urban setting and an awareness of the relationship is reflected in the emphasis placed on language in the Closed Curriculum. In addition to a separate Content Area entitled 'Language Development', an attempt was made to plan 'language across the curriculum' by incorporating specific linguistic components into objectives within the other Content Areas. For example, movement lessons offer the opportunity to teach concepts of spatial awareness (i.e. over, between, in front of, under) and the vocabulary of body parts. Within the gross motor section, therefore, objectives were included with clearly defined, built-in linguistic components. Very often the language objectives within other Content Areas are crucial in that they draw the teacher's attention to important vocabulary that the pupil will need if he is fully to understand tasks that he is required to undertake later on in the curriculum. So, for example, the following objective was included in the arithmetic section:

Uses the word 'set' in describing a collection of objects.

The implication is that the child must have mastered this language objective before he will be able to learn about building and comparing sets. A further advantage in incorporating this type of language objective is that it can help to standardize the vocabulary used by different teachers working in a team situation and thus minimize the chance of the pupil being confused.

In the development of the *senior section* of the Closed Curriculum a different emphasis emerged. Here the criterion for inclusion was related to the needs of the pupils on leaving school at the age of sixteen. The chosen Content Areas clearly reflect this emphasis. They were: Language Development, Maths, Home-making, Health and Hygiene, Do-it-yourself, Vocational Knowledge and Social Knowledge. The reader can no doubt well imagine the lively discussions that occurred when the meeting was trying to agree these sub-headings. Ask yourself, what are the most important skills for slow learners to master in order that they can successfully take up their place in adult society? There is no definitive answer, of course, but it is most important that the issue should be resolved within a school. While there will be some overlap, the nature of the answer will vary from school to school. A major factor in making the decision will be the type of environment in which the child will be likely to live. So, for example, the child being educated to live in a rural district is likely to need to master a slightly different range of skills to the child who is going to live in an inner-city area. The important thing is that teachers, taking this type of factor into account, have a responsibility to decide upon those areas their pupils will need to learn to a mastery level.

The Closed Curriculum materials appear as a series of programmes of objectives, similar to those presented in Chapter 6. Indeed, many of those examples are based upon the material developed in the project school. The essential difference in format is that in writing an individual programme we are only concerned with short-term issues; goals that will probably be achieved within a matter of weeks. When it comes to developing a curriculum which is intended to provide continuity of education over a period of many years, the issues are more complex. An obvious implication of this is the question of the relationship between the different programmes within the curriculum. Teachers need to have some guidance as to how each child should proceed as he completes a particular programme. In an ideal world each content area of the curriculum would consist of a linear sequence of programmes, with every child starting right at the beginning, on the first objective of the first programme, and working through until he had completed the final objective of the final programme. Alas, life is not so simple. Thus, there was a need to consider within each Content Area of the Closed Curriculum how the various programmes were related.

In some areas it was difficult even to speculate about any such relationship. So, for example, in Gross Motor Development, who can say whether the programme dealing with balance should precede throwing and catching balls. Commonsense would probably argue that if the teacher felt it to be appropriate they could be dealt with at the same time. Similarly, in Social Competence no useful relationship could be indicated between the programmes dealing with dressing, feeding, and toileting. In certain Content Areas, however, a useful relationship between the various programmes could be suggested. For example, in Reading, Arithmetic and Handwriting, diagrams were provided indicating the proposed hierarchical relationship between the various programmes within each of these areas. It has to be stressed that these diagrams were only meant as a guideline and that, particularly in the case of pupils being introduced to the curriculum at a later age, there was a need to use them flexibly. Nevertheless, for most of the children these guidelines do seem to have applied and the teachers have clearly found them to be of use. Figure 10 is taken from the Closed Curriculum *handwriting* section, illustrating how the five programmes should be related.

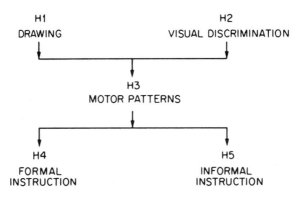

Figure 10   Relationship between the handwriting programmes

It is suggested that the programmes dealing with Drawing and Visual Discrimination might usefully be dealt with at the same time, and certainly both must be mastered completely before going on to start work on Motor Patterns.

Formal and Informal Instruction will only be introduced when the other three programmes are completed.

As the Closed Curriculum was being developed the issues of greatest debate concerned the sequences of objectives. All the issues referred to in Chapter 4 concerning the development of an individual programme had to be resolved for each area of the curriculum, taking into account the learning needs of the school's population as a whole. Thus, there was a great deal of argument about what steps should be included, what the order within a sequence should be, what the step-size should be, how much detail to include within each objective, and how generalization of new skills could be achieved. Often it was at this stage that the expertise of the educational psychologist was most useful, where he could apply his theoretical knowledge and experience to advising the staff about issues of dispute. Very often, however, complete agreement could not be achieved. At such a point the only solution was to take a vote and then, on the basis of that decision, take the particular sequence and, by trials within a number of classrooms, test the hypothesis. Over a period of time, a number of such issues were resolved, although in truth, even today, some still remain as a source of dispute within the school.

In some Content Areas within the senior part of the Closed Curriculum, the order of objectives in a sequence was not crucial. This was particularly true in parts of Social Education, where many of the objectives were concerned with basic items of general knowledge to be acquired. Take for example the following objectives from a programme dealing with current affairs:

(1) Names the four countries which comprise the United Kingdom;
(2) Names the capital city of England;
(3) Names the principal members of the Royal Family;
(4) Names the three main political parties.

It does not seem to be important that these objectives should be taught in a particular order. Knowledge of objective (1) will not necessarily make the acquisition of objective (2) any easier. Therefore, in areas such as this the objectives were sequenced in a commonsense order with, wherever possible, the simpler ideas preceding the more complex ones.

The entire curriculum, consisting as it does of 66 separate programmes of objectives, was developed, modified, and improved over a period of many months. Regular discussions and trial-and-error testing procedures led to inevitable changes being made. Early on in their development the various Content Areas were available for use in the classroom on loose, typed sheets. Eventually, however, a point was reached when it was felt that there would be a practical value in bringing together all the material in book form, in order to make classroom use easier. In fact two volumes were produced; one containing the junior section, the other the senior section. All members of staff received both books since there was obviously going to be overlap, particularly where children in the senior classes had not fully mastered all the objectives in the junior volume.

The lay-out of the two books was straightforward. Each was divided into the various agreed Content Areas. Then, after some explanation and discussion of important background issues, the programmes were presented with the goal at the top and the objectives listed in sequence below. A coding system was used to identify the various programmes and the objectives within the programmes. Thus, for example, the second programme in Home-making was given the code HM2 and so the first objective in this programme was HM2.01, and so on through the sequence. This system became useful in terms of quick reference and practical classroom use and, also, where there was a relationship between an objective in one programme and an objective in another, the code was used to draw attention to the relationship. Take this example from the area of Reading:

> R1.03 Discrimination between two spoken words which differ grossly by saying *same* or *different* (L2)

This is objective R1.03. The code L2 in brackets indicates that there is an objective in the Language part of the curriculum which is in some way related. It was found to be important and helpful that teachers were reminded of the interrelationships between objectives in different Content Areas.

All the objectives in the Closed Curriculum books were written out in clear, behavioural terms, indicating important conditions, but, in most cases, *without* any stated performance criteria. This latter omission was largely for purposes of brevity. We worked on the assumption that since there had been, and continued to be, a great deal of discussion amongst the staff concerned, the desired performance levels could be assumed. On reflection, this omission has caused some degree of continued disagreement where, for example, two members of staff have found themselves in disagreement about whether a child has, in fact, mastered a particular objective. The question left unanswered, where performance levels are absent, is what does mastery mean? Is nine out of ten good enough or must we continue for ten out of ten? It is the view of some members of staff, and we are included in this number, that the next time the curriculum is revised, explicit performance standards must be included in each objective.

One practical tip comes out of the experience of the project school that will be useful to any other special school wishing to adopt this approach to curriculum development. It is crucial to have at least one member of staff who is responsible for long-term planning, calling of meetings, and generally maintaining the impetus. It may be that the Head of the school wishes to take on this important role or it might be felt more appropriate to delegate responsibility to some other high-ranking colleague. Either way, if what is likely to be a very long-term project, perhaps over a number of years, is to be kept going, there is a need for a person who can make sure that when Christmas productions or summer camps come around, the curriculum discussions, though perhaps shelved for the time being, are not quietly forgotten.

In concluding this account of the development of an objective-based curriculum in a special school two points are of paramount importance:

(1) The strength of the entire development is *not* only the finished product but also the experience through which the staff have been. The extensive programme of curriculum development meetings has provided an excellent

basis for school-based in-service training, with a resultant increase in professional expertise. Furthermore, the staff, having been a party to the decision-making, have a high degree of commitment to the classroom implementation.

(2) The development is never finished. The curriculum material as it stands has gone through a great deal of field-testing and modification but there are many aspects that can still be vastly improved. The exciting aspect of this form of curriculum development is that it is a dynamic process, in which modification will continue indefinitely.

Implementing the Closed Curriculum

It is difficult to provide a straightforward, precise account of the classroom implementation of the Closed Curriculum. It was stressed in the earlier chapters that planning with objectives does not in any way limit the teacher's freedom to use whatever methods and resources are found to be effective. This same argument applies to the implementation of an objectives-based curriculum. Visitors to the school quite often seem to expect to see standardized teaching approaches being used. They are usually pleasantly surprised to find that very different styles can be, and are, used in conjunction with the objectives approach.

The basic issue involved in the implementation of the approach is one of individualization. Having produced a curriculum based on the teacher's predictions of the educational needs of the entire population of the school, the problem for each member of staff is to match and adapt that material to meet the needs of each individual pupil. Basically this is a problem of assessment. It is necessary to determine accurately where each pupil lies in relation to the various sequences of objectives. Which objectives have been mastered? Which have been partially achieved? And which are still to be approached? Once this information has been gathered the teacher is in an informed position to choose suitable tasks for each child to undertake. The important thing, particularly for children who in most cases have experienced a great deal of educational difficulty, is to set work at the correct level.

A major advantage of the objectives approach is that an efficient, yet simple, record system can be developed which forms a basis for continuous assessment. As note is made of the child's achievements, information is provided for choosing the next objective to work on. Furthermore, recording the date on which work commences on an objective helps the teacher to identify areas of possible difficulty. In the project school two slightly different record-keeping formats are used. In the younger classes the records consist of loose-leaf sheets bound together with plastic binders. This means that, for each child, only the current sheets need be kept and as a particular sheet becomes redundant it can be discarded. On these sheets the programmes of objectives are listed with the dating columns down the right-hand side. Four columns are used – 'initial assessment', 'working on', 'mastered', and 'checked'. The initial assessment column is only used for children new to the system who can be given a rapid screening to place them roughly at the correct places on the various programmes. The other three columns are used and dated in the manner described in Chapter 5. In the senior classes the concern is to make the record book relevant and meaningful to the pupil as well as the teacher. Therefore the objectives are written in simple language, using first-person statements (i.e. 'I can read a 24-hour clock'). Similar dating columns are used, but with an additional column in which the child writes his initials when *he* considers he has mastered an objective. These record books are small and compact, with a plastic cover, so that they can be kept around the classroom and, indeed, taken by the pupil to lessons in other parts of the school.

It must be said at this point that one of the major problems in implementing the Closed Curriculum was getting teachers to see the importance and advantages of determining a clear objective *before* deciding what teaching approach to use. Many teachers, including ourselves, were not trained to operate in this way. Instead, they have been encouraged to concentrate their planning on issues of classroom method – making the lesson meaningful, lively, stimulating, and enjoyable – leaving the question of objectives to be assumed. Similarly, some of the teachers in the project school, though committed to and involved in the curriculum work going on, found it difficult to alter their basic teaching approach. Invariably, what appeared to happen was that such teachers continued to operate in their traditional manner and then, at the end of each lesson, tried to relate the methods used to the objective of the curriculum. In other words, they were setting out on a journey with only a vague idea of where they were going and then, on arrival, they tried to determine their destination more accurately. It was interesting to observe how most of these very experienced colleagues gradually came to see the value of always starting with a clear objective in mind. It must be said, also, that once this happened the resultant classroom activity was often a joy to behold.

It is interesting to relate that inexperienced teachers rarely seem to have this adjustment difficulty. This could be because they come to the situation without predetermined ideas and, therefore, adopt the 'objectives-first' strategy quite naturally. Certainly, the presence of the Closed Curriculum has been of undoubted benefit to a whole series of teachers new to special education, including four probationary teachers, who have each in their own way relied very much on the material during their months as novices. One particular young colleague springs to mind who joined the staff at the height of the curriculum development and became very committed to the approach, knowing the sequences inside-out. He would amaze visitors, and members of staff, by holding forth in great detail about the sequences, talking solely in terms of the objectives' codes. The value of this form of curriculum when it comes to helping inexperienced teachers is immense. Too often in special schools, new teachers are dumped in a classroom without any clear guidelines and left to sink or swim.

Another difficulty that teachers new to the approach often have, concerns choice of objective. There is a danger that in her enthusiasm to see progress, the teacher will push a child on to a new objective before a satisfactory level of competence has been achieved. Over the years, the staff of the school have learnt that prematurely pushing a child forward is quite pointless. If the slow learner is to continue to progress it is necessary for a complete mastery level to be achieved and, even then, further practice, or overlearning, should be allowed. Furthermore, it is crucial that new objectives be introduced in a very careful fashion. It is not recommended that the child be bombarded with too many tasks at one particular time. Rather in any one week a pupil should be presented with only a few new steps, while spending a great deal of time on overlearning exercises. This is an important distinction and one which, when applied carefully, can assist the teacher in dealing with the important issue of how to organize her own time to best effect. What happens is that the teacher so arranges things that when a child is due to take an important new learning step, he will work either individually or in a small group under the direct guidance of a member of staff. It is at times when new learning is taking place that the slow-learning child needs the individual advice, encouragement, and confidence of the teacher. In order to make this possible, classroom resources must be developed that allow children who are on continued practice exercises to work independently. This might take the form of workcards or sheets, programmed material, audio-visual materials, or group game activities. The important point is that, whatever form the activity takes, it should give the pupil interesting and relevant practice towards complete mastery of an appropriate objective, and should require only occasional intervention by the teacher.

To make the system work well it is essential that there exists a logical arrangement of classroom resources. The coding of the objectives provides an excellent system for organizing and labelling shelves, cupboards, drawers, and other storage. Some materials will be related to a number of different objectives, possibly even from different Content Areas. Workcards and audio-visual material are more likely to be concerned with one objective. Whichever is the case, if they are marked clearly with the appropriate code, staff, and perhaps even pupils, will know where they are located and what they are for. Resources that are systematically organized are more likely to be used effectively.

Having said that questions of teaching method are left to individual teachers, over the period of years during which the curriculum material has been designed and implemented, groups of staff in the school have chosen to meet to discuss and pool their ideas on teaching method and organization. In many parts of the school, team teaching situations have necessitated some degree of agreement on these issues. Probably as a result of these discussions certain clear trends have emerged with regard to forms of organization and methods.

In the younger classes, where inevitably the children are more dependent upon their teachers and less able to work independently, there is a much greater emphasis upon group activities. This is made possible by the high staffing levels in these classes and, indeed, by the limited range of achievement within any one class. So it is viable to group children according to the objective on which they are to work. This means that a detailed system has to be arranged for grouping and then regrouping as the children work on different aspects of the curriculum. Similarly, a certain amount of on-going change between groups is necessary to accommodate pupils progressing at different rates. What is absolutely necessary is a system whereby all the teachers working with a particular class meet regularly to review progress and analyse the records in order to redefine the working groups. Some teachers find it useful to use a master record chart on the classroom wall in order to indicate visually which objectives each child has achieved.

In the senior classes (ages 12–16) different working arrangements have been developed, with a much greater emphasis on individual work. This is necessitated by the enormous range of attainment within any one class. A large cloakroom adjacent to the senior classrooms has been developed into a learning resource area. Collectively the staff concerned have developed and assembled resources related to all the objectives in the Closed Curriculum. All resources, whether made by staff, or bought commercially, are collated in terms of the objectives and coded accordingly. This approach is economic of time and effort since the teachers prepare and share materials rather than working in isolation within their own classrooms, perhaps frequently duplicating their preparations. Out of this organizational framework quite an exciting working system has emerged. The basic rationale behind the procedure is to try to involve each senior pupil in organizing his own work, leading to a greater capacity for self-management and improvements in independent work habits. It has already been explained that the senior record book is so designed as to be meaningful to the pupil. So, as the teacher chooses a new objective for the pupil, the date is entered in the 'working-on' column and the pupil is made aware of his target. The purpose is to make the pupil target-orientated, on the assumption that if he knows his objective he is likely to work in a more purposeful and effective manner.

Every week, on a Monday morning, each pupil in the senior school is given his weekly work slip. On this slip the teacher notes the objectives for the week – a few new objectives and a far greater number of objectives for continued practice. Also written on the slip are details of activities, resources, and materials for the child to follow. It is then the pupil's responsibility to organize his own work during basic learning periods to ensure that he completes all the required work by the end of the week when it will be checked by the teacher. Most of the equipment and resources are situated in the resource area and so the pupil has the task of finding these, completing the activity, having his work marked or, where appropriate, marking it himself and then returning all materials and equipment to the correct cupboard, drawer, shelf, or box in the resource area.

The basic advantage of this working system is that it places responsibility in the hands of the pupil. On a good day, when the system is working well (the school has bad days just like any other), it is marvellous to see these adolescent pupils going about their business. They seem to have few problems in finding their way around the resources and, as a result of the clear objectives that have been set, they clearly work in a very purposeful and directed manner. It is worth remembering that these are pupils who have been segregated because of their extreme learning difficulties.

Hopefully this account of the development of an objectives-based curriculum in a special school has given the reader a clear picture of the work that has been put in by the staff of the school over a period of years. It has required a high degree of commitment on their part but, of course, the benefits are now being reaped. A well-developed and structured system such as this provides the solution to many of the day-to-day problems of the classteacher and allows her time to relax and teach in a creative manner. The main advantages of the approach can be summarized as follows:

(1) It helps the teacher to plan appropriate work for each pupil;
(2) Children can be efficiently grouped according to their educational needs;
(3) Resources and equipment can be systematically arranged and coded, leading to their more efficient use;
(4) The educational process becomes more target-orientated and therefore greater progress will result;
(5) The curriculum material, and its associated record-keeping, provides an excellent basis for consistent and continuous teaching as the pupil moves from teacher to teacher.

The Open Curriculum

The danger of focusing so much attention on a limited area of curriculum within a special school is that the overall educational programme becomes too restricted. The authors know of special schools where quite excellent work goes on in the teaching of basic subjects but where little attention is given to wider aspects of curriculum. It is very dangerous, if not undemocratic, for children to be placed in a special school in order that positive discrimination can be provided and then for educational opportunities to be actually limited by their presence in such a school. Gulliford (1975) sums this issue up when he states: 'One of the problems in the education of handicapped children is how to provide them with a normal education'.

It was with this issue in mind that the curriculum model was so designed as to draw attention to the importance of providing slow-learning children with a full and rich educational diet. With the careful planning involved in the mastery areas less, rather than more, time should need to be given to this aspect of the curriculum. Indeed, it can be argued that small, regular doses of attention in basic subject areas are more efficient than having the child spend long, and often tedious, periods on these limited aspects.

Ideally, lessons can be prepared in which attention can be given to skills and knowledge from the Closed Curriculum through the enrichment experiences defined within what is called the Open Curriculum. There are two important advantages in this approach to lesson planning:

(1) When parts of the Closed Curriculum are taught within the context of aspects of the Open Curriculum, the danger that the teaching of basic subjects will become sterile, repetitive, and boring can be avoided;
(2) Lessons organized to combine both aspects of the curriculum are likely to ensure generalization of basic skills to varied situations.

To take an example, language development, in addition to being taught directly through regular group work, can be dealt with incidentally in such lessons as drama, art, or physical education. If a child is learning the terms 'under' and 'over', a physical education lesson provides an appropriate setting for practice. The child might initially be requested to go under and over the gymnastic equipment and then, as he becomes proficient, he can be asked to *state* whether he is going under or over. The terms will also need to be applied in other classroom situations in order to widen the child's mastery of their use. Thus, Closed Curriculum objectives are being developed and generalized through activities that are seen as part of the Open Curriculum.

Listening skills can be taught in a variety of settings in addition to individual instruction that may be provided in groups or by use of audio-visual machinery. In a drama session, the pupil who is being helped to improve his skills in remembering instructions can be put in a situation where he is required to obey the instructions of another pupil.

Educational visits and field trips can provide plentiful opportunity for practising and generalizing skills and knowledge being developed within the Closed Curriculum. Planning such trips may involve budgeting, map reading, writing for guide books and learning to read new sight words. A child who is learning aspects of social language, such as how to ask the way in a strange situation, may have practised the skill by role-play within the school. On a day trip to London he could be given the job of stopping a policeman and asking the way to Trafalgar Square. If care is not taken to provide varied and realistic practice of this type of skill, the child may never achieve a level at which he might apply it in everyday life.

In the senior part of the Closed Curriculum, many of the objectives, particularly in Content Areas such as Social Knowledge and Vocational Knowledge, are concerned with isolated items of knowledge. In teaching towards these very specific knowledge objectives it is necessary for teachers to be conscious of the need to provide an awareness of broader issues related to the topic; issues that might be said to be part of the Open Curriculum. Let us take as an example, three related objectives from the Social Knowledge area:

(1) Names the two principal Christian denominations and states own denomination;
(2) Names two agents who perform the marriage ceremony;
(3) States the practical functions of the Church (i.e. christenings, weddings, funerals).

In dealing with these objectives a series of lessons could be designed in which far broader aspects of the role of the church in society would be covered. Visits might be arranged, speakers invited into school and discussions held with a view to providing the pupils with a greater awareness of this important area. Such a project would hopefully stimulate interest and thought in the minds of the pupils. The point is that while a greater awareness of the topic is being developed, and interests and attitudes formed, the three Closed Curriculum objectives can be taught within a broad and enriching context and at the end of the project each pupil's retention of these specific facts can be assessed.

The development of appropriate attitudes, interests, and values is clearly an important aspect of any school's curriculum. As we have already seen, often these aspects can be dealt with in projects and activities that incorporate objectives from the Closed Curriculum. In some settings we are concerned to develop specific attitudes and types of conduct that we know will be of benefit to the pupil. Again, these are seen as being part of the Open Curriculum and can often be dealt with in an incidental manner when teaching towards Closed Curriculum objectives. In the Handicraft lesson, for example, in addition to teaching skills of using tools and equipment we are concerned to develop appropriate workshop attitudes. A form of objective can be used in this situation to aid with this development. Figure 11 is an example of a programme used in such a situation within the project school. This type of objective is sometimes referred to as an *affective objective*, and refers to feelings and emotions, such as interests, attitudes, and values rather than the intellectual and motor outcomes that are the feature of all the other objectives dealt with in this book. It is not possible to state that a child has finally mastered such an objective, since

	WORKSHOP RECORD Pupil Teacher	very good	good	average	poor	very poor
1.	I put my apron on when I came in.					
2.	I have listened carefully when told what to do.					
3.	I have used tools as I have been shown.					
4.	I have taken care with tools and equipment.					
5.	I have worked carefully on machines.					
6.	I worked without disturbing other people.					
7.	I have been able to work mainly by myself.					
8.	I tidied up well.					
9.	I put tools away carefully.					
10.	I worked cheerfully today.					

Name

Next week I must try harder on numbers _____

Figure 11   Using affective objectives in record-keeping

levels of performance may vary from lesson to lesson. Our concern is to help the child to develop in these areas. Each time the pupil works in the workshop he fills in the form for himself, judging his own performance over the whole of the lesson. The teacher discusses with the child his completed form and together they decide on aspects that could be improved on the next visit. Experience with this style of working has shown that pupils are usually very honest and realistic in their self-assessment and that this approach can be of some help in developing these affective areas. Similar forms are used in the Housecraft room and in developing appropriate work attitudes amongst the pupils in their final year at the school.

Since the Closed Curriculum was developed and implemented the staff at the school, very conscious of the need to provide a broad educational programme for pupils who in many cases have very limited experience, have given increasing attention to the Open Curriculum. The use of behavioural objectives still has a place in the development but, taking into account the previously mentioned limitations of this format, it has been necessary to make use of more generally stated objectives, expressive objectives and affective objectives. Traditional subject headings, such as Health Education, Moral and Religious Education and Science, have been used and an attempt has been made to lay-out in a syllabus format, class by class, how those subjects should be developed through the school, defining objectives appropriate for the different age groups. The assumption has been made that realistically it will not be possible accurately to individualize the teaching of these areas. The main concern is to clarify for all members of staff what their contribution should be in a pattern which is developed through the different classes. For example, in Health Education, the objectives for Class 1 are very much concerned with basic personal hygiene, but by the time the pupils reach the leavers' class the emphasis is upon parentcraft and problems of health in the home. In the other classes intermediate aspects of Health Education are dealt with. The important thing is that discussion has taken place, an agreement reached and, consequently, a developing pattern of teaching, based on clear goals and objectives, is evident.

Summary

In a special day school for children with learning difficulties the objectives approach has been used to develop a curriculum. A two-part curriculum model was adopted, taking into account the needs of the pupils and theoretical thinking on curriculum development for the slow learner. The first part, referred to as the Closed Curriculum, defines skills and knowledge to be taught to a mastery level; the second part, called the Open Curriculum, describes broader educational areas to be taught to a variety of levels, experiences that the pupils will take part in and attitudes, values, and interests that should be developed. Behavioural objectives are used where appropriate but, taking into account the limitations of this format, other kinds of objectives have been found to be necessary. The curriculum was developed over a period of years and involved staff discussion and consensus decision-making. The involvement of the staff in this development has led to a greater understanding of the material produced and, probably as a result, a high level of commitment to its implementation. In addition, the staff curriculum discussions have provided an excellent system of school-based in-service training. The implementation of the curriculum has led to a number of important improvements in classroom practice and school organization. The most important advantage, the continuity and consistency of teaching that results from such a highly structured curriculum approach, should be the major strength of a special school.

Recommended Further Reading

Blake, K. A. (1974). *Teaching the Retarded.* Englewood Cliffs: Prentice Hall.
  Lots of examples of objectives in different curriculum areas.
Brennan, W. K. (1974). *Shaping the Education of Slow Learners.* London: Routledge and Kegan Paul.
  Chapter 5 explains Brennan's view on mastery and awareness.
Bushell, D. (1973). The Behaviour Analysis Classroom, in Spodek, B. (Ed.), *Early Childhood Education.* Englewood Cliffs: Prentice Hall.
  Behavioural objectives used as a basis for a programme of compensatory education.
Kolstoe, O. P. (1976). *Teaching Educable Mentally Retarded Children.* New York: Holt, Rinehart, and Winston.
  A complete curriculum plan using objectives.
Nussel, E. J., Inglis, J. D., and Wiersma, W. (1976). *The Teacher and Individually Guided Education.* Reading, Mass: Addison Wesley.
  Using objectives to organize the school's day-to-day programme.
Stenhouse, L. (1975). *An Introduction to Curriculum Research and Development.* London: Heinemann.
  Outlines the limitations of using behavioural objectives in curriculum development.
Tansley, A. E., and Gulliford, R. (1960). *The Education of Slow Learning Children.* London: Routledge and Kegan Paul.
  The classic British work on this subject.

CHAPTER 10

The Wider Use of Objectives

Chapter Goal: *To describe the use of objectives in dealing with learning difficulties in a wide range of educational settings.*

Some years ago now, when we first started collaborating on the development of the curriculum in the special school described in Chapter 9, we believed naïvely that we had invented behavioural objectives. Only as we began to read around the literature on curriculum development did we realize that we were well behind the field and that indeed many were at the stage of doubting, or even rejecting, the value of the objectives model. While the discovery of this literature provided us with stimulation, encouragement, and greater understanding, we must admit that we were just a little disappointed that our belief in ourselves as 'pioneers' had been mistaken.

Most of this book is concerned with the need to identify children's learning difficulties as early as possible and to provide appropriate teaching in order to avoid prolonged exposure to failure. Our general orientation is towards attempting to implement this procedure, as far as possible, within the confines of normal classrooms. We believe, however, that this style of planning is germane to the needs of teachers working in special schools and units and, of course, we recommend that where possible the objectives approach should be used in the context of curriculum development as a means of providing extended special education.

We are conscious that many readers will have an interest in dealing with educational difficulties in different settings and with different age groups from those outlined above. Does the objectives approach have anything to offer in these wider contexts? We feel that it does and in this chapter we will address ourselves briefly to some of these. In so doing we will argue that our central thesis, that of defining educational problems in terms of observable, measurable behaviour and carefully planning programmes of action, is worth the consideration of colleagues dealing with learning difficulties, wherever they might be.

Inevitably, therefore, this chapter is something of a pot-pourri. Issues are raised, thoughts and ideas offered and, where possible, reference made to work already going on in the field. As we have said, we did not invent objectives, and as our involvement has grown we have become aware of an increasing number of people who are implementing this approach. Some will say (perhaps correctly, only time will tell) that it is just another 'bandwagon'. Experienced teachers, quite rightly, tend to be cynical of new ideas that appear to offer panaceas for all educational ills. Certainly there is a growing literature on the uses of objectives in wider special educational contexts. Much of this is from North America, where it is now well-established and where teachers are more accustomed to this style of working. We hope, however, that this chapter will give some idea of the excellent work going on in *this* country and provide an insight into what we believe to be a 'new wave' of thinking in British special education.

At the time of writing, the whole field of remedial and special education seems to be going through a period of trauma. A focusing of public attention has been brought about by the publication of the Warnock Report of enquiry into the education of handicapped children and young people (Department of Education and Science, 1978). As a result of the publicity surrounding the build-up to the publication of this report, many teachers, particularly those in special schools, have been going through a period of doubt and uncertainty. Speculation, rumours, and 'leaks' had created almost a sense of panic, with talk of the closing down of special schools and wholesale overnight integration of handicapped children into ordinary schools.

The actual publication of the report seems, to some extent, to have calmed the situation. While time will tell the full implications of the document's recommendations, initially at least, the reaction seems to be favourable to what is a balanced and non-controversial document. Nevertheless, the report has provoked a period of debate, questioning, and challenge. Certainly self-examination is long overdue and should lead to improvements and development. Those of us working in remedial and special education have ticked along happily for too long, apparently completely guarded from the focus of professional enquiry and public accountability. That is not to say that excellent work has not been going on, but that where it has, it has been the product of individual enterprise rather than a sustained, planned attempt to provide a comprehensive service.

The Warnock Report touches on many aspects of special education and its recommendations are wide and far-reaching. Integration of handicapped children is a pervading theme and an obvious *long-term* goal. The report sees a need for a new and wider concept of special education, in which more than one in five children may require some form of special educational provision at some time during their school career. Special education is seen as encompassing 'a whole range and variety of additional help, wherever it is provided and whether on a full or part-time basis, by which children may be helped to overcome educational difficulties, however they are caused' (para. 3.38). Because of this wider definition the report concludes that there is now no meaningful distinction between remedial and special education.

The report has a great deal to say about the categorization of handicapped children and the dangers of using educational labels, particularly in the area of learning difficulties, which is, of course, our main concern here. It summarizes the main disadvantages and concludes that the most important argument is that it perpetuates a sharp distinction between handicapped and non-handicapped children, a distinction the report wishes to eliminate.

The phrase 'children with learning difficulties', which we have tended to use in this book, is recommended by the report as a replacement term to describe children at present categorized as ESN (M) or ESN (S), and those slow learners currently dealt with by remedial services. Learning difficulties can be described as being 'mild', 'moderate', 'severe', or, in the case of children with particular difficulties, 'specific'.

It is inevitable that the Warnock Report will be a major influence on the development of special educational provision in the future. In our attempt to describe some wider implications of the use of objectives in dealing with educational difficulties, therefore, it is appropriate that we should look forward through the eyes of the Warnock Committee, picking up some of their important themes and recommendations as a basis on which to structure our discussion.

Discovery, Assessment and Recording

> We cannot emphasise too strongly ... how essential it is for a child's
> education that any special needs he has should be discovered and assessed
> as early as possible. (Warnock, para. 4.1)

In Chapter 2 we stressed the point that teachers in primary schools must be on the look-out for children with special educational needs. If in doubt, the course of action must be to refer a child who seems to be having particular difficulty to the headteacher of the school. In the past there has been a tendency for some teachers to 'soldier on' with a child in the belief that a request for help might appear as a sign of the teacher's failure or that it might result in the pupil being 'sentenced' to some form of special education. Such attitudes undoubtedly reflect a lack of understanding on the part of the teachers concerned.

In order to provide a more systematic approach to the early identification of children likely to have learning problems some authorities have over recent years introduced systems for *screening* infant age children. The Bullock Report (Department of Education and Science, 1975) was influential in promoting this idea. A useful source of information about recent developments with regard to screening is Wedell and Raybould (1976). There is a trend away from procedures based upon the use of tests towards teacher-observation approaches and 'Rating Scales' based upon behavioural statements are now an accepted means of structuring this type of observation. This approach can be a useful starting point in getting teachers to view childrens' learning difficulties in terms of observable behaviour and to use this information to plan teaching programmes. Thus a screening procedure operating within a school can be a basis for some school-based arrangement for developing and implementing teaching programmes of the type we have recommended. The information gathered by structured observation during the stage of identification will form a basis for designing programmes, and the staff, perhaps with the help of outside support agencies, can work together on programme development. Such a procedure could, incidentally, provide a platform for in-service training.

Once a child has been identified as having, or being likely to have, a learning difficulty, a careful *assessment* is necessary to determine how and, in some cases, where his needs can best be met. The Warnock Report recommends that because of the large proportion of children whose needs must be assessed, and the wide range of degree of difficulty involved, a five-stage assessment policy should be developed. The stages are to be seen as a progressive sequence, with each stage involving more refined techniques and expertise. The five stages are:

STAGE 1 – Head and classteacher gather information and discuss special arrangements that might be made within the school;

STAGE 2 – The child's difficulties are discussed with a teacher qualified and experienced in special education (either a member of staff or local advisory teacher). A special programme may be supervised by the specialist teacher;

STAGE 3 – If a satisfactory outcome does not result from Stage 2, a more detailed assessment will be carried out in the school by an outside professional, such as an educational psychologist;

STAGE 4 – A multi-professional assessment carried out at short notice, providing information on the suitability of local facilities or recommending further investigation;

STAGE 5 – More intensive multi-professional assessment, the nature of which will depend upon the special needs of the individual child.

We need only concern ourselves here with Stages 1 to 3, which are intended to be school-based. Understandably, as with many of its recommendations, the Warnock Report does not get down to practical details about the nature and form of these assessment arrangements. The Committee are concerned to outline plans which will accommodate *all* aspects of special education whereas we can relate their suggestions to a more clearly defined group of children.

At the first two levels of assessment recommended, where the classteacher is discussing with colleagues the child's difficulties, the existence of an efficient record-keeping system will be a great advantage. Records based upon dated classroom observation of objectives already achieved and teaching methods used form a factual and reliable way of focusing on the problem. Those concerned can see what the child has achieved, how long he has taken to acquire particular skills, what specific areas are causing long-term difficulty and to what methods, if any, he seems to have responded. Furthermore, these records can be passed on with little fear of their being misinterpreted.

In Chapter 5 we explained in detail the differences between norm-referenced and criterion-referenced assessment. We would support the view of Duffey and Fedner (1978) who argue that poor instruction of exceptional children may to a large extent be due to the use of norm-referenced testing as a diagnostic tool for instructional purposes. At this level, where we are concerned to help the child learn successfully in his ordinary classroom, assessment must be concerned to determine solely what the child has learned and what he should learn next. This information should provide the basis of what Warnock refers to as 'the prescription of a special programme to be supervised by the specialist or advisory teacher' (para. 4.37). We would interpret this as being a programme of carefully graded objectives designed and implemented by the classteacher with the help and assistance of whatever specialist expertise is available. This is at Stage 2, and if it does not provide a satisfactory solution to the problems then the next stage will come into effect, involving the intervention of an outside professional, possibly a peripatetic specialist teacher or an educational psychologist. We would see his role largely in terms of the strategy outlined in Chapter 7, examining the child's records, defining the problem more clearly, introducing specialist teaching procedures or modifying the programme of objectives. Once all these arrangements have been made, any child who continues to present difficulties of learning will be getting to a stage where a more intensive investigation will be required. It may well be that placement in some other educational setting has to be considered. This being the case the procedure outlined by Warnock, if implemented in the way we advise, will provide an enormous amount of data which will be of relevance to those professionals who then become involved.

In recent years some local authorities have established educational *diagnostic/ assessment units* where young children who present difficulty can be placed for a period of intensive observation. In some cases such units are attached to special schools and, indeed, many of the pupils admitted are eventually placed in special schools. Our experience of the work of some of these units leads us to believe that their overall effectiveness could be improved. A survey conducted by Brennan and Herbert (1969) found that many of the units in their sample were *not* diagnostic since no school programmes could be based on the reports made, much of their work being mainly concerned with placement recommendations. Furthermore, these decisions could often be made by use of less protracted measures. (Stories of children lingering in such units for up to three years are not uncommon.) Brennan and Herbert also commented on the problems that seemed to exist with regard to communication between units and receiving schools.

When assessment is carried out in some form of specialized unit or class with a view to eventual transfer of the child to an appropriate educational setting, the use of objectives-based procedures has the following advantages:

(1) Detailed information can be collected by teachers and parents in natural settings.
(2) Information can be gathered fairly quickly and without the use of specialized equipment.
(3) The information gathered is easily understood by professionals and parents.
(4) It has direct implications for teaching, both at school and in the home.
(5) It facilitates good communication between the unit and the receiver school.

Parents should be involved in this assessment process since it might be that the child behaves differently at home than with the teacher in the unit, and certainly the parent will be able to 'fill in the gaps' if some aspects of his behaviour cannot be observed directly. In using this system teachers are advised to note the distinction between reported observations from the parent and the teacher's own observations in the records.

One final point can be made about the passing on of information from one establishment to another. It is crucial when a child who has some special educational need is transferred, whether between special schools, or between normal and special schools, for some form of report to be passed on. Information collected by former teachers can be of help in getting the child off to a good start in his new school. Reports containing subjective opinion, vague statements or ill-defined pseudo-medical jargon, however, are *not* helpful and may, indeed, be harmful to the child. A case springs to mind of a child transferred to a special school who was reported by her primary school classteacher to have occasionally 'interfered with other children in the class'. Further enquiry revealed that the child had not been guilty of sexual malpractice but, rather, her offence was nudging other children as they were writing. There clearly are great dangers in a statement of this sort, which is easily misunderstood, being left on a child's records for the rest of her school life.

We have written in detail elsewhere of the development of a *curriculum-based assessment procedure* (Ainscow and Tweddle, 1976b). This was designed with a view to gathering relevant information on children about to be admitted to a special school for ESN (M) children. The objectives of the special school's basic curriculum were examined and key tasks identified which were to be the targets of the assessment. Together a teacher and an educational psychologist developed a system for assessing a child's functioning with regard to these tasks. The purpose was to make the procedure quick, efficient and yet pleasurable for the child. It involved a teacher from the special school visiting the 'feeder' school to work with the child within his infant classroom. There he would be asked to work on a variety of tasks from the special school's curriculum, and his performance was closely observed. It was found useful to tape parts of the assessment for analysis later. The classteacher was also asked to provide information about teaching methods used, the child's interests and any other information that might be relevant.

This procedure has been refined through use and has been found to be most beneficial. It means that the knowledge the primary school teacher has acquired from working with the child is made available to the special school. The assessment information is directly related to the curriculum of the special school and will help in the setting of objectives. Consequently, when the child does eventually transfer to his new school he is already correctly placed on the record-keeping system and can be set appropriate work immediately. Thus his initial experience should be a relatively happy one, leading him to settle quickly into his new setting. Obviously, the production of this type of assessment system is totally dependent upon the existence in the special school of a carefully worked-out, objectives-based curriculum.

The Warnock Report recommends that the progress of all children with special educational needs should be *reviewed* at least annually. We would argue that using our definition of review – that is, a detailed examination of the child's progress and reconsideration of his educational needs – it should not be an occasional occurrence but *an integral part of classroom practice.* Furthermore, where there is a need for the classteacher to discuss a child's difficulties with parents, or some outside agency, it should be done immediately and informally rather than at some predetermined date on the calendar. Of course, where a child's progress is being carefully observed, recorded and evaluated on a daily basis, review *is* an integral part of classroom life. Again, programmes of objectives facilitate all of this process.

To sum up this section we should perhaps reiterate some of the important points made in Chapter 5: Assessment should be a continuous process leading directly to classroom action. Record-keeping based on sequences of objectives provides an excellent basis for this type of on-going assessment. An assessment completed today is going to be out of date within days. It is necessary, therefore, to incorporate structured observation into day-to-day classroom practice. All these points are valid for assessment in *any* special education context.

Special Education in Ordinary Schools

> The wider concept of special education proposed in this report ... is directly in line with the principle that handicapped and non-handicapped children should be educated in a common setting as far as possible.
>
> (Warnock, para. 7.3)

A good deal of this book about special education is written with teachers in ordinary schools in mind, in the sure knowledge that there are a great many children with special educational needs in ordinary classrooms. Many of these children have what Warnock refers to as 'mild learning difficulties' but, of course, the presence of some children with 'moderate' difficulties cannot be ignored. The trend towards even more such pupils remaining within mainstream education is inescapable. Section 10 of the 1976 Education Act requires local education authorities to arrange for the special education of all handicapped pupils to be provided in county and voluntary schools, except where this is impracticable, incompatible with efficient instruction in the schools or involves unreasonable public expenditure. This provision will come into effect on a day to be appointed by the Secretary of State. So, in a sense, the long-standing argument about integration is over. The question to look at now must be *how* can the principle imbedded in the Act be accomplished successfully in practice? As Warnock says: 'The quality of special education ... cannot be guaranteed merely by legislation and structural change' (para. 2.85). As we seek to make integration a practical reality the phrase 'quality of special education' is one to keep in mind.

Four possible forms of organization for educating children with special educational needs in ordinary schools are described by the Warnock Report:

(1) Full-time education in an ordinary class with any necessary help and support provided;
(2) Education in an ordinary class with periods of withdrawal to a special class or unit or other supporting base;
(3) Education in a special class or unit with periods of attendance at an ordinary class and full involvement in the general community life and extra-curricular activities of the ordinary school;
(4) Full-time education in a special class or unit with only social contact with the main school.

Careful thought must be given to all aspects of each of these forms of integration if they are to provide adequately for children with learning difficulties, both in terms of educational and social requirements. Crucial is the question of curriculum. Basically, wherever possible, we are seeking to help the child to participate fully in the curriculum of the school, although implicit in the variety of forms of organization referred to above is the need in some cases to modify or supplement that curriculum.

As we seek to make our procedures for providing special education within normal schools more effective it may be that we can learn from the American experience. The trend towards integration – often referred to as 'mainstreaming' in the USA – is much further forward there, and we could do well to observe their development. A major stage in their development will be achieved this year with the coming into force of Public Law 94 – 142, 'The Education for all Handicapped Children Act'. Readers interested in following the legal and historical aspects of this are advised to consult Abeson and Zettel (1977) and Zettel (1978).

One interesting aspect of this American legislation is worth our consideration at this point. The new law requires that a written individualized educational programme (IEP) be prepared for every handicapped pupil. It should be designed by teachers, signed by the parent, and be a precise statement of what will actually be provided for the child, as opposed to a general plan. Turnbull *et al.* (1978) suggest that an IEP will consist of seven components:

(1) A statement of the pupil's current level of educational performance;
(2) Annual goals to be accomplished by the end of each school year;
(3) Short-term behavioural objectives indicating intermediate steps towards the goals;
(4) Dates on which the programme will start and end;
(5) An account of the extent to which pupils will take part in normal classes;
(6) Special education services needed by the child;
(7) Evaluation criteria and procedures to be used for determining mastery of goals and objectives on at least an annual basis.

These components bear some resemblence to the strategy outlined in this book for designing a teaching programme. It is perhaps a little sad that the American setting necessitates teachers being compelled to plan in this way when teaching handicapped children but, nevertheless, on the positive side, it is a development that must lead to a more individualized and systematic approach which, in the long run, must be of considerable benefit to a lot of children. Furthermore, the requirement of teachers to work out their intermediate steps in terms of behavioural objectives will provide a platform for school-based research, in-service training, and curriculum development. The important issues of evaluation and accountability, both implicit in the IEP procedure, were dealt with in Chapter 8. Certainly this approach of requiring individually designed programmes for children with special needs is one we in the United Kingdom should watch with interest.

It is probably at the secondary stage that the education of children with learning difficulties in ordinary schools presents more problems. Factors not present in primary schools, such as large classes, complicated timetables, specialist subjects and teachers, pressure of exams, widening range of pupil attainments and the tradition of more formal class-teaching styles make it difficult to provide flexible provision. It may be that to accommodate children with special needs many of our secondary schools will have to consider radical modifications to their existing practices. Let us examine some of the current approaches evident in secondary education and consider ways in which the objectives approach might be of some help.

McCall (1977) suggests that three forms of remedial organization are predominant in secondary schools: (i) special classes, (ii) group or individual withdrawal, and (iii) mixed ability teaching. In many schools a mixture of these arrangements is used, with, for example, mixed ability teaching in the first two years and then group withdrawal in the older forms. It is difficult, therefore, to present a clear picture of the usual style of organization or to provide evidence as to how successful these styles are. Garnett (1976), Fisher (1977), and Webster, *et al.* (1977) all describe impressive arrangements for dealing with slow learners, and more handicapped pupils, within comprehensive schools. However, the picture is by no means uniformly bright. Stephen Jackson, in a book review which appeared in the journal *Special Education, Forward Trends* in 1976, referred to 'the motley practices that go under the banner of remedial education' and suggested that there seemed to be a paradox in a situation where research casts serious doubts about the value of remedial education and yet 80 per cent of remedial teachers found their job 'challenging', 'fascinating', and 'giving tremendous job satisfaction'. As a result of a recent survey Kerry (1978) suggests that 'neither heads nor teachers (in secondary schools) appear in general to have a systematic approach to identification and special treatment'.

Special classes – This may take the form of a remedial class providing block instruction in the basic subjects, or a special unit where pupils are provided with an almost completely separate curriculum. In some cases these classes are used flexibly, with a great deal of movement in and out, while in others the classes are very much self-contained. Many special classes seem to suffer the negative features of segregation that are often attributed to special schools.

It may be that some of the pupils placed in a special class cannot benefit for the most part from the main curriculum of the school and so the staff will be concerned to develop a separate curriculum to meet their needs. In this situation the ideas outlined in Chapter 9 concerning the use of objectives in curriculum development should be of use.

A different approach is necessary, however, if we are to meet the needs of children who might, with help and support, be reassimilated into the ordinary classes. In any segregated provision where reintegration is seen as a goal, attention has to be given to the question of curriculum matching. It is necessary to analyse carefully the curriculum into which we are seeking to readmit the pupil, and to determine the skills he will require if he is to do this successfully. The objectives of the ordinary classes must be made explicit and the staff of the special class must develop effective programmes to help the pupil catch up. It is essential that great care be taken over developing and monitoring the success of this type of curriculum matching procedure otherwise it is very easy for a pupil's presence in the special class to mitigate against a successful transfer back. Our suggestion would be, therefore, that entry to a special class should be as a result of a pupil's inability to benefit from the curriculum being offered, the programme should then be carefully structured to bring the child to a necessary level in those objectives necessary for successful reintegration and the child should be helped and encouraged to work his way out of the special class by achieving the required criteria for reassimilation. This may seem a tall order, and indeed, experience suggests that unless a clear and systematic plan of action is worked out immediately the child is placed in a special class, reintegration into the main curriculum is going to be increasingly difficult for him.

Group or individual withdrawal – The strategy of allowing slow-learning children to take part in the normal class activities of the secondary school with withdrawal for special help in areas of weakness with a remedial teacher, is still very common practice. It has the advantage of keeping the child in touch with his peers and, to a large extent, the normal curriculum of the school. There is, however, some evidence indicating that despite the short-term gains that can be achieved by this approach, long-term effects are disappointing (Sampson, 1975). It may be that effectiveness could be improved by a more systematic approach.

A referral for remedial help should be specific, stating in behavioural terms the child's precise area of difficulty. Thus the remedial teacher should be asked to deal with a clearly defined problem rather than, as is often the case, being sent a pupil because he is said to be 'struggling', 'thick', 'unable to cope', or 'incapable of paying attention'. Given a specific problem to deal with, the remedial teacher can design a programme of objectives, provide appropriate teaching and, where possible, follow-up work that can be carried out within the normal classroom. In addition the remedial teacher should look at the situation in which the child has previously had difficulty. It may be that advice can be given to subject teachers as to how curriculum objectives and pupil materials can be modified to allow the slow-learning child to take part in the normal class activities. Certainly it seems possible that the lack of long-term success of remedial interventions may be due, at least in part, to a lack of continued support for the pupil when he returns to normal class activities.

Mixed ability teaching – This is the most integrated approach but, also, the one that presents the greatest challenge to the teachers involved. The other two organizational arrangements to which we have referred rather assume that the special needs of children with learning difficulties will remain largely the responsibility of a specialist teacher, whereas, in a mixed ability class, the subject teacher is responsible for the progress of all the children, whatever their level of achievement.

Kerry (1978) studied 21 'good' teachers of mixed ability classes, covering a wide range of science and humanities subjects, and found that 19 of these reported difficulties caused by the presence of slow learners. Therefore, if children with learning difficulties are to learn successfully in mixed ability settings the subject teachers taking the classes must be provided with some form of specialist support. This will probably mean that remedial teachers will have to switch their operation away from working with individuals or small groups removed from normal classes, to providing a support service. Flexible approaches will, no doubt, be necessary. The remedial teacher may spend time at the preparation stage, helping the teacher to analyse the syllabus into graded steps suited to the needs of the slow learner. The teacher will also need advice and help in designing methods and materials suitable for use with the programmes of objectives that are produced. There are an increasing number of studies available indicating that successful practice of this form of curriculum adaptation is being undertaken at the grass-root level. For example, Wood (1975) describes how objectives were used to structure a science course to make it relevant to less able pupils. Another account of objectives being used successfully to adapt a science curriculum is reported by Mitchell and Kellington (1978). Larcombe (1977) describes how maths materials were modified for use with slow-learning pupils in mixed ability classes, using careful analysis of the structure, the stating of clear objectives, and well-designed materials. Evans (1976) also describes, enthusiastically, how the needs of slow-learning children can be met in mixed ability classes. Some of the material related to various of the Schools' Council curriculum projects would be well worth the consideration of teachers interested in developing work for slow learners (Gulliford and Widlake, 1974).

To all teachers interested in developing courses for mixed ability teaching we would recommend a close study of the literature on Bloom's mastery learning strategies, referred to in earlier chapters. Essential to the approach is the structuring of school courses into teaching units based upon behavioural objectives, the regular and systematic use of pupil evaluation and the provision for extra instruction if required. Thus, an entire class are given instruction on a unit, working towards explicit objectives. When instruction and follow-up work is completed all the pupils are tested to see if they have mastered the objectives of the unit. Children who are having difficulty in achieving the desired criteria are identified at this point and given additional help and further time to master the objectives. All pupils must master the objectives of this unit before going on to the next. Where a wide range of pupils are in one class the approach can be used effectively in conjunction with individualized instructional approaches. A great deal of the literature, however, assumes a more traditional, class-teaching approach and is well worth the consideration of teachers in secondary schools. Useful source books are Block and Anderson (1975), and Bloom (1976). Readers interested in the teaching of reading are advised to look at Smith and Katims' (1977) account of how mastery learning approaches are being used to develop a reading programme in Chicago.

Where children with learning difficulties are being taught in a mixed ability class the remedial specialist may find it necessary, in addition to helping with modification of curriculum and preparation of materials, to go into the class and work side-by-side with the subject teacher, providing extra help to those children who need it. Certainly a willingness to assist in this way is likely to enhance the remedial teacher's credibility in the eyes of her colleagues and a close working liaison is likely to be professionally beneficial to both parties.

The Warnock Report recommends the establishment in large secondary schools of some form of resource centre to promote the effectiveness of special educational provision. Such a centre would be the focal point of *all* aspects of special education available in the school, whether it be as a base for special classes, a source of special materials and equipment, a centre for advice for teachers or a base in which visiting specialists may work with children. The resource centre idea is growing in popularity in the USA, where the main responsibility of the centre staff is to develop ways of supporting the child with special needs within the ordinary classes, and a great deal of attention is being given to evaluating the effectiveness of this type of approach (Jenkins and Mayhall, 1976; Sindelar and Deno, 1978). Again, we in Britain would do well to observe this development.

Advice and Support

> Every local education authority should restructure and, if necessary, supplement its existing advisory staff and resources to provide effective advice and support to teachers concerned with children with special educational needs through a unified service. (Warnock, para. 13.3)

Within any local authority there should be some overall framework evident in which all members of the special education service have a clearly defined role. This is particularly important with regard to an authority's support service outside the schools. Warnock stresses the importance of support for teachers dealing with children who have special needs, particularly those in ordinary schools, and proposes changes of organization in this direction. Implicit in the recommendation is the availability of an armada of advisors and consultants. Already in too many authorities there exists a variety of advisory and support services tripping over one another's feet, and a lack of role definition resulting in different services attempting *independently* to deal with the same situations in different ways. It is crucial that such situations are sorted out and, in particular, *teachers in the schools made clearly aware of the areas of responsibility of each of the available support services.* For example, Gray and Reeve (1978) describe a system established in one authority for identifying educationally 'at risk' children at an early age with a view to providing teachers in ordinary schools with support programmes. While we find ourselves doubting the theoretical orientation to learning difficulties inferred by the authors of the article, the approach is commendable in its organization across a large authority.

It is not our role here to examine the roles of the various agencies in the advisory and support services with a view to making detailed organizational recommendations. No doubt, whilst Warnock's view of this will be debated nationally, decisions and working arrangements will be determined at local level, taking into account the needs and existing provision within each area. Our concern is to suggest ways in which the objectives approach may have implications for working practice.

Certainly the use of objectives would be beneficial in ironing out some of the difficulties of role definition referred to above. Let us take an example to illustrate how this *could* work. A school seeking to make suitable arrangements for its slow learners might seek the advice of three outside agencies – the adviser for special education, a specialist teacher from the remedial services, and an educational psychologist. But is it necessary to consult all three? Might their advice be conflicting? If an objectives approach to learning difficulties is taken by *all three* consultants it is possible that each could offer his own component of advice which could be fitted together to provide a cohesive policy for the school. Each would be offering suggestions at a different level, although inevitably overlap must occur. The special education adviser's contribution would include advice on matters of curriculum balance and which subjects should be emphasized. In other words he would be helping in determining appropriate teaching goals. The educational psychologist, on the other hand, would be more concerned in helping the staff to generate programmes of objectives from the teaching goals. Finally, the remedial teacher would contribute his knowledge of methods and materials, helping the classteacher to implement the programmes. It can be seen that an arrangement such as this would provide a school with a coherent support service, with each agency offering a distinct yet related contribution.

Intervention of this kind would require major changes in the working style of many of us in the field of special education. Increasingly teachers dealing with children with learning difficulties will need advice on how *they* might cope with the situation rather than having the child taken out of the class for assessment and/or treatment. The teacher will need help in problem definition, structuring programmes, analysing learning targets, writing objectives, and developing appropriate teaching strategies. Where a pupil is having a particularly long-term difficulty the teacher needs someone to turn to who can bring experience and expertise to bear on the situation, spotting where a programme might be improved.

Already in many authorities teachers in the remedial service are giving thought to how they can alter their working style. Traditionally they have tended to work with individual children, either visiting the school to see the pupil, or having the pupil attend the remedial centre, once or twice a week. Increasingly they are being required to act as advisers and consultants, a role for which in many cases they are ill-prepared. Very often they have vast knowledge of teaching methods, equipment, and materials, but much of their work could in future be concerned with advice about the implementation of programmes of objectives and the suitability of resources. It seems likely that some in-service training provision would be required to prepare these teachers for this wider role.

We have referred previously to the role of the educational psychologist in helping teachers to deal effectively with children with learning difficulties (Ainscow and Tweddle, 1977). The psychologist's theoretical expertise is likely to be of particular benefit in designing programmes and strategies for assessment and evaluation. Elsewhere we have described how the psychologist might be involved in a special school in attempting to work 'through' the teachers as opposed to concentrating attention on the problems of individual children (Ainscow and Tweddle, 1976a) and this general approach could be taken in dealing with slow-learning pupils in all settings. It is only fair to add that some psychologists are unhappy about this drift away from the traditional client-centred approach, and examination of the professional journals confirms a continuing debate on role definition – a debate which is likely to persist in the wake of the Warnock Report. However, teachers *need* specific, dejargonized, practical advice on how best to serve their slow learners. As Watts (1977) states: 'Instead of merely assessing the child and confirming that he needs help, more educational psychologists could help teachers to devise suitable programmes for use in class'. We would suggest that the objectives approach meets these needs more comprehensively than any other contemporary approach to the problem.

A notion which has grown in support during recent years, and is supported by the Warnock Report, is that of developing the role of special schools as a resource centre of advice and help for teachers in ordinary schools. Special schools do tend to be isolated and a closer interaction with ordinary schools would be beneficial for both staff and pupils. Ainscow *et al.* (1978a) argue that if a special school is to take on the role of resource centre it should have expertise in curriculum design, assessment procedures, specialist teaching methods, and techniques of progress-monitoring for children with exceptional educational needs. A good special school should be involved in developing and evaluating new techniques and materials, and its work in curriculum development should develop staff expertise about the sequencing and grading of learning steps which can be shared with teachers in local schools. In taking on an advisory role, special school teachers will find that they have a credibility that grows out of the fact that they teach, on a daily basis, children with marked learning problems. They can talk from experience and, of course, their classrooms can be used to illustrate the actual use of techniques that may be being recommended. Consideration will have to be given to developing effective strategies of dissemination. How will the special school provide help and support? Will it run courses, or will the spreading of expertise be based on teachers working together in classrooms? Again, special school teachers who are required to take on these extra duties will need in-service training and support.

One area of support for teachers in dealing with learning difficulties which is sometimes overlooked, and which should not be underestimated, is the provision of classroom ancillaries. Many of the ideas presented in this book for implementing programmes of objectives are dependent upon time being available to work individually with the child occasionally and for his progress to be monitored constantly. In classes where an extra person is available to help, more efficient arrangements can be made. We are not arguing for the replacement of qualified teachers by unqualified ancilliaries but rather for the improvement of the teacher's work by the relatively inexpensive provision of classroom assistants. Bijou (1977) supports this view and suggests that classrooms operated on an objectives approach are best able to utilize the extra help fully since teaching procedures are made explicit and the objectives format is easily understood. Hulbert *et al.* (1977) stress the value of having assistants to help deal with children who might be presenting problems of management.

A feature of many inter-professional working arrangements is difficulty of communication. The classroom assistant needs to understand the teacher, the classteacher must understand the remedial adviser, and the remedial adviser must have clear communication with the psychologist. Possible misinterpretation that can result from the use of vague statements or jargon in written reports has already been mentioned. In situations where the emphasis is placed upon the use of behavioural statements, many of these difficulties can be avoided. Furthermore, talking about pupils' needs in terms of objectives is more likely to lead to action. Gregory and Tweddle (1978) recommend that objectives should be stated for case meetings in order to make them purposeful and decision-orientated. Klein and Jones (1977) provide an interesting account of the case meetings held in a residential special school. Members of a number of professions attend the meetings and they have attempted to remedy what they regard as the main weaknesses of many such meetings (i.e. poor communication between disciplines, lack of evaluation, tending to use global and 'fuzzy' aims) by concentrating attention on agreeing goals and strategies of action.

In-service Training

> In-service training will be vital if teachers are to help effectively in recognising the children who have special educational needs and in making suitable provision for them.   (Warnock, para. 12.4)

It may seem strange to find a section on in-service training in a book about teaching children with learning difficulties. Increasingly, however, it is being accepted that teachers need, as part of the advice and support service mentioned above, a range of training opportunities to teach them techniques and strategies for dealing with slow learners. Warnock lays emphasis on the need for aspects of special education to be part of initial training courses and, undoubtedly, this is long overdue. Nevertheless, for years to come the schools will be staffed by many teachers who feel unsure about how to deal with children who have difficulty in learning.

The area of in-service training is one which the various agencies responsible for advising and supporting teachers will need to consider carefully. It cannot be assumed that because a person is an expert in his field he is necessarily proficient in the techniques of dissemination.

An essential primary feature of any programme of in-service training, whether it be a course, a workshop, or supervised classroom training, should be the determining of objectives. Only when clear objectives are made explicit can an effective in-service package be developed, methods and arrangements considered and the whole procedure evaluated. We shudder at the memory of meetings of course-organizing committees at which planning was commenced with questions such as: 'How long will the course be?', 'Who shall we get to speak?', 'Do we need discussion groups?' and, without fail, 'What time will the coffee breaks be?'. All questions to do with methods and arrangements can only be answered meaningfully when the purpose of the programme has been agreed. Thus, course planning must commence with a statement of objectives based upon a sound assessment of the needs of the trainees.

Determining the in-service needs of teachers working with slow-learning children is not always so simple. Two main sources of information are available to the course planner: (i) the teachers' own observations about gaps in their expertise, and (ii) the observations of other professional groups who visit the schools regularly. Ideally an assessment of needs should be based on both of these sources. Thus in developing a course to improve the skills of primary school teachers in teaching slow learners, the teachers might be asked to fill in a questionnaire about which areas they would like help with and, in addition, the head of the school, the local inspector, visiting remedial teachers, and educational psychologists might be asked to suggest areas of weakness that would warrant attention. All the information thus gathered is then used to formulate the objectives for the course.

A procedure for designing and evaluating in-service courses using objectives is described in Ainscow *et al.* (1978b). The procedure was developed as a result of a course that was staged to teach infant school teachers how to design and implement programmes of objectives in dealing with learning problems. It was found useful for the course tutors in encouraging the students to use objectives with their pupils, to indicate the use of the course objectives in their own teaching. Pascal (1976) employed a similar rationale (that a person tends to teach in the way he has been taught) in using behaviour modification to teach techniques of behaviour modification. In recent courses in which we have been involved we have found it helpful to give the students a list of objectives, with record-keeping columns (Figure 12). The objectives are carefully sequenced and are used to illustrate the point that proceeding to the next objective before achieving mastery of the previous one is a recipe for educational difficulty. This simple procedure seems to get the point home.

Once course objectives have been agreed the organization of the actual course can go ahead. Teaching methods can be as varied as is required. There are indications that interesting new techniques may be useful, supplementing or even replacing the standard format of lectures and discussion groups. Hargie (1977), for example, describes one experiment using micro-teaching with special education teachers. The idea is to break teaching down into discernible skills. These are then practised in isolation with small groups of children and the student-teacher's performance is recorded on video-tape so that it can be examined later with a view to self-evaluation and improvement.

One important aspect of in-service work which needs considerable attention is the question of the transfer of skills learnt on a course back into actual classroom practice. Evaluation of a number of courses with which we have been involved has indicated that even where a student had mastered the course objectives little evidence of classroom implementation was apparent. To get over this major hurdle we would suggest that in designing a course the organizers should write their objectives in a way that requires evidence of classroom implementation in order for the student to be said to have achieved a mastery level. In doing this we are modifying the stated conditions within our objectives in order to make the course more effective. Consequently, some form of structured follow-up to help the teacher to implement the skills he has learned on the course is important, and indeed it may in future be found useful to focus some in-service training courses on individual schools, rather than on teachers' centres, so that extended work in the classrooms can be incorporated.

Goal: To teach some techniques of using goals and objectives to write teaching problems.

1. When asked to define the term 'behaviour' *states* that it is 'any observable act'	6. When asked to define the term 'goal', *states* that it is 'a statement of the teacher's priority teaching intentions'
2. Given a list of 10 printed verbs, *ticks* those which are suitable for use in behavioural statements, with no more than one error or omission	7. Given 10 printed statements, *ticks* those which are goals, without error or omission
3. Given a list of 10 printed statements, *ticks* those which are behavioural, without error or omission	8. Given 3 different printed goals, *writes* one or more 'target objectives' for each, to include at least an appropriate verb
4. When asked to define the term 'objective', states that it 'is a behavioural statement which describes the end product of learning'	9. Given 3 different printed goals, *writes* one or more 'complete target objective'
5. Given a list of 10 printed statements, *ticks* those which are objectives, without error or omission	10. Given a goal and details of current competence levels, *writes* a programme of objectives, each to include at least an appropriate verb

Figure 12   An in-service training programme

In concluding this short section it is clear that in-service training is an important aspect of improving the educational opportunities open to children with learning difficulties. If teachers in ordinary school can be given a positive attitude, brought about as a result of providing them with the skills necessary to modify their lessons to meet the needs of exceptional children, great progress will have been made. The danger is that a growing awareness of the need to make this type of provision could provoke a rush of poorly designed and ill-prepared courses that may leave some teachers even more confused than they are at present. To all those concerned we say two things:

(1) Plan in-service training programmes carefully, stating clear objectives on the basis of a needs assessment;

(2) Include a procedure for systematically evaluating the course. Only through careful self-examination can modifications and improvements be made.

Children with Severe Learning Difficulties

> It is now recognised that the tasks and skills to be learned by these children have to be analysed precisely and that the setting of small, clearly defined incremental objectives for individual children is a necessary part of programme planning. (Warnock, para. 11.57)

It seems likely that the education of children previously referred to as mentally handicapped or educationally sub-normal (severe) will continue to be provided for in special schools or hospital schools, although there are examples of units attached to ordinary schools (Fisher, 1977).

Since the transfer of responsibility for the education of ESN(S) children from the Ministry of Health to the Department of Education and Science in 1971 there has been increasing interest and attention given to meeting their needs. Much discussion and research has taken place with a view to improving the quality of education provided for these children and this is gradually influencing practice in the schools. The notions of stating precise objectives for instruction, analysing learning targets, and using many of the behavioural teaching strategies described in Chapter 7 are becoming increasingly popular.

An important contribution to recent developments is made by McMaster (1973) who argues that there is a need for a theoretical framework as a basis for thinking about the education of mentally handicapped children. After suggesting that the field is 'fragmented, unstructured and largely chaotic' he suggests that there are two major issues to be resolved:

(1) How to decide what kind of education is best for the mentally handicapped child;
(2) How to systematically plan and implement the educational programme.

The solution he proposes is an approach to educational planning involving the use of objectives which he relates to five categories: knowledge, comprehension, increasing intellectual abilities, perceptual motor skills, and attitudes. Three main reasons are given for the emphasis placed on the use of objectives:

(1) They are essential for assessment and evaluation;
(2) They provide a 'common' language for discussing in detail the content of the educational programme;
(3) They help to determine appropriate teaching methods.

These arguments are valid not only in the education of mentally handicapped children but with regard to all the programmes presented in this book.

Some special schools for ESN(S) children are seeking to use the objectives approach to develop a curriculum plan. Many of the practical suggestions with regard to the organization of staff involvement that were given in Chapter 9 will, no doubt, be relevant. As with an ESN(M) school, a school for children with severe learning difficulties should provide a consistent and continuous educational programme.

In commencing a curriculum development programme the staff of a school for ESN(S) children will need to give thought to the first of McMaster's issues, concerning the nature of the education that is to be provided. Only when suitable aims have been agreed can specific objectives be generated. Williams (1978) suggests that in determining objectives careful investigation should be made of the childrens' problems. Pupils can be observed in terms of three classes of behaviour: assets, excesses, and deficits. These observations should provide the information required for choosing objectives – asset behaviours should be developed to an appropriate level, excess behaviours should be decreased, and deficit behaviours should be remedied by the teaching of new skills.

A useful source of information with regard to curriculum development for children with severe learning difficulties is Bender *et al.* (1976) who have produced a very detailed, three-volume curriculum guide containing objectives, strategies, and activities. An important aspect of any curriculum for ESN(S) children will be language development and readers interested in this aspect should look at Snyder *et al.* (1975) who have analysed twenty-three accounts of language training programmes used with the severely retarded, Swann and Mittler (1976), which includes a survey of the language skills of 1400 ESN(S) children, and Williams (1973), a language programme designed for use with young mentally handicapped children. An excellent detailed account of the development of a sequenced maths curriculum for severely handicapped pupils is given in Williams *et al.* (1977). Publications by the Hester Adrian Research Centre at Manchester University will also be valuable references.

An important trend in the education of ESN(S) children has been the increasing emphasis placed upon the parents' role. The Warnock Report stresses the need for a full involvement of parents in the education of handicapped children, particularly during the earliest years when they must be seen as the main educators of their children. Attention has been given recently to devising ways of supporting and helping parents dealing with severely subnormal children at the pre-school stage. These have usually taken one of two forms:

(1) Workshops in which parents meet together to receive some form of group training; or
(2) Individual support programmes given to families in their own homes.

The work of the Hester Adrian Centre, at Manchester, has been influential in spreading ideas for providing pre-school parental support. In their 'Parental Involvement Project' described in McConkey and Jeffree (1975), parents are required to gather detailed information about their child through structured observation using developmental charts. On the basis of this information specific teaching objectives are chosen and a teaching scheme devised. One difficulty that has become evident as a result of running this type of group activity is that some parents are unable or unwilling to take part (Sandow and Clarke, 1978).

The use of clearly stated objectives is also a feature of the 'Portage Project' (Shearer and Shearer, 1972). Here parents of young handicapped children are visited once a week, individual target objectives are prescribed, and teaching methods demonstrated to the parents by the home teacher. During the week the parent teaches towards the target and records the child's progress on a daily basis. Four main advantages are claimed for this approach:

(1) Learning occurs in the natural environment of the home and therefore problems of transfer of learning from the classroom or clinic to the home are avoided;

(2) There is direct and constant access to behaviour as it occurs naturally;

(3) Maintenance of new behaviours will more likely be enhanced if they are learnt in a natural environment;

(4) The training of parents will provide them with the skills necessary to teach further behaviours at a later date.

A curriculum kit has been devised as part of the project consisting of: (a) a developmental checklist grouped in five areas – cognitive, language, self-help, motor, and socialization, and (b) a set of cards to match the behaviours listed in the checklist which use behavioural objectives to describe the required skill and suggest teaching methods. This kit is available from Wisconsin and is being used in a number of authorities in this country.

Once the ESN(S) child is admitted to the school the need for a close parent–teacher partnership is essential. Ballard (1975), the parent of a mongol boy, writes: 'The achievement of educational objectives, however defined, closely depends on the relationship between home and school'. Where teachers are working towards stated objectives these can be the focus of the parent–teacher liaison. Meetings can be held to discuss implementation of the programme and then informal systems arranged for passing back and forth progress reports. McCall and Thacker (1977) describe a project at an ESN(S) school where a workshop format was used to develop the co-operation of teachers and parents in designing and implementing programmes of objectives. These then formed the basis for a continued home/school communication system.

In concluding this section on the education of children with severe learning difficulties we must make brief reference to the situation in subnormality hospitals. Penfold and Corrie (1978) discuss the conflict that often exists between nursing staff and teachers. They argue that the two professions must work together to provide continuity of education, which should be a positive feature of the residential setting where, given good communication and co-operation between staff, the child's education can continue on a 24-hour basis. They quote as an example of good practice in this field the work of Luke Watson in America, who uses the objectives format to structure the hospital setting, thus producing a totally integrated educational process involving both teachers and nurses.

Summary

Defining problems carefully and planning programmes of action using explicit objectives are recommended when dealing with learning difficulties in any context. The report of the Warnock Committee, which has enquired into the education of children with special needs, has recommended a number of changes that should be made. Increasingly, in the future, children with learning difficulties should be educated in ordinary schools and teachers there must be given support in terms of modifying curriculum and developing appropriate teaching materials and methods. Those working in the field of special education will need to consider ways of providing this support. Members of the advisory and support services may also have to redefine their working roles. The effectiveness of in-service training, which will have an important contribution to make in the development of special education, can be improved by the use of objectives in planning courses and workshops. Finally, the needs of children with severe learning difficulties, who will probably continue to be educated in special schools, should be met by the development of curricula based upon carefully graded sequences of objectives. Objectives will also provide a basis for closer parent–teacher co-operation.

Recommended Further Reading

Leach, D. J., and Raybould, E. C. (1977). *Learning and Behaviour Difficulties in School.* London: Open Books.
A useful source book for teachers in ordinary schools concerned to provide special education.
McMaster, J. M. (1973). *Towards an Educational Theory for the Mentally Handicapped.* London; Edward Arnold.
Describes a plan for curriculum development using the objectives format.
Sampson, O. C. (1975). *Remedial Education.* London Routledge and Kegan Paul.
Examines in detail the development of remedial education.
Wragg, E. C. (1978). Training teachers for mixed ability classes: A ten point attack, *Forum* **20**, 2, 39–42.
Outlines the professional skills needed for successful mixed ability teaching.

References

Abeson, A., and Zettel, J. (1977). The end of the quiet revolution: The Education for All Handicapped Children Act, 1975, *Exceptional Children*, **44**, 114–128.

Addison, R. M., and Homme, L. E. (1966). The reinforcing event (RE) menu, *National Society for Programmed Instruction Journal*, **5**, 8–9.

Ainscow, M., Bond, J., Gardner, J., and Tweddle, D. A. (1978a). A new role for the special school? *Special Education, Forward Trends*, **5**(1), 15–16.

Ainscow, M., Bond, J., Gardner, J., and Tweddle, D. A. (1978b). The development of a three part evaluation procedure for inset courses, *British Journal of In-Service Education*, **3**, 184–190.

Ainscow, M., and Tweddle, D. A. (1976a). A new role for the psychologist? *Special Education, Forward Trends*, **3**(2), 11–12.

Ainscow, M., and Tweddle, D. A. (1976b). The ascertainment of mild subnormality in education, *Association of Educational Psychologists Journal*, **4**(1), 50–52.

Ainscow, M., and Tweddle, D. A. (1977). Behavioural objectives and children with learning difficulties, *Association of Educational Psychologists Journal*, **4**(5), 29–32.

Anderson, S. B., Ball, S., Murphy, R. T., and Associates (1975). *Encyclopaedia of Educational Evaluation*, San Francisco: Jossey-Bass.

Ausubel, D. P., (1968). *Educational Psychology: A Cognitive View*. New York: Holt, Rinehart, and Winston.

Ballard, R. (1975). Special parents, special relations, *Special Education, Forward Trends*, **2**(3), 10–12.

Bateman, B. (1974). Educational implications of minimal brain dysfunction, *Reading Teacher*, **27**, 662–668.

Bender, M., Valletutti, P. J., and Bender, R. (1976). *Teaching the Moderately and Severely Handicapped* (3 Vols), Baltimore: University Park Press.

Bereiter, C., and Engelmann, S. (1966). *Teaching the Disadvantaged Child in the Pre-school*. Englewood Cliffs: Prentice-Hall.

Bessent, W., and Moore, H. (1967). The effects of outside funds in school districts, in Miller, R. (Ed.), *Perspectives on Educational Change*, New York: Meredith.

Bijou, S. W. (1977). Practical implications of an interactional model of child development, *Exceptional Children*, **44**, 6–15.

Block, J. H., and Anderson, L. W. (1975). *Mastery Learning in Classroom Instruction*, New York: Macmillan.

Bloom, B. S. (1975). Mastery learning and its implication for curriculum development, in Golby, M., Greenwald, J., and West, R. (Eds.), *Curriculum Development*, London: Croom Helm.

Bloom, B. S. (1976). *Human Characteristics and School Learning*, New York: McGraw Hill.

Bloom, B. S., Hastings, J. T., and Madaus, G. F. (1971). *Handbook on Formative and Summative Evaluation of Student Learning*, New York: McGraw Hill.

Brennan, W. K. (1974). *Shaping the Education of Slow Learners*, London: Routledge and Kegan Paul.

Brennan, W. K., and Herbert, D. M. (1969). A survey of assessment/diagnostic units in Britain, *Educational Research*, **12**, 13–21.

Broden, M., Bruce, C., Mitchell, M. A., Carter, V., and Hall, R. V. (1970). Effects of teacher attention on attending behaviour of two boys at adjacent desks, *Journal of Applied Behaviour Analysis*, **3**, 199–203.

Bushell, D., Wrobel, P. A., and Michaelis, M. L. (1968). Applying group contingencies to the classroom study behaviour of pre-school children, *Journal of Applied Behaviour Analysis*, **1**, 55–61.

Carrillo, L. W. (1972). The language-experience approach to the teaching of reading, in Melnik, A., and Merritt, J. (Eds.), *The Reading Curriculum*, London: University of London Press.

Charles, C. M. (1976). *Individualizing Instruction*, Saint Louis: C. V. Mosby.

Cleugh, M. F. (1968). *The Slow Learner*, London: Methuen.

Collins, J. E. (1961). *The Effects of Remedial Education*, London: Oliver and Boyd.

Corey, J. R., and Shamow, J. C. (1972). The effects of fading on the acquisition and retention of oral reading, *Journal of Applied Behaviour Analysis*, **5**, 311–315.

DeCecco, J. P., and Crawford, W. R. (1974). *The Psychology of Learning and Instruction*, 2nd Edn., Englewood Cliffs: Prentice-Hall.

Department of Education and Science (1975). *A Language for Life. (The Bullock Report)*, London: HMSO.

Department of Education and Science (1978). *Special Educational Needs*. (The Warnock Report), London: HMSO.

Duffey, J. B., and Fedner, M. L. (1978). Educational diagnosis with instructional use, *Exceptional Children*, **44**, 246–251.

Durrell, D. D. (1956). *Improving Reading Instruction*, New York: World Books.

Eisner, E. W. (1975). Instructional and expressive objectives, in Golby, M., Greenwald, J., and West, R. (Eds.), *Curriculum Development*, London: Croom Helm.

Evans, G. W., and Oswalt, G. L. (1968). Acceleration of academic progress through the manipulation of peer influence, *Behaviour Research and Therapy*, **6**, 189–195.

Evans, T. (1976). Teaching children of mixed ability, *Special Education, Forward Trends*, **3**(3), 8–11.

Fisher, G. (1977). Integration at the Pingle School, *Special Education, Forward Trends*, **4**(1), 8–11.

Frostig, M. (1964). *The Developmental Test of Visual Perception*, Palo Alto, California: Consulting Psychologists Press.

Gardner, W. I. (1977). *Learning and Behaviour Characteristics of Exceptional Children and Youth*. Boston: Allyn and Bacon.

Garnett, J. (1976). 'Special' children in a comprehensive, *Special Education, Forward Trends*. **3**(1), 8–11.

Givner, A., and Graubard, P. S. (1974). *A Handbook of Behaviour Modification in the Classroom*, New York: Holt, Rinehart, and Winston.

Gray, D., and Reeve, J. (1978). Ordinary schools: Some special help, *Special Education, Forward Trends*, **5**(1), 25–27.

Gregory, R. P., and Tweddle, D. A. (1978). Planning and evaluating meetings, *Social Work Service*, **16**, 21–25.

Gronlund, N. E. (1976). *Measurement and Evaluation in Teaching*, New York: Macmillan.

Gulliford, R. (1975). Enrichment methods, in Wedell, K. (Ed.), *Orientations in Special Education*, London: Wiley.

Gulliford, R., and Widlake, P. (1974). Schools Council curriculum materials, *Special Education, Forward Trends*, **1**(4), 13–15.

Hammill, D. D., and Larsen, S. C. (1978). The effectiveness of psycholinguistic training: A reaffirmation of position, *Exceptional Children*, **44**, 402–414.

Hargie, O. E. W. (1977). Micro-teaching with pre-service special education teachers, *Remedial Education*, **12**(1), 22–26.

Haring N. G., and Bateman, B. (1977). *Teaching the Learning Disabled Child*, Englewood Cliffs: Prentice-Hall.

Hayman, J. L., and Napier, R. N. (1975). *Evaluation in the Schools: A Human Process for Renewal*, Belmont, California: Wadsworth.

Holland, J. G., Solomon, C., Doran, J., and Frezza, D. A. (1976). *The Analysis of Behaviour in Planning Instruction*, Reading, Mass: Addison-Wesley.

Homme, L. (1976). *How to use Contingency Contracting in the Classroom*, Champaign, Illinois: Research Press.

Hulbert, C. M., Wolstenholme, F., and Kolvin, I. (1977). A teacher-aid programme in action, *Special Education, Forward Trends*, **4**(1), 27–31.

Jeffree, D. M., and McConkey, R. (1976). *P.I.P. Developmental Charts*, London: Hodder and Stoughton.

Jenkins, J. R., and Mayhall, W. F. (1976). Development and evaluation of a resource teacher programme, *Exceptional Children*, **43**, 21–29.

Johnston, M. K., Kelly, C. S., Harris, F. R., and Wolf, M. M. (1966). An application of reinforcement principles to development of motor skills of a young child, *Child Development*, **37**, 379–387.

Karnes, M. B. (1972). *Goal Programme: Language Development*, Wisbech, Cambs: Learning Development Aids.

Keogh, B. K. (1975). Social and ethical assumptions about special education, in Wedell, K. (Ed.), *Orientations in Special Education*, London: Wiley.

Kephart, N. C. (1971). *The Slow Learner in the Classroom*, 2nd Edn., Columbus, Ohio: Merrill.

Kerry, T. (1978). Remedial education in the regular classroom, *Remedial Education*, **13**, 117–121.

Kirk, S. A., and Kirk, W. D. (1971). *Psycholinguistic Learning Disabilities, Diagnosis and Remediation*, Illinois: University of Illinois Press.

Kirk, S. A., McCarthy, J. J., and Kirk, W. D. (1968). *Illinois Test of Psycholinguistic Abilities*, Illinois: University of Illinois Press.

Klein, M., and Jones, M. (1977). Case conferences at Meldreth, *Special Education, Forward Trends*, **4**(3), 23–25.

Larcombe, T. (1977). Using the Kent Mathematics Project, *Special Education, Forward Trends*, **4**(2), 12–15.

Lerner, J. W. (1976). *Children with Learning Disabilities*, 2nd Edn., Boston: Houghton Mifflin.

Lindsley, O. R. (1974). Precision teaching in perspective, in Kirk, S., and Lord, F. (Eds.), *Exceptional Children: Educational Resources and Perspectives*, Boston: Houghton Mifflin.

McCall, C. (1977). Remedial strategies in secondary schools, *Forum*, **19**(2), 44–47.

McCall, C., and Thacker, J. (1977). A parent workshop in the school, *Special Education, Forward Trends*, **4**(4), 20–21.

McConkey, R., and Jeffree, D. (1975). Partnership with parents, *Special Education, Forward Trends*, **2**(3), 13–15.

MacDonald-Ross, M. (1975). Behavioural objectives: A critical review, in Golby, M., Greenwald, J., and West, R. (Eds.), *Curriculum Design*, London: Croom Helm.

McKenzie, H. S., Clark, M., Wolf, M. M., Kothera, R., and Benson, C. (1968). Behaviour modification of children with learning disabilities using grades as tokens and allowances as back up reinforcers, *Exceptional Children*, **34**, 745–752.

McMaster, J. M. (1973). *Towards an Educational Theory for the Mentally Handicapped*, London: Arnold.

Marshall, C. P. (1976). Screening procedures for the early identification of children in need of help, *Association of Educational Psychologists Journal*, **4**(2), 2–12.

Meacham, M. L., and Wiesen, A. E. (1974). *Changing Classroom Behaviour*, 2nd Edn., New York: Intext.

Mehrens, W. A., and Lehmann, I. J. (1973). *Measurement and Evaluation in Education and Psychology*, New York: Holt, Rinehart, and Winston.

Miller, L. K., and Schneider, R. (1974). The use of a token system in Project Head Start, in

Ulrich, R., Stachnik, T., and Mabry, J., *Control of Human Behaviour*, Vol. III, Illinois: Scott, Foresman.

Mitchell, A. C., and Kellington, S. A. (1978). Integrated science for the less able, *Remedial Education*, **13**, 129–134.

Mordock, J. B. (1975). *The Other Child: An introduction to Exceptionality*, New York: Harper.

Nash, R. (1973). *Classrooms Observed*, London: Routledge and Kegan Paul.

Neisworth, J. T., and Smith R. M. (1973). *Modifying Retarded Behaviour*. Boston: Houghton Mifflin.

O'Leary, K. P., and O'Leary, S. G. (1977). *Classroom Management; The successful use of behaviour modification*, 2nd Edn., New York: Pergamon Press.

Pascal, C. E. (1976). Using principles of behaviour modification to teach behaviour modification, *Exceptional Children*, **42**, 426–430.

Penfold, J., and Corrie, C. (1978). Rethinking the teachers' role? *Special Education, Forward Trends*, **5**(2) 8–9.

Pidgeon, D. A. (1970). *Expectation and Pupil Performance*, Slough: NFER.

Popham, W. J. (1972). Probing the validity of arguments against behavioural objectives, in Gnagey, W. J., Chesebro, P. A., and Johnson, J. J. (Eds.) *Learning Environments*, New York: Holt, Rinehart, and Winston.

Popham, W. J. (1975). *Educational Evaluation*, Englewood Cliffs: Prentice-Hall.

Poteet, J. A. (1974). *Behaviour Modification: A Practical Guide for Teachers*, London: University of London Press.

Premack, D. (1959). Towards empirical behaviour laws: 1. Positive reinforcement, *Psychological Review*, **66**, 219–233.

Rosenthal, R., and Jacobsen, L. (1968). *Pygmalion in the Classroom*, New York: Holt, Rinehart, and Winston.

Ross, J. A., and O'Driscoll, J. (1972). Long-term retention after use of a free time contingency to increase spelling accuracy, *Behaviour Research and Therapy*, **10**, 75.

Sabatino, D. A., and Dorfman, N. (1974). Matching learner aptitude to two commercial reading programmes, *Exceptional Children*, **41**, 85–91.

Sampson, O. C. (1975). *Remedial Education*, London: Routledge and Kegan Paul.

Sandow, S., and Clarke, A. D. B. (1978). Home intervention with parents of severely subnormal, pre-school children: An interim report, *Child: Care, Health and Development*, **4**, 29–39.

Shearer, E. (1977). Survey of ESN(M) children in Cheshire. *Special Education, Forward Trends*, **4**(2), 20–22.

Shearer, M. S., and Shearer, D. E. (1972). The Portage Project: A model for early childhood education, *Exceptional Children*, **39**, 210–217.

Sheridan, M. D. (1973). *Children's Development Progress from Birth to Five years: The Stycar Sequences*. Slough, Bucks: NFER.

Sindelar, P. T., and Deno, S. L. (1978). The effectiveness of resource programming, *Journal of Special Education*, **12**, 17–28.

Skinner, B. F. (1953). *Science and Human Behaviour*, New York: Free Press.

Skinner, B. F. (1972). *Beyond Freedom and Dignity*, London: Cape.

Smith, J. K., and Katims, M. (1977). Reading in the city: The Chicago Mastery Learning Reading Programme, *Phi Delta Kappa*, **59**, 199–202.

Smith, R. M. (1974). *Clinical Teaching: Methods of Instruction for the Retarded*, New York: McGraw-Hill.

Snyder, L. K., Lovitt, T. C., and Smith, J. O. (1975). Language training for the severely retarded: Five years of behaviour analysis research, *Exceptional Children*, **42**, 7–15.

Stephens, T. M. (1977). *Teaching Skills to Children with Learning and Behaviour Disorders*, Columbus, Ohio: Merrill.

Stott, D. H. (1974). *Inappropriate cognitive styles as immediate causes of learning failure* (Unpublished), Centre for Educational Disabilities, University of Guelph, Ontario.

Sulzer, A., Zaroff, B., and Mayer, G. R. (1977), *Applying Behaviour Analysis Procedures with Children and Youth*, New York: Holt, Rinehart, and Winston.

Swann, W., and Mittler, P. (1976). Language abilities of ESN(S) pupils, *Special Education, Forward Trends*, **3**(1), 24–27.

Tansley, A. E. (1967). *Reading and Remedial Reading*, London: Routledge and Kegan Paul.

Tansley, A. E., and Gulliford, R. (1960). *The Education of Slow Learning Children*, London: Routledge and Kegan Paul.

Thorne, M. T. (1978). Payment for reading. The use of the 'Corrective Reading Scheme' with junior maladjusted boys, *Remedial Education*, **13**, 87–90.

Turnbull, A. P., Strickland, B., and Hammer, S. E. (1978). The individualised education programme, *Journal of Learning Disabilities*, **11**, 40–46, 67–72.

Ulrich, R., Stachnik, T., and Mabry, J. (1974), Control of Human Behaviour, Vol III: Behaviour Modification in Education, Illinois: Scott, Foresman.

Vargas, J. S. (1977). *Behavioural Psychology for Teachers*, New York: Harper and Row.

Watts, C. (1977). A primary approach to encopresis, *Special Education, Forward Trend*, **4**(2), 25–26.

Webster, G., Forder, M., and Upton, J. (1977). Action for the vulnerable child, *Special Education, Forward Trends*, **4**(4), 26–28.

Wedell, K., and Raybould, E. C. (1976). *The Early Identification of Educationally 'At Risk' Children*, University of Birmingham.

Williams, C. (1973). *A Language Development Programme*, Bromsgrove: Institute of Mental Subnormality.

Williams, C. (1978). An introduction to behavioural principles in teaching the profoundly handicapped, *Child: Care, Health and Development*, **14**, 21–27.

Williams, W., Coyne, P., Johnston, F., Scheuerman, N., Swetlik, B., and York, B. (1977). Skill sequences and curriculum development: Application of a rudimentary developmental math skill sequence in the instruction and evaluation of severely handicapped students, in Haring, N. G., and Brown, L. J. (Eds.), *Teaching the Severely Handicapped*, Vol. II, New York: Grune and Stratton.

Wood, J. W. (1975). Curriculum design for ROSLA pupils, Part 2. *Remedial Education*, **10**, 67–71.

Ysseldyke, J. E. (1973). Diagnostic-prescriptive teaching: The search for aptitude-treatment interactions, in Mann, L., and Sabatino, D. A. (Eds.), *The First Review of Special Education*, Philadelphia: JSE Press.

Ysseldyke, J. E., and Salvia, J. (1974). Diagnostic-prescriptive teaching: Two models, *Exceptional Children*, **41**, 181–185.

Zettel, J. (1978). America's new law on integration, *Special Education, Forward Trends*, **5**(2), 13.

Author Index

Subject Index